APOSTLE TO ISLAM

A Biography of
Samuel M. Zwemer

by
J. CHRISTY WILSON

BAKER BOOK HOUSE
GRAND RAPIDS 6, MICHIGAN
1952

Printed in the United States of America

SAMUEL M. ZWEMER AND AN INQUIRER
In His Study in Cairo, 1921

INTRODUCTION

It is eminently fitting that there should be a biography of Samuel M. Zwemer and that it is under the title *Apostle to Islam*. It is also highly appropriate that it is by one who succeeded him in teaching missions at Princeton Theological Seminary and whose own years of missionary service were spent among Moslems.

No one through all the centuries of Christian missions to Moslems has deserved better than Dr. Zwemer the designation of Apostle to Islam. Indeed, if one means by these words to include all of Islam and all Moslems, it is doubtful whether they could so aptly be applied to any one since Raymund Lull. In his young manhood Dr. Zwemer joined in initiating a mission in that most difficult of all Moslem fields, Arabia, the very home of Mohammed and Islam. In later years he travelled through most of the lands where Islam is found seeking to stimulate a comprehensive approach to it by the Evangelical forces. He long attacked the problem from Cairo, the intellectual center of Islam. It was appropriate and characteristic that the journal which has been so closely identified with him that it is difficult to mention the one without immediately thinking of the other should bear the comprehensive title *The Moslem World*. Through the years Dr. Zwemer sought to enlist youth for missions to the Moslems. For a generation he was a familiar and beloved figure with his stirring voice on platforms and in Christian assemblies in many countries.

Yet even the vast and urgent challenge of Islam was not enough for Dr. Zwemer. Like all great missionaries, he was true to the commission of his Master and dreamed and labored for the proclamation of the Gospel to every creature. As one long closely identified with the Student Volunteer Movement for Foreign Missions he embodied its watchword, "the evangelization of the world in this generation." It will never be known, unless God himself discloses it in "that land of large dimensions," how many missionaries either first heard the call or had their purpose crystallized through the compelling, loving appeal of Dr. Zwemer. Nor until that roster is revealed will it be clear how many countries have been touched by them or how many thousands have been introduced to eternal life by their witness.

During his years at Princeton not only were scores of young men prepared under him for missionary service abroad, but through his classes and his personal contacts hundreds of future pastors had their horizons lifted to the entire world and through them the missionary impulse has been aroused or strengthened in hundreds of congregations. Dr. Zwemer has reached an even wider public through his books. Some of these have been primarily for those specializing on missions to Moslems. Others have been for a still more inclusive constituency and have covered wide ranges of the Christian faith.

There was something of the Old Testament prophet about Dr. Zwemer. He had the prophet's fearlessness and forthrightness, the burning conviction which would brook no compromise. That, indeed, must be true of any who would across the years present the message of Christ to adherents of so sturdy a faith as Islam. Yet there was in him much more than the Old Testament. It was the Old Testament fulfilled in the New. Dr. Zwemer was frankly a conservative Evangelical. In him there was no wavering or hesitation in the proclamation of the historic Evangelical faith. Yet he never forgot that Evangel means Good News, and that the Good News is the Gospel of God's love. His zeal was always transfigured by love and it was not only for his simple, unquestioning faith that those who were honored to be in the circle of his intimate friends will best remember him, but it will be also and primarily for his loving heart that they will recall him, a loving heart which was the reflection of God's love in Christ.

KENNETH SCOTT LATOURETTE
Sterling Professor of Missions and
Oriental History and Fellow of Berkeley College
in Yale University.

CONTENTS

Part One

As the Twig is Bent

I
Prologue

"In the realm of biography there is always place for the work that is not so much a creation as a chronicle by someone in possession of the facts. What the best biographical writing of recent years can truthfully claim is that it has turned wholesomely away from the falsified 'character' and the exaggerated 'funeral oration,' and has tried to depict human beings instead of frigid types."

GEORGE SAMPSON,

in Encyclopedia Britannica.

CHAPTER ONE

PROLOGUE

With its background of mosque and minaret the life of Samuel Marinus Zwemer is one of the most colorful and interesting missionary epics of our time.

A moving picture script of this life would be stranger, and we dare say in many cases more interesting than fiction. There is romance on the Tigris and trips to far-away places, desert sheikhs and veiled women—but these are only incidental to the real passion of a man to plant the Cross wherever the Crescent holds sway.

The modern missionary movement of the nineteenth and twentieth centuries has extended the Christian Church to all the world. Many sober historians view this as the greatest enterprise of modern times in any field. In the latter part of the nineteenth century a group of young men were inspired by this cause of taking the Christian Gospel to the world. Among them were Robert Wilder, John R. Mott, Robert E. Speer and others. Zwemer was also one of this group who dared to attempt:

"The evangelization of the world in this generation."

The miracle was that they all but succeeded. The Church was established all over the world. Zwemer more than any other man called the Church seriously to preach the Gospel in the most difficult and unrewarding field of all—the Moslem world. In Arabia and Egypt, as well as in travels over the length and breadth of the Mohammedan world, he was the blazing herald of the Gospel as well as keeping this field before the Church in Europe and America.

Second only to his passion for evangelism was his zeal for writing and the distribution of Christian literature. The books he wrote in English make far more than a "five-foot shelf," and there are also many titles in Arabic that came from his pen, which had been touched by his Master and was constantly guided by prayer. Aside from the two main languages of his literary endeavor, his books have been translated and published in Chinese, Danish, Dutch, French, German, Persian, Spanish, Swedish and Urdu.

Zwemer always looked upon the book room and Bible depot as the dynamo of the mission station, and his conferences with missionaries in many of the Moslem fields resulted in remarkable increases in the program of Christian literature. The printed pages were the "leaves for the healing of the nations" in his program of mission strategy.

He was the founder and for thirty-six years the editor of *The Moslem World*, a quarterly review of current events, literature and thought among Mohammedans as well as a source book concerning missionary work in this field. In addition, from his pen there was a constant flow of articles, editorials, book reviews and tracts. In the volume of his literary production, as well as in many other ways, Zwemer resembled his predecessor, the earliest well-known missionary to Moslems, Raymund Lull.

Sherwood Eddy concludes, "Zwemer was a prophet to challenge Christendom to confront Islam." As a missionary statesman, he believed that the Christian Church could not as a matter of conscience or missionary policy afford to neglect its greatest rival to the claim of finality as a world religion. From the time that he went out as a founder of the Arabian Mission he became a leader and organizer in many of the conferences on Moslem work and represented this field in ecumenical gatherings such as those at Edinburgh and Jerusalem.

Zwemer was the founder of a small organization which gave more than a quarter of a million dollars for work among Moslems, principally in the production of evangelical Christian literature. He was the inspiration for brotherhoods in the great Mohammedan fields which had as their purpose leading Moslems to Christ and was also the founder of prayer groups in Britain and America for this work which consumed his heart and soul.

It was one time while with a picnic party on the island of Bahrein that Zwemer discovered what he took to be indications of oil, but not until years later was actual exploration done, and now that part of the world has developed into one of the largest producers of oil with untold reserves, and derricks and refineries dot the field of his labors, the islands of the Persian Gulf and the Arabian shore.

The constant ready humor which he displayed on all occasions and his burning zeal offer abundant illustrations and quotations. Certainly no missionary of our time has been more widely quoted. It is a fortunate fact that Zwemer kept diaries and journals throughout much of his life, which were made available to the writer. In addition, many facts have been gleaned from his books, the *Moslem World*, the files of *Neglected Arabia*, as well as from the family history of his father, the history of the Arabian Mission, correspondence and conference records— all contributing to what we trust may be a definitive biography of a man who is certainly one of the truly great missionaries.

Our purpose here is to present an objective book which may show the facts of a life and its significance to posterity and to throw light upon the person and his accomplishments. Dr. Zwemer has himself stated that in addition to heredity, environment, and personality there is an additional fourth factor in every Christian life—it is the power of God. In the life at which we look there are constant reminders of the generating and impelling power of prayer and the direction of the Holy Spirit.

Here we shall attempt what is not a chronological biography but rather an endeavor to open some of the windows through which the sunlight may fall upon one of the great lives of our time, remembering that God's sunlight is always more important than the windows through which it falls.

II

Of Huguenot-Dutch Descent

"But the emigration of the Huguenots. while to France it proved an injury that has not even yet been fully made up, must be viewed in the larger relations of world history, wherein the advantages accruing to the Netherlands, to Switzerland, to Germany, to England, to the United States, and to other countries, far more than offset the damage received by the land which the fugitives forsook."

The Huguenots and the Revocation,
BY HENRY M. BAIRD,
Vol. II, Ch. XX, p. 579.

CHAPTER TWO

OF HUGUENOT–DUTCH DESCENT

Providence must have decreed something special for Samuel M. Zwemer, for he came into the world as the thirteenth of fifteen children!

The Zwemers were descended from French Huguenot ancestors who fled to the Netherlands shortly after the revocation of the Edict of Nantes in 1685. After the usual course in the common schools, Adriaan Zwemer, the father of Samuel M. Zwemer, was drafted and served in the Dutch army. He had learned tailoring with an elder brother, but after his military service he accepted a position as teacher and later entered the tax and customs service of his country.

While thus employed he met and fell in love with Catherina Boon of German descent, the daughter of a blacksmith in the village of Buttinge, near Middleburg on the island of Walcheren, in the province of Zeeland. Soon after his engagement, Adriaan Zwemer was taken with the idea of emigration to America. Catherina Boon was at first opposed to this venture, but she finally agreed, and the young people joined the party of the Reverend H. G. Klyn, a pastor who had been called to a church among his compatriots in Michigan.

The ancestors of these strong people were Calvinists who having left their native land because of religious persecution were welcomed by the Reformed Church in Holland. The strain of deep faith and virtuous life from both sides of the family was reflected in their children. Samuel Zwemer also inherited those characteristics, and wherever he went, through a long life of Christian service, he depended constantly upon the power of prayer and the guidance of God.

In the month of July, 1849, some 128 Hollanders under the leadership of pastor Klyn set out from Rotterdam. The passage on the sailing ship *Leyla* took thirty-eight days. For four weeks the ocean was calm and the weather pleasant for the passengers in the hold and on the rear deck. The emigrants took with them all of their own food and bedding. Later there came an experience to try the fortitude of these hardy souls from Holland on the way to the New World. Let Adriaan Zwemer describe the incident in his own words:

"On Saturday, the 28th of July, there were indications not only of gathering clouds and wind, but the activity of the sailors proved that they expected bad weather. Mother was preparing some rice cakes for the invalid Mrs. Klyn when suddenly a wave dashed over the ship, put out the fire, and

19

carried away the open hearth. The scattering of the firebrands over the deck almost caused an alarm of fire.

"Shortly after, all passengers were ordered below. The ship continued to toss from side to side. Although we were below deck the water leaked in profusely .... most of the emigrants spent the night in prayer . . . when morning came the only light we had was through one of the port-holes near the gangway. In the hold the water was as high as the lower bunks. Some said the ship was sinking. It was a terrible day, but the following night, toward morning, the wind grew less, and some of us found sleep. Even the invalid wife of Mr. Klyn seemed to have suffered no more than the other passengers. Monday morning at eight o'clock we saw light and breathed air again, for they opened the hold." [1]

Seven little children of the Dutch emigrants died during the voyage and were buirèd at sea. This company, however, included many of the Dutch pioneers who did so much to build the communities in Michigan and Iowa as well as other states of the East and West. Seven of those on board later became ministers, and sixteen children of these families entered full-time Christian service at home or abroad. Many years later the Reverend J. Van der Meulen wrote in the magazine *De Hope*, "No other ship of emigrants sailed which had so many future ministers of the Gospel as this ship, the *Leyla*."

After debarking at the port of New York the emigrants started on the journey west to Michigan. When they reached Rochester, by the Erie Canal, they met members of the Dutch colony, and Adriaan Zwemer and Catherina Boon decided quite suddenly to remain there rather than continue to Michigan. They were married and established their humble home in one back room. By diligent labor and frugal living they were able not only to get along but to save regularly and to give to those in greater need. Four children were born in their days at Rochester, one of whom died in infancy. They also undertook the care of an orphan boy.

Before leaving the Netherlands, Adriaan Zwemer had been recommended by his church as a student for the ministry, but he did not learn of this until his plans had been made to sail for America. In this country he gradually became convinced of his call. He was accepted for help by the Board of Education and arrangements were made for him to attend Hope Academy and College at Holland, Michigan.

The family moved at once to the West where severe trials awaited them. Adriaan Zwemer obtained lumber and materials on credit, dug a cellar, and built a small house with his own hands while keeping up his work in school. In addition to his regular academic work, he studied theology with local ministers. In June, 1857, he was asked to preach in the church at Vriesland, Michigan. He must have been a satisfactory preacher, for a few days later the church issued him a call.

---

1. **Genealogy and History of the Zwemer-Boon Family.** Written by Adriaan Zwemer in Dutch. Translated and privately published by S. M. Zwemer, 1932.

It was accepted on the condition that the church allow him another year of study. He was examined, duly ordained and installed at Vriesland. It was there in the manse that Samuel Marinus Zwemer was born on April 12, 1867.

In 1870 the family moved to another church in Milwaukee, Wisconsin. Samuel Zwemer had learned to read Dutch and English by the time he was five years old. He began school in Milwaukee and learned German. To the fact that he spoke three languages as a child may be attributed something of his facility in acquiring other tongues later in life.

The mother had been in failing health for several years, but she continued to care for the household with an indomitable spirit. She had been a strong force in keeping her husband true to his conviction of a call to the ministry over the years when Providence seemed to close the way. Samuel Zwemer remembered his mother as one who was always busy with hand and heart in the service of others and who made many rough places smooth with a wonderful sense of humor. Eventually there were six sisters in the household, and they were taught the care of the kitchen, the laundry and all the work of the home. All six became public school teachers in the state of Michigan. Two of them had a record of over thirty years service in this capacity. Nellie Zwemer, after special training, went to Amoy, China, and spent forty years as a missionary in that country. Of the five brothers, four entered the Christian ministry.

The major decisions of the home were all made after seasons of prayer, and there was a constant feeling of fellowship with Christ and Divine guidance in the family. As a boy Samuel Zwemer loved Fox's *Book of Martyrs* and *The Pilgrim's Progress;* both had colored illustrations. He also read many times over *The Family Fairchild* in Dutch. It was a story of the adventures of a pious family and was written in a style to appeal to youngsters. Three times a day, at each meal, there was Bible reading and prayer. In such a home it is little wonder that the youth felt himself committed to Christ from the time of his earliest reflection on the subject. Nor was it out of the ordinary that he should join the church and hear the call to the Gospel ministry and later enter foreign service. The father had at one time hoped to go to Africa as a missionary; although kept by Providence in the home field, he was always a leader of his congregations in missionary zeal.

Pastorates followed—in Albany, New York, beginning July 6, 1873. There Samuel attended the public schools. Then came another change in 1876 when the family moved to Graafschap, Allegan County, Michigan. There the children studied at the typical "little red schoolhouse" of the frontier community. It was at a later date during this pastorate that Samuel attended the preparatory department of Hope College and continued until he received from the college the A.B. degree.

In 1886, before his son's graduation, the father had accepted a call to Middleburg, Iowa, and in 1891 he returned to a church in Spring Lake, Michigan. It does not seem strange that Samuel later covered so much of the world, for his travels had begun as a boy following his peripatetic father.

Samuel inherited from his father a love for tools and carpentry. The elder Zwemer generally had a shop in the shed or barn and at one time he made a complete croquet set, including the mallet and balls, for the children. For the most part, however, Samuel did not engage in sports. He was frequently found in his father's study reading books of a type far above his age, this often being the case when there was work to be done; he came to be known as "lazy Sam" by the other boys.

Several of the children died in infancy. The oldest brother, James Frederick, had a notable career, and, among other positions, he was president of Western Theological Seminary at Holland, Michigan. Frederick James Zwemer also was a minister and a pioneer evangelist in the Dakotas. Peter John Zwemer, who was a year and a half younger than Samuel, followed his brother to Arabia. There "the precious cruse of his strength was broken for the Master's service" after a few short years in the rocks and hills and awful heat of Muskat in the Persian Gulf. He was forced to return to America and died in the Presbyterian Hospital in New York on the eighth of October, 1898, just six weeks after his thirtieth birthday.

Such was the family of Dutch pioneers who conquered the wilderness of the West and sent their lines out to Arabia, that most difficult of mission fields. In the father and mother and children one can trace that faith in God and indomitable power of will which have built America and have sent the Gospel out from these shores to the far corners of the world.

In late life Samuel Zwemer said, "I understood the loving fatherhood of God as Jesus taught it because of what I saw in my own father." When the son published his book on *The Moslem Doctrine of God*, it was dedicated to his father. He said that the entire absence of the idea of fatherhood in the Moslem doctrine turned his thoughts to his own father. The title page of the book bears the quotation:

> "Yet most I thank thee, not for any deed
> But for the sense thy living self did breed
> That fatherhood is at the great world's core."

III

Girding On His Armour

"At about the time of the graduation of the first class, in 1866, a theological seminary was started in the little city of Holland, which remains
today under the name of Western Theological Seminary. So great was
the enthusiasm for higher education that the people dared almost anything, under the spur of the eloquence of their leaders. It was not considered fantastic to establish a post-graduate school the moment the college turned out its first class. The whole system — academy, college, seminary — was thought of as one training school. So great was the people's
zeal that at one of the early commencement exercises six hundred persons
assembled to listen to the oratory. The program that faced them, and
that apparently they absorbed with relish, began at eight o'clock in the
evening and continued till two in the morning!"

Americans from Holland,
BY ARNOLD MULDER,
p. 209.

Chapter Three

GIRDING ON HIS ARMOUR

Henry van Dyke in his *Spirit of America* says, "The typical American is a person who likes to take care of himself, to have his own way, to manage his own affairs . . . . He is an individual, a person, and he feels very strongly that personal freedom is what he most needs, and that he is able to make good use of a large amount of it." This was certainly the feeling of the Dutch pioneers and much of this spirit in American life came from their contribution. While certain forces operated to keep them within their own community and to maintain the language and the ways of the Netherlands, there was always more than enough of individualism to balance the former spirit; it has been aptly said that "stars were constantly shooting out into the life of the lusty young nation growing up around them."

These men from Holland were for the most part extremely conservative; however, the one adjective most often used to describe them is possibly "solid." Their historian Mulder has remarked that like the Scotch, they have often been charged with penuriousness or parsimony, or they have been called plain "tight." But their attributes in this regard may better be linked to "common sense." They were ready to support the cause in which they believed and they would give with liberality and self sacrifice to education, to missions, and to their church.

Dr. Zwemer himself paid them tribute in an address he gave in 1937 at an anniversary of Hope College. He said, "They never steered by the weather-vane of public opinion, but by the compass of conviction . . . The whole policy in the new colony was based on thrift and industry, on education and self reliance, on a home and a church and a state where true liberty was enthroned."

The pioneers in Michigan redeemed the wasteland as well as the good, and from the black ooze of the swamps they cut out year after year the roots that had grown through centuries and finally gave celery to the American table and to much of the world. Arnold Mulder tells us in his book *Americans from Holland,*[1] that almost before they had a roof over their heads they would begin to build their church. Of the specific project which resulted in the schools at Holland, Michigan, he goes on to say that the famous Dutch pastor, Dr. A. C. Van Raalte, began talking of a college as the first blows of the ax fell in the wilderness.

Soon he was instrumental in getting an academy under way. This he wished to enlarge looking toward a college. When a call came for him to go

---

1. **Americans from Holland,** by Arnold Mulder; J. B. Lippincott Co., New York, 1947, pp. 320.

to Iowa he used the occasion to give his compatriots just twelve days to raise $12,000 for a new building—or he would leave. They pledged the money.

Though $12,000 was a large amount in those days, Van Raalte was by no manner of means satisfied. He continued to think and talk of a "university." He had the name, "Hope Haven University," and often used the phrase: "This is the anchor of my hope." It was natural, therefore, that the institution of higher learning should eventually be known as *Hope College*. The first college class was graduated in 1866 and at about this time the Western Theological Seminary of Holland, Michigan, came into being.

I

From the manse at Graafschap, Michigan, four miles from Holland, trudged the boy Sam Zwemer at the age of twelve. In the autumn of 1879 he entered the first class of the preparatory school which was a part of Hope College. The school was co-educational and there were about twenty boys and girls in each class. The four-year course was the equivalent of high school.

The only brick building of the institution at this time was Van Vleek Hall. Its woodwork had been painted by Adriaan Zwemer when it was first constructed, and the three coats of paint lasted until many years after the son, Samuel, attended the Academy and College. The building is still used as a dormitory for girls.

Graafschap was one of the early points established by the Dutch settlers. Each Monday morning the boys, for Samuel after one year was joined by his younger brother, Peter, in the Academy, walked in to the house in town where they boarded with friends. Then on Friday after school they would trudge back to the home in Graafschap. There they attended two church services and Bible School each Sunday. The rate of board and room in the town home was two dollars and a half a week.

The four years in the preparatory department passed by swiftly with little out of the ordinary school routine except the summer jobs, where an effort was always made to earn and save for school expenses. On one vacation Samuel worked with the village blacksmith and wagon maker in Graafschap; another vacation he clerked in a grocery store. There were also many other kinds of employment.

One wonders how the father and mother, on the very small salary of a minister, managed to educate eleven of the fifteen children who grew up to reach manhood or womanhood. It is at least a near miracle but the chief secret lies in the help of the sisters. It became almost a proverb in the Dutch community that the older sisters by teaching enabled the Zwemer family to send the boys through preparatory school and college.

While in the academy the young Samuel was taking his first flights in literary composition for the school paper called *Excelsior*. He contributed both prose and verse. As an example of his thought while in his junior teens we may quote a few lines from a blank verse poem *True Courage*.

> "True bravery never seeks the laurel-crown,
> Her fame extends into a higher sphere,
> Her praise is sounded through eternity!
> He, who, when plodding on life's thorny path
> As oft as care or want his way oppose,
> Doth overcome these obstacles and rise again
> And still march on, is truly brave."

I I

The year 1883 saw the successful completion of the preparatory school and entrance in the freshman year of Hope College at the age of sixteen. There were seven members of the College class in freshman year and all remained through the four years to graduate, five men and two girls. One of the young ladies after graduation married a local business man; of the men, one became a lawyer and another a photographer—four members of the class went to the foreign mission field. They were the Reverend Albertus Pieters and his wife, née Emma Kollen, who was the other young lady of the class. Their mission service was in Japan. The Reverend H. V. S. Peeke also went to Japan and Samuel Zwemer went to Arabia and the Moslem World. All saw long service in their respective fields.

These pioneers, with what Mulder terms "fantastic audacity," decided to build a missionary ship to carry members of their colony to Africa and other far away lands. Adriaan Zwemer had charge of a lengthy program when the keel was laid. Though the ship was never completed, the spirit shown by this undertaking sent ambassadors of the Cross out to the four corners of the world.

Those in charge of Hope College maintained a rather rigid curriculum in the classical tradition. Most of the course was prescribed and there were few electives. Latin and Greek were continued in college; German and French were required; Dutch was elective. There were courses in Philosophy and related subjects. The program in mathematics included the subject of surveying, taught by the college president and no doubt of great practical importance in the frontier days. There was chemistry, geology and botany in the sciences. The woods, which were still all around the town of Holland and near at hand when Zwemer was in college, offered many fine specimens of plants and flowers, and he acquired an interest often displayed in other lands in later years.

As much as sixty years later Dr. Zwemer remembered incidents of these courses which he would tell with great glee. Professor "Billy" Shields required an essay every Friday from each member of the class. They got their heads together and figured out that if the first member to be called upon wrote a paper which would take an hour to read the others would not have to write for that week! One member of the class wrote a paper on the subject of "Pottery," which took the full hour. The second week Sam Zwemer took the whole period with a dissertation on "George Washington," but by that time the professor caught on and broke it up.

The buildings were all heated by iron stoves, under the care of a janitor named Peter De Witt, whom most of the students remembered all their lives. Members of the upper classes at one time removed all the stoves and placed them in a huge snowdrift with stovepipes sticking out. Early in the morning all the stoves were lighted; with a great display of smoke the snowdrift melted, but classes had to be cancelled for the day.

The first active religious leadership in which Zwemer engaged was the teaching of a district Sunday School in Pine Creek schoolhouse, across the Black River. This was volunteer work and the young leader walked from college, a couple of miles, and returned. A page from a Bible used at this time is inscribed "Joined church March 9, 1884."

In spite of all her indomitable energy and strength of will, the mother of the Zwemer family had been growing steadily weaker. She passed on to her reward on August 25th, 1886. Before she died she told Samuel that he had been placed in the cradle with the prayer that he might be a missionary. She was buried in the Pilgrim Cemetery at Holland.

During vacations the young college boy whom we are following did all kinds of work to make money for the ensuing year. He worked with a threshing gang that went from farm to farm after the grain harvest. The work was hard and the dust was often terrible, but the wages were very good. He was also a notable book agent; this type of work was to his liking both because of his love of books and his flare for the circulation of literature. The farmers and townsmen of the West in the eighteen eighties were not the easiest prospects in the world by any means, but the stubborn characteristics of the Dutch gave him great success in the overcoming of sales resistance. The books he handled were family Bibles, a volume with the title, *Mother, Home and Heaven,* and *Lives of the Presidents.*

During his senior year in college Zwemer heard Robert Wilder speak and became a Student Volunteer. He was one of the first thousand to enter the movement and became one of its leaders. Under date of March 22nd in his senior year he records in his diary, "Six boys of our Mission Band came to spend the evening. Read paper on the Belgian Congo."

In March young Zwemer applied to the American Bible Society for work during the summer as a colporteur. He was appointed and began this service before the graduation and commencement. In May he bought a horse for $70.00 and a cart for $26.00 to furnish transportation in his Bible distribution. He must have been a good worker for only a few days had passed before he was arrested for selling Bibles without a license.

Not to keep the reader in suspense, our hero did not remain in *durance vile*, for he got off a telegram at once to the Bible Society in New York and they were able to convince the over-zealous local authorities that a peddler's license was not necessary for the sale of the Bible by a regularly appointed agent of the Society.

The graduation exercises took place on June 22, 1887. Like all such they were very long, but the friends and supporters of Hope College seemed to relish a program of several hours and would probably have felt a bit cheated if the ceremonial had not been long enough to make it impressive.

With his bachelor of arts degree in hand at the age of twenty Zwemer went back to the labor of selling Bibles and covered much of several Michigan townships in an attempt to put a Bible in every home. The work occupied May, June and July, and in addition to travel in his cart, involved plenty of walking, sometimes as much as twenty miles in a day.

While engaged in this work he wrote a missionary article each month for the magazine "De Hope" and among other books read *Sartor Resartus* by Thomas Carlyle, which he notes in his diary was "very fine."

The service with the Bible Society was completed on August 10th. The horse and cart were sold at a profit and the colporteur headed across the lake and on to Middleburg or Free Grace, Iowa, where his father had gone as pastor of the Reformed Church. The son remarked that in Sioux County at this time his father was in the midst of primitive pioneer life.

There was a family reunion at Alton, Iowa, where James F. Zwemer, an older brother, had formerly been pastor of the church. Frederick J. Zwemer, the noted pioneer home missionary to the Dakotas had come in from his field. A friendly argument ensued as to where the recent graduate of Hope College should take his theological course. Fred had gone to McCormick Seminary in Chicago and insisted Sam should go there. James was a professor at Western Seminary which was a part of the same training institution as Hope College. He felt that the younger brother should continue where he had so successfully completed academy and college. Samuel argued for New Brunswick Seminary, where his father had intended to go and which he felt would give him a broader outlook because located in the East. Following the contest of the three brothers and no little thought and prayer the decision was reached in favor of New Brunswick.

After a bit of a vacation in Sioux County, Iowa, during which he did carpentry work—always a hobby—repaired a pump, and canvassed for his father's book of poems in Dutch, selling as many as seventeen copies in one small village; Samuel then took his way back to Michigan and was off for Seminary in New Jersey. He went by day-coach all the way; the ticket from Grand Rapids to New Brunswick cost $18.50. Having been delayed by a wreck, his train finally arrived at New Brunswick at three o'clock in the morning.

III

On September 19, 1887, he entered the Seminary and was assigned Room 32 in Hertzog Hall. Queen's College had been founded by the men from Holland in New Brunswick as a college of liberal arts; it had also been intended as "a school of the prophets in which young Levites and Nazarites of God may be prepared to enter upon the sacred ministerial office." The name was later changed to Rutgers College and finally Rutgers University, which has become the State University of New Jersey. The divinity school became a separate institution known as The Theological Seminary of the Reformed Church in America at New Brunswick.

Samuel Zwemer entered upon his theological course with zest and attacked all of his work with characteristic ardor. The members of the faculty were professors Samuel M. Woodbridge, D. D. Demarest, John G. Lansing, John De Witt, and W. A. V. Mabon. From the very beginning the Gardner-Sage Library was a source of real joy to the boy from the West and his place of study. A deep friendship sprang up with the librarian, John Van Dyck, which was to grow stronger through the three years of the seminary course.

He joined the Suydam Street Church under the pastorate of Dr. William H. Campbell and later under Dr. W. A. V. Mabon, where he sang in the choir and taught a class in the Sabbath school. He also worked in the Throop Avenue Mission with Alfred Duncombe, winning men to Christ and visiting the poor.

In October of 1887 Zwemer was a delegate to the Inter-Seminary Missionary Alliance which met in convention at Alexandria, Virginia.

In preparation for the mission field he began this same month, October, 1887, a special study of medicine. He read Gray's *Anatomy* and a manual on therapeutics and other medical texts. At a later period in his course he went on weekends to New York where he worked in Dr. Dowkontt's clinic with a young doctor named Wanless who was doing graduate work but later became Sir William Wanless of India and one of the best known missionary physicians in the world. Wanless gave him lessons in medicine and Zwemer acted as assistant and druggist. He put the medicine in bottles and according to the rules of the Bleecker Street Mission always stuck a Scripture text on each. One day in his haste he forgot to look at the label but gummed on a text, and the greatly upset patient brought back the bottle which had a "FOR EXTERNAL USE—POISON" label on it and beside it the text "Prepare to meet thy God"! This study of medicine was later to create openings for the Gospel in Arabia.

The theological student notes that with a number of others he took "Professor Loissettes" memory system but didn't seem to get much good out of it. His seminary work was going along well, however; he preached his first sermon in class on January 24th. It was the same day that he conceived the idea of the seminary students and faculty supporting their own missionary. He proposed it that evening and by 11:00 p. m. had $150 pledged, which was raised to $700 in a few days and the Reverend Louis R. Scudder, M.D., of India was supported as the missionary of the Seminary.

His diary shows that the regular habits of personal devotions and prayer had been established, which were his abiding source of power. He writes, "George Muller's life of trust makes one feel the power of prayer. Why can we not all live in that way?"

On Sunday, March 11, 1888, he preached his first public sermon to a congregation of colored people in a small church. Not that there was any connection, but the next day the famous blizzard of '88 hit the town and the school. He notes that he helped a milkman out of snowdrifts, that all trains were stopped and no mail was delivered. The classes were discontinued; on Tuesday, as the storm did not abate, five of the students had their pictures taken in a large drift. This photograph was reproduced half a century later on the cover of the *Intelligencer Leader* published in Grand Rapids, Michigan, the issue being that of February 24, 1939. The students in the picture were Frank S. Scudder, James Cantine, Philip T. Phelps, George W. Furbeck and Samuel M. Zwemer.

The accounts in the Zwemer diary show a great and growing interest in and zeal for the cause of foreign missions. He was in correspondence with Robert Wilder and went to Princeton and other seminaries to speak on missions. In November of 1888 he cast his first vote; it was for the candidates of the Prohibition party. The family had always been rock-ribbed Republicans. The reasons for his vote as he sets them down were two: a protest against anti-Chinese legislation and the feeling that the Republican party might be in secret league with the "rum power."

There follow in November some diary references which are of vital interest in view of subsequent events. On November 13th we read: "Had a talk with James Cantine in evening and he says he will go to the foreign field. God has answered my prayer." The next day we find the entry: "Had a short talk with Phelps and Cantine on the choice of a field of work. We spoke of the idea of forming a self-supporting mission of the Reformed Church." On November 15 he writes: "Called on Dr. Lansing with Mr. Phelps. Spoke of practicability of starting a mission in Arabia independent of church boards. He seemed to favor it. After a social hour we left, all resolving to think and pray over the matter again."

Dr. J. G. Lansing was the professor of Hebrew and Arabic and the idea caught fire and resulted the next year in the formation of the Arabian Mission. The symbol of the Mission was a wheel with three double spokes; the original three spokes were Zwemer, Cantine and Phelps.

About this time Zwemer was appointed secretary of the mission band and arranged for a district meeting of the Student Missionary Alliance. He wrote to all the seminaries in New York, New Jersey and Pennsylvania and arranged for the gathering. A few days before the meeting a member of the faculty found out about it and made some very pointed remarks about the arrangements having been made without faculty permission. However, Robert P. Wilder and other speakers and the delegates arrived. The secretary met them at the train, was up early in the morning and hung maps and charts for the meeting. The conference was a great success and the young student had been responsible for the first of many such meetings he was to organize the wide world over.

Vacation periods were now given over largely to speaking on Foreign Missions and work for the Student Volunteer Movement. He attended the meeting of the General Synod of the Reformed Church at Peekskill, New York. The communities at Albany and Rochester were visited and in the latter place he preached in Dutch.

During the summer the theological student canvassed in Michigan for *The Christian Intelligencer* and spoke many times on missions in that state, the region of Chicago, and in Iowa. At Wheaton College thirteen new names were added to Student Volunteer declaration cards after his address on September 11, 1888.

Throughout the Seminary course, though he was a good student and always put his academic work in first place, he yet found time for a great deal of missionary activity and continued the medical studies.

As a student he continued to write articles in Dutch for the weekly magazine "De Hope," most of them on missionary subjects. The project of the self-supporting mission in Arabia gradually took shape and his life was dedicated to that call.

We find that he continued the hour of prayer and Bible reading from noon to one o'clock, which had been established the first year in Seminary. Before a major address for the Student Volunteer Movement he records, "Felt very weak spiritually but prayer was strengthening." Again and again he notes that he was greatly helped in speaking, as an answer to prayer.

Finally the day arrived for graduation from the Seminary at New Brunswick. There were seven in the class; one of them was Frank Scudder who became a missionary to the Far East and Hawaii. Another was George F. Talmage who was subsequently to be the pastor of Theodore Roosevelt at Oyster Bay, Long Island. Two members of the class later entered the ministry of the Protestant Episcopal Church.

The Arabian Mission had been launched. James Cantine graduated a year before Zwemer and was to precede him to the Near East to begin the study of Arabic. Philip T. Phelps, the other "spoke" of the wheel which was the symbol of the new Mission, because of health and family circumstances went into a pastorate at home and continued in this country to support the project. The prayer of Abraham, "Oh that Ishmael might live before thee," was adopted as the motto of the Mission, since the people of Arabia were largely descended from that son of Abraham and "Ishmael" was taken to represent the Moslem world in general. Following the graduation, Samuel M. Zwemer was ordained as a missionary by the Classis of Iowa on May 29, 1890.

Professor John C. Lansing, D.D., and the three students laid their plan before the Board of Foreign Missions and the General Synod of the Reformed Church. The Board was having difficulty in supporting its existing missions and was in debt. Zwemer said later, "We took the matter up with the Board step by step (or was it stop by stop), but we remained fully persuaded that God wanted us in Arabia." *Constant persuit.*

Before sailing for the field Zwemer had made a tour of churches in the West to secure support for the new mission venture. Of churches and friends interested at the time he said fifty years later, "One marvels at their faith in continually sowing on such desert soil when all evidence of a visible harvest was absent." Dr. J. G. Lansing was also active so that his follower as treasurer of the Mission could state, "He secured money and pledges of annual gifts to such an extent that when the Mission was incorporated, Cantine had been sent to Beirut and maintained there and the money for Zwemer's support was in hand."

Part Two

To the Heart of the Moslem World

IV

Pioneering in Arabia

"If I can get no faithful servant and guide for the journey into the interior, well versed in dealing with Arabs and getting needful common supplies (I want but little), I may try Bahrein, or Hodeidah and Senna, and if that fails, the North of Africa again, in some highland; for without a house of our own the climate would be unsufferable for me — at least, during the very hot months — and one's work would be at a standstill. But I shall not give up, please God, even temporarily, my plans for the interior, unless, all avenues being closed, it would be sheer madness to attempt to carry them out."

Last letter of
BISHOP VALPY FRENCH
from Muscat,
February 13, 1891

CHAPTER FOUR

PIONEERING IN ARABIA

Arabia is the homeland of Islam, and that religion was the chief rival of Christianity and the most difficult problem in the world missionary strategy; so Zwemer and Cantine decided to apply the antidote of the Christian Gospel at the very source, where the Mohammedan religion saw its birth, where its adherents were the most fanatical, where there was little hope of numerical success in converts, and where the climate was all but impossible. The young pioneers were fully aware that it would take much in funds and life to establish a witness here in the stronghold of Islam. They had what it takes, and from the beginning they had in their vision not only Arabia but the whole Moslem world.

Zwemer remarked, "A reception was given to Cantine before sailing and the students presented him with a pair of field glasses. He surely needed them for he went to spy out the land." He sailed for Beirut on October 16th, 1889, where he was engaged in the study of Arabic until joined by Zwemer who sailed on June 28th, 1890. The departure was on the steamer *Obdam* of the Holland American Line. He was accompanied by his father and older brother, Frederick, who desired to visit in Holland.

The missionary recruit went to Scotland where he conferred with the only society that had work in Arabia; he also met the family of Ian Keith Falconer, the brilliant young Britisher who died at Sheikh Othman, near Aden, May 10, 1887, a martyr to mission work in Arabia.

Years later Zwemer noted, "I spent a few days in London where I bought, among other books, Doughty's *Arabia Deserta!* Those two volumes were to me a second Bible for many years, until I sold them at Cairo during the World War to Colonel Lawrence."[1]

After contacts with other Societies in England he returned to Holland, said farewell to his father and older brother after a boat trip up the Rhine to Mainz, took the train to Trieste and sailed from there to Beirut.

The young missionaries were shown great hospitality and courtesy by such great Arabic scholars as Dr. Cornelius Van Dyke, translator of the Bible, Dr. James Dennis and Dr. H. H. Jessup. They met many other members of the Syria Mission of the Presbyterian Church, U.S.A., and were invited to sit in on some of their mission meetings. Most important, the American missionaries secured for them language teachers. Zwemer wrote: "Cantine, Phelps and I began to study Arabic at New Brunswick Theo-

1. **The Golden Milestone**, Samuel M. Zwemer and James Cantine, Fleming H. Revell Co., New York, 1938, p. 33.

logical Seminary. Dr. Lansing's *Manual for Classical Arabic* had just been published, and our teacher was enthusiastic, but his frequent illness and our other studies, which were *not* elective, interfered with any great progress. At any rate, I knew the alphabet and elementary rules before reaching Beirut. Professor Lansing's brother, Dr. Elmer Lansing, who had lived long in Egypt, was at that time practicing medicine at Haverstraw, New York, and I recall how he drilled me in some of the gutturals during a weekend visit. Both Cantine and I procured excellent native teachers in Syria, and for a short time I sat at the feet of that prince of Arabic scholars, Dr. Cornelius Van Dyke. He told me it was a seven-day-a-week job and that one could become proficient only by neglecting all English papers and books!

"This so-called 'language of the angels' is celebrated among those who know it for its beauty and, among all who try to learn it, for its difficulty . . .

"The first difficulty is its correct pronunciation. Some Arabic letters cannot be transliterated into English, although certain grammars take infinite pains to accomplish the impossible. The gutturals belong to the desert and, doubtless, were borrowed from the camel when it complained of overloading. There are also one or two other letters which sorely try the patience of the beginner and in some cases remain obstinate to the end."[2]

Before the close of the year 1890 the two pioneers left Beirut; we may let Cantine speak:

"At Cairo we met Dr. Lansing, whose health had broken down and who was seeking its renewal in the environment of his old home city. Together we threshed out all possibilities for our location, finally holding to our early hope of working with the Scotch Mission at Sheikh Othman. In June I took a direct steamer from Suez to Aden, Zwemer remaining longer with Dr. Lansing and then taking a coasting steamer down the Red Sea, which allowed him to go on shore at various ports. A memorable experience of his was having as a fellow passenger the venerable Bishop French of the Anglican Church, one-time missionary Bishop of the Punjab, India, and always very jealous for the evangelization of the Moslem world. At this time he was travelling around the Arabian peninsula, looking as we were, for the best location in which to establish a new mission."[3]

I

It is no doubt best to let Zwemer describe his own first journey along the Red Sea coast of Arabia:

"It has been my choice, or my fate, to be the 'Flying Dutchman' of the Arabian Mission. In our adventure it seemed the part of wisdom to both of us to gain some knowledge of those areas on the coast that were accessible. So, in travelling from Cairo to Aden, where Cantine had preceded

2. Ibid., pp. 34, 35, 36.
3. Ibid., pp. 27, 28.

me, I took a small coasting steamer. These 'tramp' ships, as they were
called, offered few comforts but plenty of adventure. One was never sure
at what ports the captain would call for cargo, how long there would be
delays, or what fellow passengers would be encountered. I remember, a
few years later, travelling from Basrah to Aden on the S. S. Gorgi loaded
with dates for London and pilgrims for Mecca. By the time we got to
Aden there were sick pilgrims and dead pilgrims. The food was bad and
the voyage rough. I was the only English speaking passenger and received
as a gift from the captain 'a book someone left on board, of which none of
us can make any sense.' It was Carlyle's *French Revolution* and it was a
godsend on that lonely voyage!

"On January 8, 1891, I left Cairo for Suez, paying seven pounds for
a second-class ticket to Aden. The Rt. Rev. Thomas Valpy French and
his chaplain, Mr. Maitland, were the only other European passengers —
the rest mostly were pilgrims for Jiddah. It was a great experience to meet
this saintly Bishop who, after long years of service at Lahore, was on his
way as pioneer to Muscat, where he died soon after.

"On January 12 we went ashore at Jiddah (my first sight of Arabia) and
visited the tomb of Eve near the Mecca gate. 'From the immense length of
the grave, 110 paces,' I wrote in my diary, 'the apple tree must have been
a giant poplar.' We saw the bazaar and made some purchases. Meanwhile,
the Bishop had taken his large Arabic Bible on shore and was preaching
to the Arabs in a café. His venerable appearance and high classical phrase-
ology doubtless preserved him from the fanaticism of his listeners. At Suakin I met General Haig.[4] His dromedary was tied to the door of an old,
rambling house. He lived in camp style, however; 'a table, chair, and camp
bed, books scattered everywhere — Arabic and missions on the top.' He
was engaged in relief work for the famine-stricken and orphans. Some
sixty orphans were cared for in one large tent, and Dr. Harpur was teaching them the Lord's Prayer. On Sunday the Bishop held a Communion
service for us all at the home of the Belgian consul. From Suakin we sailed
for Massawah through a heavy sea, and I was seasick even after landing.
Just outside the city, at the Swedish mission house, we were entertained and
saw something of their work in Ethiopia. At Hodeidah we saw the bazaars
and learned that the way to Sana's was open for merchants. I met an Italian trader who was very friendly later when I travelled inland. Through
the straits of Bab-el-Mandeb, after passing the island of Perim, we reached
Aden fifteen days after leaving Suez. Cantine had rented some rooms in
the Crater,[5] and a convert from Syria, Kamil Abdul Messiah, was already
busy winning friends and preaching. Alternately, according to my diary,
we were down with malarial fever, and our finances were never before or
since in such straitened condition. We prayed and even fasted one whole
day — and the answer came in a long overdue remittance for salaries. How

---

4. Major General F. T. Haig who made explorative journeys in Arabia and elsewhere for the
Church Missionary Society.
5. A name given to the old native part of the town for obvious reasons, Aden having a climate
of terrific heat, and is also on the site of an extinct volcano.

well I recall those two months at Aden together, climbing to the top of Shem-Shem, reading Arabic, visiting the Scotch missionaries at Sheikh Othman, planning for the future and preaching in the Institute for nonconformist soldiers. With Ibrahim, a colporteur of the Bible Society, I also went inland as far as Lahej where a number of sick folk welcomed treatment and Scriptures were sold.

"While Cantine was in correspondence with Syria and planning to go up the Gulf, it was agreed that Kamil and I should tarry at Aden and if possible study openings on the coast. The south coast of the Arabian peninsula, from Aden to Muscat, measures 1,480 miles, and includes the three provincial divisions of Yemen, Hadramaut and Oman, whose names have come down from the earliest times. Aden commands the commerce of all Yemen on the south; Muscat is the key to Oman and its capital; Makallah is the great seaport of the central province."[6]

In consultation the young missionaries decided that since the Scotch Mission was in occupation at Sheikh Othman nearby, they should seek another location for the beginning of their work. It was decided that Zwemer and the young convert from Syria, Kamil Abdul Messiah, should explore the southern coast as far as Makallah, while Cantine would visit the coasts of the Indian Ocean and the Persian Gulf to the east and north.

The travelers, on the expedition along the southern coast, had a most adventurous time visiting a number of towns skirting along the shore in a small native boat. Zwemer describes part of that journey. "Troubles never come singly. Our boat was having a rough time with the waves; baggage and passengers were fairly drenched; and, to add to the general fear, a couple of sharks made their appearance. The 'shark drum,' a skin stretched over a frame of wood and struck with a stick, was called into service, and the boatman said the sharks were now afraid!

"Nevertheless he turned the rudder, but not for Makallah. Instead, he put back to Bir Ali, saying that the sea was too high to proceed any further. No sooner were we in sight of Bir Ali than a large sailing vessel bound for Makallah and Muscat sailed into the harbor. Could anything have been more to our desire? So we paid the fare and went on board. It was a Muscat trader, large, clean and full of passengers from the various towns on the coast. The captain and crew were very kind to us in many ways. Before next morning Kamil had sold thirty parts of Scripture in Arabic to the passengers and crew and I had treated some ten people to eye lotion and other simple remedies; the captain purchased all the Arabic books on medicine we had with us for study and gave orders for other scientific books to be sent to him at Muscat, and three Moslems who had heard us at evening prayers came to ask for copies of these prayers to use themselves, as they said they liked them better than those they used. Next day they were reading and learning the Christian prayers that Kamil had copied for them.

6. Ibid., pp. 48, 49, 50.

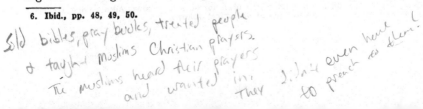

"After all our delays and continual contrary winds, we came in sight of Makallah on Friday evening. It is a second Jaffa, with high and well-built houses, two prominent mosques, and a large Bedouin encampment west of the city. The harbor and docks would do credit to a European government, while the row of fortresses, the public wells, and the large market place prove that the ruler of Makallah is a sultan in more than name. We had letters of introduction to him, obtained through Ibrahim, the Bible Society agent at Aden, from the native governor at Camp. The sultan found a lodging for us near the sea and provided for all our wants. For a Moslem he is a man of liberal ideas. Before the second day of our stay had closed, all our Arabic Bibles were sold. Kamil was busy all the time in the house and in the market, proving from the Scriptures (theirs and ours) that Jesus Christ is the Prophet Who has come into the world and that salvation is in Him alone."[7]

On the return to Aden Kamil wrote to Dr. Henry H. Jessup in Syria:

"From Mejrud, the limit of British jurisdiction, to Makallah, in the wild there is no safety for travellers except by paying money to each sultan to take you through his territory to the next, and so on. From Belhaaf to Makallah there is less danger. From Makallah to the east it is remarkably safe.

"But the best and the sweetest and the most delicious of all the glad tidings which we have written is this: We have planted in the Lord's vineyard, in this blessed journey, one hundred and ten copies of the Arabic Scriptures. Eight remained over, which I have sold in Aden."[8]

Bishop French left Aden before Cantine and said to the latter, "I understand that you also are intending to visit Muscat and the Persian Gulf coast of Arabia. Do not let the fact that I am preceding you change your plans. I am an old man, and it may be God's will that I can only view the promised land, while it is for you to enter in."

These words were indeed a prophecy for upon Cantine's arrival in Muscat he learned that Bishop French had passed to his reward. We read later in Cantine's narrative of his journey:

"I was naturally much interested in the story of the last days of the good old Bishop. He had utterly refused to trade upon his rank and reputation, refusing to accept the hospitality of the English political agency, preferring to live among the Arabs with whom he soon gained a reputation for great sanctity. Unfortunately, his Arabic was of too classical a brand to be understood by the common people, though they listened most courteously as he gathered groups about him in the city gate. I was told that he was not very tolerant of advice and persisted in wearing his black clerical hat. It was midsummer and exposure, perhaps unavoidable, in a trip by small sailing boat up the coast resulted in sunstroke from which he did not recover. He was buried in a nearby small, sandy cove, only a few

7. *Ibid.*, pp. 53, 54.
8. *Kamil Abdul Messiah*, H. H. Jessup, the Westminster Press, Philadelphia, 1898.

yards distant from the wide sea, but not wider than was his love for his fellow men; and now lies within sound of its ceaseless waves, a fitting accompaniment for his ceaseless prayers for the children of Ishmael."[9]

Having visited Muscat the young pioneer decided to explore further. He went ashore at Bahrein during the stop of the steamer and went on to Bushire on the Persian side of the Gulf. While there, a letter came which had much to do in the decision as to the location of the Mission.

The letter was from Dr. M. Eustace, who had been a member of the C.M.S. Mission in Isfahan, Persia, and was then acting as resident physician for the British Community in Basrah and carrying on a dispensary for the poor. He had heard that the two young men were looking around Arabia and the Gulf for a place to open Mission work and he invited Cantine to come to Basrah. Of this invitation Cantine said: "He wrote very cordially, saying that he had heard that I had been visiting the Gulf ports with a view to the location of a new mission and that he hoped I would come on and be his guest while I looked over the possibilities of Basrah. Of course I went, and it did not take many days to realize that his invitation had been providentially inspired, and that I should write to Zwemer to come on and see for himself. He at once agreed with me. The trustees at home took our word for it, and the Arabian Mission had at last taken root."[10]

II

Basrah then was a city of some 60,000 inhabitants about sixty miles above the Persian Gulf on the Shatt-el-Arab, which is the great river formed by the confluence of the Tigris and Euphrates. The Station was opened in August, 1891. Zwemer had made a difficult journey of twenty days in late June and July to Sana'a in the highlands of Yemen and found that an attractive place, but everything considered he agreed that Basrah was the best situation for the opening work of the Arabian Mission.

At the beginning the young missionaries lived with Dr. Eustace and his wife. The latter was called, however, by the C.M.S. to work in Quetta, Baluchistan, while Zwemer and Cantine continued to occupy the commodious Eustace home. They moved later to a small house in the Arab part of town but when the lease expired they encountered great difficulty in getting another place. It was finally ascertained that an order had been issued by the government forbidding anyone to rent them property. At last they obtained a house, built for them by a contractor who was a member of a nominal Christian group. Later they found that this man had placed a small bribe with the proper authorities and had the building and rental contract ratified. It turned out — to their dismay — that the bribe had been a case of whiskey!

Soon after his arrival in Basrah Cantine made the journey up to Baghdad and came to know missionaries of the C.M.S. and others there. Zwemer

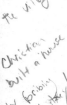

Handwritten margin notes: Moved into the village / Christian built a house by (bribing) with whiskey!

9. *Ibid.*, pp. 41, 42.
10. *Ibid.*, p. 44.

Had men an extreme love for his with a passion for always Muslims, whom the pray! for!

yards distant from the wide sea, but not wider than was his love for his fellow men; and now lies within sound of its ceaseless waves, a fitting accompaniment for his ceaseless prayers for the children of Ishmael."[9]

Having visited Muscat the young pioneer decided to explore further. He went ashore at Bahrein during the stop of the steamer and went on to Bushire on the Persian side of the Gulf. While there, a letter came which had much to do in the decision as to the location of the Mission.

The letter was from Dr. M. Eustace, who had been a member of the C.M.S. Mission in Isfahan, Persia, and was then acting as resident physician for the British Community in Basrah and carrying on a dispensary for the poor. He had heard that the two young men were looking around Arabia and the Gulf for a place to open Mission work and he invited Cantine to come to Basrah. Of this invitation Cantine said: "He wrote very cordially, saying that he had heard that I had been visiting the Gulf ports with a view to the location of a new mission and that he hoped I would come on and be his guest while I looked over the possibilities of Basrah. Of course I went, and it did not take many days to realize that his invitation had been providentially inspired, and that I should write to Zwemer to come on and see for himself. He at once agreed with me. The trustees at home took our word for it, and the Arabian Mission had at last taken root."[10]

II

Basrah then was a city of some 60,000 inhabitants about sixty miles above the Persian Gulf on the Shatt-el-Arab, which is the great river formed by the confluence of the Tigris and Euphrates. The Station was opened in August, 1891. Zwemer had made a difficult journey of twenty days in late June and July to Sana'a in the highlands of Yemen and found that an attractive place, but everything considered he agreed that Basrah was the best situation for the opening work of the Arabian Mission.

At the beginning the young missionaries lived with Dr. Eustace and his wife. The latter was called, however, by the C.M.S. to work in Quetta, Baluchistan, while Zwemer and Cantine continued to occupy the commodious Eustace home. They moved later to a small house in the Arab part of town but when the lease expired they encountered great difficulty in getting another place. It was finally ascertained that an order had been issued by the government forbidding anyone to rent them property. At last they obtained a house, built for them by a contractor who was a member of a nominal Christian group. Later they found that this man had placed a small bribe with the proper authorities and had the building and rental contract ratified. It turned out — to their dismay — that the bribe had been a case of whiskey!

Soon after his arrival in Basrah Cantine made the journey up to Baghdad and came to know missionaries of the C.M.S. and others there. Zwemer

9. Ibid., pp. 41, 42.
10. Ibid., p. 44.

many who witnessed to the purity of his life and motives. He was far above the average of native workers, in ability and earnestness and was thoroughly magnanimous. His loss to our work will be great.' "[12]

In December, 1892, Peter J. Zwemer, younger brother of Samuel, arrived in Basrah to assume his duties as a member of the Mission. That same month Samuel made a visit to Bahrein and these islands, with some 50,000 population, were occupied as a second station of the new mission.

The members of the young mission kept always before their mind the intention to occupy the Arabian mainland and to reach the interior when the way should open. Samuel Zwemer made a journey to the interior province of Hassa, west of the Bahrein islands in October.

In November, 1893, Peter Zwemer visited Muscat and a third station of the Mission was established there. From here camel journeys were made to other points in the province of Omah. In a little more than two years after the occupation of Basrah the Mission had been established at three points. During these early years the whole region of the Gulf was visited by a severe epidemic of cholera. Many people fled from Basrah and Zwemer estimated that at least 5,000 died of the dread disease in Bahrein.

In 1894 another physician, Dr. James T. Wycoff, was appointed and joined the Mission. His work was most encouraging, but after a few months he had to go to India because of ill health and returned from there to America. Early in the year Samuel Zwemer was also ill with pleurisy followed by pneumonia, but made a rapid recovery.

III

During this year the independent Arabian Mission was taken over by the regular Board of the Reformed Church in America. Some members of this church had from the beginning referred to the founders of the Arabian Mission as "cuckoos," because, as the critics maintained, they laid their eggs in other birds' nests. At any rate, though the Church had at first refused to sponsor the new Mission, it was going on nevertheless and since much of the support was coming from the Reformed Church, the Mission was regularly adopted and the Board issued the following statement, "From henceforth the Arabian Mission will have a peculiar claim upon the members of the Reformed Church. The appeal of Arabia, its millions and its missionaries should come home to them with no less force than that which comes from our older Mission fields." So the new arrangement was made to the satisfaction of those on the field as well as to the Board and Church at home.

Meanwhile, two young ladies had been appointed as pioneer missionaries from Sydney, Australia, to join the C.M.S. in Baghdad. Since they were expected to arrive in Basrah the members of the Baghdad Mission

12. **The History of the Arabian Mission**, Alfred DeWitt Mason and Frederick J. Barney, Reformed Board, New York, 1926.

asked the two young bachelors, Cantine and Zwemer, to meet them and see them safely on their way to Baghdad.

They arrived on the first of April, 1895. The house of the young men had been put in order, their furniture, made from packing cases largely, was covered with attractive shawls. The few dishes were set out on a table cloth with a heavy fringe. One of the young women, a most attractive nurse with rosy cheeks, was asked to pour tea. Just then Zwemer called her to see a passing caravan. As she rose her foot caught in the fringe and most of the dishes came down with a smash onto the hard floor. The chagrined young lady rushed out onto the balcony in tears but Zwemer was after her like a flash, and it has ever since been reported in the Mission that he suggested it would be fine should she stay on and break the remainder of the dishes at her convenience.

In those days the C.M.S. had very strict rules about their young lady missionaries having gentlemen friends visit them, but "love laughs at locksmiths" and Samuel Zwemer had never shown himself one to give up easily. After a friendship in correspondence, he arranged to visit Baghdad, where he acted as teacher of Arabic for the young ladies. There romance blossomed into a love which was to guide and mold the life under review. Amy Elizabeth Wilkes and Samuel M. Zwemer were married on May 18, 1896, in the British consulate in Baghdad. Thus took place in actual fact a romance which few would be so bold as to construe even in fiction. Certainly the ends of the earth united to form this happy household which was to be of such great service to the kingdom of our Lord.

True it is that the Church Missionary Society did not surrender their prize without something of a struggle. As is the custom with most Societies, a portion of transportation cost must be refunded if a new person does not remain a certain time on the field. It was necessary to meet this rule, so that even unto this day members of the Mission maintain that Samuel Zwemer purchased his wife in true oriental fashion.

It was indeed a great thing to have a real trained nurse in the household when they had returned to Bahrein. Zwemer had done much to relieve illness and pain from his knowledge of medical treatment gained during his seminary course. He had also been a dentist of sorts, extracting teeth and relieving pain. As he said, "In a place where dentistry is practiced by the use of wedges, hammers and tongs and where they fill a hollow tooth with melted lead to ease pain, I have won a score of friends by less painful methods."

In January, 1897, Mr. Cantine visited the Zwemers in Bahrein. Of his stay he said, "Two weeks at Bahrein passed very quickly. It was the only one of our stations blessed with the presence of a woman, and you may see that it had possibilities of entertainment far above those of less fortunate Basrah and Muscat. While I was there P. J. Zwemer also come up from Muscat and together we had a very busy and withal pleasant time, looking over reports of work done during the year past and planning for that tò come. The Mission House in Bahrein is pleasantly situated on the sea-shore, comfortable and well adapted to our needs. I could not help con-trasting my surroundings with those we endured in '93 when, during a bad epidemic of cholera, we were shut off from communication with the out-side world, with only one room to live in and that wholly unprotected from the August sun."[13]

Later in the year 1897 the Zwemers left for furlough in America. Their daughter, Katharine, was born at Spring Lake, Michigan, May 23rd of this year. The father was active among the churches in creating interest and raising funds for the Mission in Arabia.

The following year the family returned from furlough, bringing with them two new recruits. One of them was Miss Margaret Rice who became the bride of the Reverend F. J. Barny, already on the field. The other re-cruit was the Reverend George E. Stone, who was to give his life at Mus-cat after a short period of service. Two doctors also joined the Mission in 1898; they were Dr. Sharon J. Thoms and Dr. Marion Wells Thoms, who were sent out by the University of Michigan.

Peter Zwemer had founded a school for freed slave boys in Muscat and was like a father to some eighteen of these little fellows who had been rescued from the hold of a slave trader, "dispirited in mind, broken in body and warped in morals."

We have the following description from Robert E. Speer: "Six years ago I stopped from a British India steamer at Muscat to visit Peter Zwemer who was working there alone, the signs of fever plain upon his face so that any man might read but abiding still by his work. He took us up to the house where he was living and into the room where he said his family would be found. There, sitting on little benches around the room, were eighteen little black boys. They had been rescued from a slave ship that had been coming up the Eastern coast of Arabia with these little fellows and other slaves to be sold on the date plantations along the Tigris and the Euphrates rivers. The British consul had gone out and seized them from the slavers and had delivered them to Mr. Zwemer to keep until they were eighteen years of age, when they were to be given their manumission papers. They sat in the plain room, dressed in their brown khaki garments with their little red fezes on their heads, just as happy as the children of a king. 'They were not so,' said Mr. Zwemer, 'when I got them. The eighteen of them huddled together in the middle of the floor just like rabbits, and every time I came close they huddled nearer together. They distrusted everyone. For months they had known nothing but abuse and cruelty, and had been shut down in the hold of the slave ship in order that they might not betray their presence.' I saw on the cheek of each child a little mark about the size of a silver half dollar on the cheekbone, and I asked Mr. Zwemer what that curious scar was. 'Why,' he said, 'that is the brand of the slaver's iron.

Every one of these little boys was burned that way.' I understood something standing in the presence of those eighteen little black boys with the brand of the slaver's iron on their cheeks, of what it was that nerved Wilberforce and Clarkson to endure ignominy and shame and social octracism until at last they had stricken the shackles from the wrists of the last British slave and reinstated him in his rights as a man."[14]

A hospital building had been added to Bahrein station but in spite of better medical attention Ruth Zwemer died on July 7th, 1904, at the age of four, and Katharina, the eldest daughter, passed away at the age of seven, on July 15th. Thus within about a week these two young lives were given to add to those of missionaries who had sacrificed themselves. On the graves of the two little daughters was recorded, "Worthy is the Lamb that was slain to receive riches." Even such a severe loss could not in the least shake the dauntless faith of these pioneers and the proclamation of the Gospel in this most difficult field went on — with increased zeal.

At one time I asked Paul Harrison why more missionary societies were not at work in Arabia; he replied, "I don't believe God has given enough divine stubbornness to anyone except Dutchmen to stay on and work in Arabia."

To celebrate fifty years of the Arabian Mission, Zwemer and Cantine joined to write *The Golden Milestone* which has been much quoted here. In the introduction to that book Lowell Thomas wrote:

"The names of great explorers are usually emblazoned across the pages of history. Not so with the missionary. But in the region where he spends the active years of his life the great missionary is often a legendary figure, and frequently exploration is his sideline.

"Among the names now a legend along the romantic coast of Arabia are the two Americans who are the authors of this book. From the Straits of Bab-el-Mandeb to the Gulf of Oman, from Mokka to Muscat, from the mysterious Arabian city of Sana'a to Basrah the home of Sinbad the Sailor, from Aden to Baghdad, the names of Zwemer and Cantine are now a part of the Arabian legend.

"Today along the whole Persian Gulf coast the shieks of Araby still talk of these two pioneer missionaries who had the courage to tell the story of Christianity to the fanatical Moslems, Musulmen who believe that to kill 'a dog of a Christian' is one sure way of earning admission to the paradise of the Prophet.

"In the white coral skyscrapers of the seaport of Makallah and among the pearl fishers of Bahrein, Zwemer and Cantine accomplished missionary miracles. And this is the intimate story of their voyages, voyages as interesting and romantic as those of the fabled Sinbad.

"Ever since my own visit to Arabia, twenty years ago, I have dreamed of visiting the forbidden city of Sana'a. So the chapter describing Zwemer's

---

14. **Missionary Principles and Practice**, Robert E. Speer, Fleming H. Revell Co., New York, 1902, pp. 462, 463.

two successful journeys to that mysterious Arab capital was of particular interest to me.

"*The Golden Milestone* is a story of dauntless courage and high adventure."[15]

---

15. The Golden Milestone, pp. 5, 6.

V

Arabian Nights—and Days

"We who love them see the possibilities of sacrifice, of endurance, of enthusiasm, of *life,* not yet effaced. Does not the Son of God who died for them see these possibilities too? Do you think He says of the Mohammedan, 'There is no help for him in his God'? Has He not a challenge too for your faith, the challenge that rolled away the stone from the grave where Lazarus lay? 'Said I not unto thee, that, if thou wouldst believe thou shouldst see the glory of God? Then they took away the stone from the place where the dead was laid.'"

I. LILIAS TROTTER
Missionary to Algiers

CHAPTER FIVE

ARABIAN NIGHTS — AND DAYS

The Arabian Mission was launched and expanding—the romance and glamor of the Arabian Nights had now become real toil and hardship and endurance of days in fearful heat.

Soon after the occupation of Bahrein Zwemer sent out the first printed letter telling of his journey around the islands and of the work. It was printed in Bombay.

I

"Half way down the Persian Gulf from Basrah, off the East Arabian Coast and between the peninsula of El Katar and the Turkish province of El Hassa, are the islands of Bahrein. The islands have a long history; they are identified by Sprenger with Dedan of Scripture, and were known to the Romans by the name of Tylos. In Niebuhr's day, the principal island was called Owal and this name is still known. Properly Bahrein or 'the two seas,' is the name of the opposite coast triangle between the salt sea of the Gulf and the fresh-water flood of the Euphrates, but it has for many years been the collective name for Owal and the smaller island of Moharrek.

"The main island is about thirty miles long and six to nine miles in breadth; the northern part is well watered by natural springs of slightly brackish water, and abounds in gardens and palm groves. Toward the south of the villages of Rifa,' near which there are ancient sepulchral tumuli, probably of Roman date[1], the land rises, becomes rocky and barren, and stretches from the extinct volcano, Jebel Dokhan, to the coast. Moharrek has a town of the same name and is the residence of the ruling Sheikh, 'Isa bin 'Ali, but Menameh on the large island is the centre of trade, and the harbour for the pearl fisheries and the steamers from the Gulf ports. The total population of the islands is estimated at 50,000 *(Persian Gulf Pilot)*, all of which is Moslem with the exception of about sixty resident Hindu traders.

"The pearl-fisheries are carried on from June to October, and nearly all the island population are engaged in the work in one way or another. During the height of the season more than four thousand boats are said to visit the pearl-banks, and the total number of fishermen is over 30,000. They come from Lingah and other parts of the Gulf; but that the control of the work is mostly in hands of Bahrein fishermen can be judged from the fact that of the total export of Gulf pearls in 1889, valued at £ 430,000, two-thirds passed through the Bahrein customs. The pearl divers do not, however,

1. Two were opened by Theodore Bent in 1889.

receive the fair profit due their costly toil. A clothes-pin-like clasp, called *ftam*, holds the nostrils, wax protects the ear, while strong, claw-like gloves, a basket and a rope of date fibre completes their diving suit; then they plunge down, remain two or three minutes, and return with a basketful of hope.

"My first visit to the islands was on December 7th, 1892, and I remained there until the end of the year; a second visit was made in February for a longer time, and now we can call Bahrein the first out-station of the Arabian Mission from Basrah, our head-quarters. On a first visit we were in doubt whether it would be possible even to remain on the island, not to speak of carrying on Gospel work; now a Bible and book-shop has been established, and we believe God has opened this door not to close it again.

"When I came on shore from the mail-steamer in December, the English Government postmaster, a Portuguese, welcomed me and showed me much kindness. Two weeks after I obtained upper rooms in a house adjoining a Mosque and could receive visitors on my own account. The Arabs received me with less prejudice than I expected. I suppose the medicine-chest I carried, and a wonder-working electric-machine were the indirect cause of their kindness. All Arabs are hospitable to strangers, but on the whole Arabian coast they have learned to suspect Christians who come with the Book. Great numbers came for treatment every day, and many of them I was able to help in some way or other. Fever, rheumatism, and ulcers were most common.

"Two weeks before my arrival, colporteurs of the British and Foreign Bible Society from Bushire met with rough treatment in the bazaar and had to leave; on this account I was perhaps too cautious at first in selling Scriptures openly. However, of the sixty portions of the Word of God which I took with me on my first visit forty-four were sold before I left. Since then two large boxes of books and Bibles have come to our Bahrein depot, and by arrangement with the British and Foreign Bible Society the work is now in the hands of our Mission.

"Mission work has begun at Bahrein. Those who had never seen, now buy and read the Word of God, many, we hope, intelligently. Opposition here, although expected and even inevitable, can never reach that stage possible in places directly under Turkish rule. Will you not pray earnestly for these islanders that in their search after pearls they may seek and find the Pearl of Great Price?

"In the early morning of last Christmas-day at Bahrein there was a light shower of rain from the West; the sun arose over the Gulf without a cloud, and then I saw for the first time and in Arabia a double rainbow, two concentric arches, perfect and beautiful above the lime-stone houses and palm-trees of Menameh. Was it not the bow of God's promise, sure and precious, Christ's Christmas greeting to Behrein: 'He shall set judgment in the earth: and the isles shall wait for his law'?"

It is a far cry from the pearl divers and medieval life of the bazaar in those days to the oil wells and great refineries, the port facilities and air-cooled houses of our own day on Bahrein! Yet, in spite of all the opposition and the small outward results that were apparent, in spite of the sacrifice of life and the intense heat and fever and loneliness, Zwemer could exclaim as he looked back fifty years later, "But the sheer joy of it all comes back . . . . How gladly would I do it all over again in some unoccupied seaport of Western Arabia."

I I

Since the Old Testament Samuel is not mentioned in the Koran and the name Zwemer seemed difficult for the Arabs to remember or pronounce the young missionary adopted the name Dhaif Allah, meaning the Guest of God, which seemed the more appropriate since the bearer of the name was a guest in Arabia. This was the name of an Arab who had befriended the great explorer Doughty, and Zwemer got the name from his account.[2] (The Arabs, when sometimes unfriendly, called him "Dhaif Shaitan"— guest of the Devil!) Strangely enough a son of the original friend of Doughty later came to the Mission hospital.

Very early in his career he began the travels over the territory of the Mission which lay outside the occupied station. The new mission had scarcely been settled in Basrah when Zwemer left to visit points in central Iraq. The country was still generally known at that time as Mesopotamia, or the land between two rivers—and two mighty rivers they are, the Tigris and Euphrates.

He took the river steamer to Baghdad, arriving there in late July, 1892 and left that city on the 27th to visit the shrine city of Hillah and go on down the Euphrates. Friends in Baghdad endeavored to persuade him to postpone the journey for three reasons. It was the very hottest season of the year, it was the Mohammedan month of Muharram when Shiah Moslems would be in fanatical mourning for their saints Ali and Hussain, especially in the shrine cities of Iraq, since Hussain is buried at Kerbela; and there were known to be river pirates and robber bands at various places on the proposed route.

None of these considerations daunted the young missionary. In company with a Moslem who had been interested in Christianity in Baghdad he set out; we may quote from his own account of the journey: ". . . . We hired two mules and left the city of the old caliphs with a caravan for Kerbela, at four p.m., July 27, and made our first halt that night four hours from Baghdad, sleeping on a blanket under the stars. An hour after midnight the pack-saddles were lifted in place and again we were off. It was a mixed company: Arabs, Persians, and Turks; merchants for Hillah, and pilgrims to the sacred shrines; women in those curtained, cage-like structures called *Taht-i-vans*—two portable *zenanas* hanging from each beast; derwishes on foot with green turbans, heavy canes and awful visages; and, to complete the picture,

---

2. Doughty's **Arabia Deserts,** Vol. I, p. 390.

a number of rude coffins strapped crosswise on pack-mules and holding the remains of true believers, long since ready for the holy ground at Nejf."

Because of the intense heat the caravan traveled mostly at night. Zwemer made friends in villages wherever they stopped, sold some copies of Scripture and helped people by dispensing simple remedies like quinine. The traveler continues:

"At three o'clock in the morning we left Haswa, and, because of a delay on the road, it was nearly noon when we reached the river. The bazaar and business of Hillah formerly were on the Babylonian side of the stream, but now principally on the further side of the rickety bridge of boats, four miles below the ruins of Babylon. After paying toll, we crossed over and found a room in the Khan Pasha—a close, dirty place, but in the midst of the town and near the river. The two and a half days at Hillah were very trying because of the heat." [3]

Concerning similar heat the traveler quoted one of his comrades in the Arabian Mission as writing:

"June 10.—I write; it is too hot to do anything else. I cannot sleep, nor read, nor do anything; it is 107 in the coolest part of the veranda. The pen is hot, the paper is hot and the ink won't run. I am sitting with a wet towel on my head to prevent my being overcome with the heat. Oh, it is nice and comfortable here, but you have to be very fond of heat to enjoy it. My head feels as big as a barrel, and the wet towel is all that keeps me from having another sunstroke . . . . When we use a medical thermometer we are obliged to put it in a glass of water to bring it down to normal temperature."

On the last day of July the missionary and his companion left Hillah in a native boat to sail down the Euphrates. They found this river more muddy than the Tigris and at various places there are shallow rapids. When boats are held up at these points they are often set upon and robbed by the pirates who live in mat huts in the glades of tall reeds along the many side channels where it is all but impossible to reach them.

The native boat traveled mostly at night to avoid the heat, but made some progress in the daytime. A stop was made at Diwanieh where the missionary was a guest of the Turkish governor. There were large groves of palm trees and a customs house and toll bridge. The customs was largely for the wheat trade down the river. The governor, when asked, said that the river was unsafe but he would supply the traveler with a guard.

Two soldiers were added to the party who shared the dates and bread of the American and took the occasion of the boat ride to patch their uniforms and polish their single shot rifles which bore the mark "U.S. Springfield. Pat. 1863" and may have been relics of the Civil War.

The missionary noted that the Arab tribes along this part of the river were not true nomads but lived in settled villages on fish and the products of the

---

3. This and subsequent references, unless otherwise noted, are from **The Golden Milestone**, 50th anniversary volume of the Arabian Mission.

huge black river buffalo. After watching a herd of these animals swim the river with shouting and swearing herdsmen after them in the water, he ejaculated, "And this was once the home of Abraham, the friend of God!"

The journey continued down the river through dangerous rapids to the town of Samawa. The missionary obtained a room in a caravansarai and writes of his experience:

"I remained at home, therefore, until the following day and saw the confusion of the night of Ashera from the window, the tramp of a mob, the beating of breasts, the wailing of women, the bloody banners and mock-martyr scenes, the rhythmic howling and cries of 'Ya Ali! ya Hassan! ya Hussein!' until the throats were hoarse and hands hung heavy for a moment, only to go at it again.

"The following day I went about the town freely and spoke and sold books to those who came to the khan. Samawa is smaller than Hillah; four-fifths of the population, I was told, are Shiah, and there are forty Jews, but no Christians. A bridge of boats crosses the river and leads from the Serai to the Sunni coffee houses on the eastern bank. West of the town stretches the open desert plain, fourteen camel marches to Hail, the capital of Al Nejd." How Zwemer longed for the interior!

On the fourth of August the travelers took another boat loaded with barley for Basrah. The only place where shade could be found was a low cabin at the rear filled with boxes, ropes, lanterns and other paraphernalia of the ship. Here the missionary gave the first lessons in reading to his companion who was an inquirer. He also read to him the entire Gospel of John.

The river becomes broader below Samawa and is more easily navigable. With stops at one or two places they reached the government center Markaz, also called Nasiriyeh, which latter name may signify that there had formerly been a number of Christian inhabitants. There were still a few nominal followers of Christ in the town. The missionary had dinner with the head of the telegraph who invited several other Christians and they had fellowship in Scripture reading and prayer. There were also members of the Sebean sect, or Disciples of St. John, in Markaz and at other points further down the river. In his careful diaries which the traveler kept there is still an accurate plan of Markaz with the location of all principal points of interest.

Three hours to the west of the town lie the ruins of Ur of the Chaldees but the missionary did not have the opportunity to visit these mounds, which many years later would yield so much of interest to the excavator.

On down the river went the boat to Suk Al Shiukh or "The Bazaar of Old Men." Here friends were made but a letter of introduction to one of the Sebeans was torn up after he had read it and thrown away. Later all the people of this sect in the place were called up for entering into a plot with an Englishman. The itinerant missionary was finally able to explain that he was not an Englishman and had no part in a political plot, but he was forbidden to sell books in the town.

There was a delay over this incident and the travelers ran short of provisions. The boat crew were fanatical Moslems and not willing to share their food or cooking arrangements with a Christian.

fanatical
Muslims.

As they went on down the river the marsh lands increased, with great areas covered with reeds and rushes, inhabited by tribes who kept their large black buffalo cattle, and who were known as the Ma'dan pirates—the terror of the river boatmen. The traveler recounts that many of these Bedouins of the swamps live a large part of their time in the water and have not even arrived at the loin cloth stage of civilization. There were also great clouds of insects along the river in this marshy country.

A change was made to another boat at Kurna on August 11th and by an overnight trip to Basrah. On arrival there the young missionary wrote in his diary:

"Seven hundred miles of touring along populous rivers and historic ruins; seven hundred miles of Moslem empire awaiting the conquests of the Cross; one missionary at Baghdad and two at Basrah; what are these among so many? The Euphrates and Tigris are the natural highways for the Gospel in North Arabia, even as the Nile is for that other land of the patriarchs, Egypt. And even so should they be occupied, village after village, by schools and Gospel agencies."

III

In late September, 1893 Cantine came down from Basrah to take over the work in Bahrein and Zwemer left a few days later, for a journey inland to Hassa, Hefhuf and other points.

Aside from exploration of the field there was a desire to find a place inland where members of the Mission might go in summer to escape the terrific heat of the Gulf; cholera was also raging at the time of this journey and it was thought an inland place might be free from this epidemic which was claiming thousands of victims at Bahrein and other points around the Persian Gulf.

The journey started by donkey caravan down to the southern point of the island. There the various members of the party paused at a coffee house for a very leisurely farewell. Finally they waded out several hundred yards through shallow water and reached their boat which left about sunset and with a fair wind reached Ojeir on the mainland coast the next morning.

At this point there was no town but a large Turkish customs house, as much trade in cloth, rice, sugar, coffee and other commodities comes to the interior by this port, from which dates and other products are also shipped.

Around the customs house there was the tumult and the shouting of loading seven hundred camels for the journey to the interior. After some difficulty concerning his passport the missionary joined himself to the caravan of one named Salih of Nejd. The party was off without great delay over the typical desert, broken only here and there by ridges of sand. That night certain of the Arabs dug shallow wells with their hands in the bottom of a wady and obtained drinking water. The traveler slept on the warm sand under the stars, rolled in a blanket. After the high temperatures of the day the nights seemed cold by comparison.

About noon of the second day they sighted the palm groves that surround the city of Holhuf. Zwemer cites the famous description of this city by Palgrave who says from afar it has "the general aspect of a white and yellow onyx chased in an emerald rim."

On reaching the section of palms and gardens the caravan stopped where its leader and the missionary were welcomed by a friend of Salih and served a very fine meal.

At sunset they started again and passed on through gardens and other villages. There were small rushing streams of tepid water which made a contrast to the arid desert over which they had so recently passed. The night was spent in one of the suburban villages where the missionary sold some Scriptures and had interesting conversation for several hours.

An early start was made and the caravan passed through gardens and date groves, over all hung the morning mist. The traveler comments, "At seven o'clock the mosques and walls of Holhuf appeared right before us as the sun lifted the veil; it was a beautiful sight."

The American went directly to the government headquarters and was received with great politeness and given a room in the government buildings. There he was able to entertain visitors and worked for several days visiting the bazaars and coffee shops. He sold all the Scriptures he had brought along, even his own New Testament, and upbraided himself for lack of faith in not bringing more copies of Scripture. As it was, all of his outfit for the road, including food, bedding and books, had been packed in one pair of camel saddlebags.

The return was planned by an overland journey northward to Kateef. He was forced to sign to the effect that the government would not be responsible for any harm which might befall him, as he was warned that the road was unsafe.

The caravan passed gardens and fields of rice and swamps which the missionary records were very unlike the descriptions of Arabia in the geography books. However, within a few hours they were again on the desert.

Although there was no attack from robbers, the beating sun on the desert proved too hot for the American travelers and a fever came on which he could not shake off until his return to Bahrein. With a handwriting that shows the effects of the fever he records, "It's fearfully hot. With my umbrella and blanket I have made a sort of tent under a bush." The caravan traveled mostly at night and on the fourth day they came to the palm groves, wells and ancient aqueducts of the Kateef environs. At last they saw the sea. The price of the camel ride from Hofhuf to the sea was four dollars.

After a bit of rest and refreshment a boat was hired and the return trip was made to Bahrein. The traveler was still suffering from fever and at times had a temperature of more than 104°F.

I V

Though Lowell Thomas was never able to get to Sana'a in Yemen, Zwemer visited the closed city twice in the early days of the Arabian Mission.

The first journey was made in 1891. On the twenty-seventh of June he left Aden on the little freight steamer *Tuna* and made the first leg of the journey in two days around through the famous straits of Bab-el-Mandeb and up the Red Sea coast to Hodeida. There had recently been a rebellion against the Turkish authority in the region of Sana'a but the young missionary adventurer hired a mule and set out.

Yemen, or Arabia Felix of the ancients, is a land of mountains and productive terraced hillsides. We should have Zwemer's own description of the journey:

"I found no trouble or difficulty, however, anywhere on the road to Sana'a, although the country generally was unsettled. The journey took six days on mule-back. The natural scenery all the way up to the mountains is beautiful, and the terraced hills are covered with vegetation. When I left Aden the temperature was 104°F. but halfway to Sana'a, at Suk-el-Khamis, it was 58°F. at sunrise. The plateau around Sana'a is pasture land. We saw camels, cows and sheep by hundreds. But the mountainsides are cultivated for coffee, millet, grapes and other fruit. I am still surprised, as I look back, that the Turks were so friendly and the people so hospitable at that time. God tempers the wind to the shorn lamb . . . . and I was then only a kid!" [4]

It should be noted that this is the region of Arabia where the finest Mocha coffee is grown. Temperatures change very rapidly and there were very hard downpours of rain accompanied with lightning and thunder on the journey.

In Sana'a after the usual formalities of government inspection the missionary had a good deal of freedom to work about the city; though his passport was held until the time of his departure. He met a Syrian convert who seemed to be a devoted Christian and a man of prayer. He found a few other Christians and visited a large colony of Jews; he notes in the diary that they had some thirty-nine synagogues in the region.

The journey was made back over the same route to Hodeida. The missionary was especially impressed at Bajil on the way when an old Sheikh kissed the book that was handed him when he found it was the *Injil*, or New Testament. After a few days' wait the streamer came and the return was

---

4. **The Golden Milestone.**

made to Aden. There, however, the passengers were kept on board seven days in quarantine because there was news of cholera at some of the Red Sea ports.

The second journey to Sana'a was made at the request of the Mildmay Mission to the Jews. This London society had heard of the earlier visit and Zwemer was asked to distribute two boxes of New Testaments to Jews in Yemen. The society undertook all expenses for the journey.

This time it was made overland from Yemen as it was desired to reach Jews of intermediate towns with Scriptures.

The cavalcade started with a caravan on July 2, 1894. The early stages were through barren desert country but when the mountains were reached there was rich vegetation and a much cooler climate.

Trouble awaited the party at the first customs house they encountered at a small place named Mufallis. They were informed by the very bad mannered man in charge of the station that no books were allowed to enter Yemen. All the Scriptures, as well as maps and other literature, were taken and held. The party went on to Taiz to make an appeal to the governor.

On the road they were overtaken by a severe downpour of rain followed by hail. The donkey of their Arab guide was carried away by a torrent, where a short time before there had been only a dry wady. The camels were stampeded by the hail and only after a great deal of trouble the party finally found a house, after a steep climb up a hill through the mud. They were kindly received by the owner of the house, one Sheikh Ali.

A war party of some sixty wild Bedouins descended on a village where they were staying the next night, but after butchering a cow belonging to one of the villagers and eating to their full of this and other food they demanded, the raiding party left.

After reaching Taiz the governor sent for the books but the missionary had to pay for the camel to bring them and give money for customs duty to a soldier who went to get them. The first man was waylaid and robbed of his rifle, a second soldier finally brought the books and they were sent on to Sana'a under guard which the traveler later discovered was also a guard over him. The soldiers carried a letter which informed the authorities, "This is a converted Jew, Ishmail, who is corrupting the religion of Islam, and sells books to Moslems and Jews."

Sana'a was reached on August 2nd, just one month after the departure from Aden. He was at first held in the care of a policeman and finally released when a Greek friend from Aden went bail for him. Then began a series of trips from office to office until ten days later the books were finally released. The governor sent word that he must not remain in the city more than a week. As a recapitulation of the reasons for this venture let us quote a hitherto unpublished letter from Zwemer to his sister Nellie in China. It it dated August 9, 1894, Sana'a, Yemen. He writes:

"My dear Sister:

"The way here from Aden did not lack in adventure. Some of it only trying to my patience, other to my purse, but most of it was free from danger. It took us eight days of climbing to reach *Taiz* the first big city of Yemen. On the way we had a heavy hail and thunder storm that filled all the wadies, swept away the donkey of our guide and when the camels stampeded I lost my umbrella and part of my outfit! It was the worst storm in which I ever had to sit under a bush! At night we found a house. The next day all my books were seized at the Customs, in spite of every effort I could only get back Sprenger and the German authority as guides. All the rest were declared 'forbidden.'

"I went on to Taiz to enter complaint. The day before we arrived I sprained my ankle pretty badly in climbing and so was a sort of prisoner on board a camel ship only dismounting to limp with a cane. At Taiz I waited in a dirty coffee shop 15 long weary days on the red-tape government. One soldier who was sent for my books was attacked on the road, stabbed, and robbed of his rifle! The next messenger brought the books at my expense of course even for the sealing wax with which the boxes were sealed. Again I plead in vain and was sent with the books under guard to Sana'a. While at Taiz I tried to preach a little bit but a mob went to the governor's house and demanded my expulsion. I was warned not to speak to any Arab under penalty of being sent a prisoner to the coast. Finally we started off, I on a mule and my soldier guard on fine white horses, my servant on foot, and the books of Hebrew Scriptures on a camel. At the first station Ibb my servant was put into jail because he gave the name of some villages en route to me! After an hour walking about in the rain, from official to official, I got him free. No adventure after that up to Sana'a except that a poor Jew with whom I tried to speak was beaten and cursed because he ventured near the "guard." At Sana'a I obtained liberty through my passport. But I believe I am very closely watched and so I 'walk with wisdom toward those that are without,'—sometimes I fear to the discredit of my Captain in Chief who feared not the face of man.

"The Scriptures are still being inspected and this is the eighth day I am here! Job himself would grow weary of seeing Turkish officials. What is worse, I am bankrup—at Yermin in the 'kawah' I was robbed of 3 pounds which I had kept to the last. With some difficulty I have borrowed a little of a Greek merchant and now must wait for word from Aden. The road onward is *open* but whether I shall go I know not.[5]. These delays were not in my program. My health is excellent; foot better; food plentiful; fruit cheap; and lodging clean though naked and bare. Have read over ⅔ of my English Bible on route, not a bad job for vacation. God bless you; I *pray* for *all* every day but still feel lonesome. Yours, 'Sam.'"

The object of his journey having been accomplished he reteurned to the coast and on to Aden by steamer. The journey had not been easy. The

<hr>

5. Zwemer had planned if possible after visiting Sana'a to make the long caravan journey right across central Arabia to the Persian Gulf somewhere in the vicinity of Bahrein.

only places to stay in the villages were filled with vermin and few things to eat were found aside from bread and dates. Zwemer carried a box of cocoa and hot milk was often obtainable. Indeed it seems a wonder that he was able to make the journey at all. At one place he was only saved by his guide taking a three-fold Bedouin oath that he was not a government agent or an Englishman. At another point there was a lively argument as to whether or not he should be taken and held for ransom.

An account in the *Edinburgh Scotsman* was printed under the title, "A Dauntless American." It told of his journey and commented "A Dutch-American like this young fellow, with a good Arab tongue in his head, is not easily daunted." It is quite true that one who combines the stubbornness of the Dutch and the inquisitive American spirit and the zeal of a pioneer for Christ is not easy to stop.

VI

Seeking Recruits and Funds

"If these great things are to be achieved we must pay what it costs. What will be the price? Undoubtedly it involves giving ourselves to the study of missionary problems and strategy with all the thoroughness and tirelessness which have characterized the intellectual work of those men who have brought most benefit to mankind. It will cost genuine self-denial. In no sphere so much as that of extending the knowledge and sway of Christ is the truth of His own word illustrated, 'Except a grain of wheat fall into the earth and die, it abideth by itself alone; but if it die, it beareth much fruit.'"

The First Two Decades of the
Student Volunteer Movement,
by JOHN R. MOTT

CHAPTER SIX

SEEKING RECRUITS AND FUNDS

Once, while in the capital city of Yemen, Sana'a, Zwemer was attempting to sell Scriptures. He was advised by a man whom he met on the street to go to the Casino where he could sell a number of books, the informer thought, to the Turkish officers. This proved true and he had soon disposed of some half dozen New Testaments.

The officers had not had them long, however, when they wanted to return them and get the money. The missionary on asking the reason was told that the bartender was a Christian and he had said these books were not the genuine *Injil* but only an imitation put out by the Protestants. Zwemer asked who this man was and where he was from. It turned out he was a Greek from Crete.

The young distributor of the Bible said at once, "No wonder he speaks against this book, because of what it says about the people of Crete. Whereupon he read to the officers, "One of themselves, even a prophet of their own, said, the Cretans are always liars, evil beasts, slow bellies. This witness is true."[1]

The bartender contended that this was merely one of the corruptions of the New Testament and the real Greek New Testament contained no such statement. The missionary had the answer for this. He produced a Greek Testament and convinced the bartender, who bought and paid for the Greek Testament . The laugh was on him and the Turkish officers kept their Scriptures, all the more anxious to read a book that was so applicable to present situations.

Zwemer used to say that from this and many similar happenings he believed in "verbal inspiration." Certainly the Master Himself told his followers not to fear when called before authorities, as what they should say would be given unto them. The pioneers of the Arabian Mission depended upon such guidance at every step.

In spite of heavy sacrifice of life in the early years,[2] the Arabian Mission was well established with four stations, several doctors and a number of

1. Titus 1:12-13.
2. Seven lives were sacrificed in the Arabian Mission in a period of about seven years. They were as follows:
   Rev. Peter J. Zwemer, died of effects of fever and debility, October 18, 1898.
   Rev. George E. Stone, died from heat apoplexy, June 28, 1899.
   Rev. Harry J. Wiersum, died a victim of smallpox, August 3, 1901.
   Ruth Zwemer, aged 4, died of dysentery, July 7, 1904.
   Katharina Zwemer, aged 7, died of dysentery, July 15, 1904.
   Mrs. Marion Wells Thoms, M.D., died of typhoid, April 25, 1905.
   Mrs. Jessie Vail Bennett, died of typhoid, January 21, 1906.

Second time home/ for a to seek support
This time few years

women missionaries by 1905. In March of that year the Zwemer family left for their second furlough in America. Though on leaving they little realized the fact, it would be several years before they returned to their home in Bahrein.

Upon arrival in the United States they went to Holland, Michigan and took up at once the task of raising money in the churches for the Arabian Mission and other work of the Reformed Board. He proposed at this time a system of specific support of missionaries by individual churches. He delved back into the history of Missions and found that such an arrangement had been proposed by leaders of the Church Missionary Society more than sixty years before this time. Baptists and Presbyterians had also used such a plan. Zwemer went forth to tell the churches:

"People can be interested in men easier than in machinery. By raising a special sum, in addition to their usual offerings, for their 'own missionary,' the contributors cannot help but feel that in a special way they have hearkened to the command, 'Go ye into all the world and preach the Gospel.' The personal equation counts for much, not only in the matter of finance but in the stimulus it gives to prayer. And who can tell how much strength it gives to a missionary to know that there is a company of believers whose thoughts and efforts and prayers are focussed on his field of work? In addition there comes to him the stimulus of the fact that those who deny themselves for his sake, nay for Christ's sake, are considering him their representative. *Nobless oblige.*"

Along with speaking and writing along these lines the furloughed missionary distributed a small tract he had written with the title "Per Capita." On the cover was a picture of Christ wearing the crown of thorns. Statistics were given as to the Per Capita giving of the Reformed Church in the various Synods. He then went on to comment:

"It is perfectly evident from such statistics that we are facing an arbitrary standard, that is, a PER CAPITA — per head. By derivation, PER CAPITA evidently has little to do with the heart, and yet until our PER CAPITA gifts come EX CORDE we cannot expect them to rise to a much larger amount. If, as a denomination, we are to cease living at this 'poor dying rate,' we need God's Spirit to give us a new dynamic for denominational benevolences.

"We shall never understand the real significance of PER CAPITA until we stop counting heads in the congregation, and gaze upward to see the head of our Lord.

> 'O sacred Head, now wounded
>   With grief and shame weighed down,
> O kingly Head, surrounded
>   With thorns, Thine only crown . . . .'
>
> 'O make me Thine forever;
>   O may I faithful be;
> Lord, let me never, never,
>   Outlive my love to Thee.'

"These words go back to Bernard of Clairvaux, and the days of the Crusades, when men sacrificed all to win an empty sepulchre. How much do we sacrifice to proclaim a living Saviour? Or is it possible that some of us have 'outlived' our love for Him?"

Two incidents illustrate Zwemer's ready wit and ability to raise money for missions. He visited an Iowa farmer who declined to give because he thought some in the mission or Board did not hold the proper view of *Inspiration*. The missionary asked the farmer for a statement of what he believed inspiration to be. He replied that Zwemer knew better than he and that he had heard him preach and thought he was all right. So Zwemer asked, "Do you believe God inspires people *now?*" The farmer said he did not. Zwemer said, "I'll prove it to you. Let me see your check book. Now write the date, you know what date it is don't you? Now write your name." The farmer did so. "Now," said Zwemer, "God will inspire you as to what amount you should write in there in figures and in words, let us pray." The amount was not small.

At the time of the second incident Zwemer was at dinner with a Dutch family. He asked the husband directly for a contribution to mission work, but he declined to give. The wife urged him, however, to give something. Zwemer asked, "Who is the head of this house anyway?" The wife replied that her husband was, but he modestly said his wife was head of the house. The visitor then pointed to a wall plaque which read, "Christ is the Head of this House." He asked, "Now is that true or is it not?" The contribution was made.

Aside from the general promotion of missionary giving, and response for the other missions of the church, he kept careful account of gifts he raised for the work in Arabia. They amounted in that first year at home to $32,886. The salary of a missionary on the field at this time was $900 a year.

About this time Zwemer and his family had a very sobering experience which cast a shadow over their life and work, yet in the end gave a great and abiding assurance of the power of prayer. In Arabia and especially after his return to America Zwemer's eyes had been giving him considerable trouble. He had consulted an oculist in Grand Rapids, Michigan, and by reference from him had visited a noted specialist in New York City. The latter wrote in part as follows:

May 15, 1905
New York

"Dr. J. G. H.
Grand Rapids, Michigan

"My dear Dr. H.:

"Many thanks for your kindness in advising Dr. Zwemer to consult me regarding his eyes.

"Your diagnosis of insipient atrophy of the optic nerves is perfectly correct. I am at a loss to know what has occasioned it . . .

Very sincerely yours,
J. E. W——, M.D."

Things went along with continued examinations, but the following letter came like something of a bombshell:

6/1/06

"Rev. S. M. Zwemer,
My dear Sir,
    "After a careful examination of your eyes I am of the opinion that the atrophy of the optic nerves is progressive and that therefore the prognosis is very unfavorable and that in the usual course of events you may expect to gradually lose your sight. This may take years but would be hastened by your return to Arabia. I am extremely sorry to have to make so gloomy a report.

Cordially,
J. G. H.——, M.D."

In hopes that this might not be the last word in the case there were other consultations in New York and finally the suggestion that there did not seem any escape from the blindness gradually creeping on through the hardening of the optic nerves, yet to leave no stone unturned a world-famous German specialist might be consulted.

As at every crisis in the life of Samuel Zwemer there was a friend ready to send him on this journey of last hope. In fact Mr. E. E. Olcott, who with his wife were great and good friends of the Arabian Mission, was willing to send his wife along and to pay the expense of a serious operation if there should be a possibility in that way of saving the eyesight.

When confronted with the fact of possible loss of vision Zwemer prayed that in any case, if it should be the Lord's will, he might continue his missionary service. He called his oldest daughter and asked her, "Will you be my right hand if later I become blind?" Nothing could daunt his spirit!

When the book *Islam A Challenge to Faith* was published, the dedication to his wife was in Greek, in reference to her as "My companion in tribulation" the author referred to the approaching blindness with which he was threatened.

The Specialist in Grand Rapids was consulted in regard to the trip and he replied in part:

"There is no reason why you should not accept the very kind offer. . . I am not sure that there is anything to be gained by it so far as your eyes are concerned and yet we must not be too sure on that point.

"But it will be a matter of considerable satisfaction to yourself and friends if you have done *all* that could be done, and principally for this reason would I advise the trip.

"I cannot praise Dr. Pagenstecher's ability as an oculist too much. He is one of the world's great men and I am sure you will profit by meeting him in more ways than one."

Arrangements were made for the journey and early in March they arrived in Wiesbaden and consulted Professor Dr. Hermann Pagenstecher. There was a series of examinations and the noted specialist took Zwemer before the class in his clinic to show the unusual condition of the optic nerves, not easily diagnosed.

On March 16th, 1907, the specialist was able to write

> "I must write to you a few lines about Mr. Zwemer. I am glad to say that there is no danger that he will lose his sight, which is now good and which will always enable him to go on with his work. His general health has suffered a little by the hot climate . . . In consequence of that his optic nerves are a little pale in the center, a symptom which is not alarming.
>
> "I gave him a remedy to strengthen his general health and his nerves and he begins to look and to feel better. Besides that I am treating a chronic infection of the nervous membranes of the eyes which is making good progress and will come to a healing. With kind regards,
>
> Yours very truly,
>
> HERMANN PAGENSTECHER."

With this letter was kept as a prize possession and a trophy of grace the noted doctor's receipted bill for 160 marks, the total cost of his treatment and "cure." By the third of April the Zwemers were back in New York with hearts full of thankfulness and praise that the cloud had passed and the sun was shining in all its glory again.

It was shortly after this that Zwemer began the practice which was to characterize him for the balance of his life as a man with many irons in the fire — when he was not busy with one thing he was busy with several. He was asked to accept a three-year appointment as traveling secretary for the Student Volunteer Movement to visit the colleges, universities and student conferences to inspire and to recruit for the missionary enterprise. It was some years later that Cleland McAfee said, "The consecration of young life is the vital nerve of the missionary enterprise." Zwemer felt this same truth and so he was constrained to accept this call. About the same time he was asked to become Field Secretary for the Reformed Board of Foreign Missions. This was work in which he had proven his usefulness and which he was, perhaps, better qualified than any other to do. It included, moreover, the support of the Arabian Mission — his own Mission in a very true sense and the cause nearest his heart.

It was evident that the choice between these two calls would be most difficult, so he accepted both. Shortly after the birth of their daughter Mary the Zwemers moved from Holland, Michigan, to Mount Vernon, New York, to be near the headquarters of the organizations he was to represent.

The year 1908 began with visits to Yale, Auburn, Virginia and other universities and seminaries throughout the East. When he was advertized in the colleges the initials F.R.G.S. were often added to his name, the meaning of which even some of the college students had to inquire. There is, in fact, quite a story connected with these letters. When returning from a visit to Sana'a on the boat to India there were several British officers and Government officials on board. In the course of conversation the young missionary described his trip to the capital city of Yemen. They were at first reluctant to believe that he had actually made his way alone to Sana'a, but when they were convinced one of them asked if he would accept a nomination to the Royal Geographical Society, and the questioner turned to another of the party asking, "Colonel, would you second the nomination?" The Colonel was willing, and so some time later the news came that he had been elected a Fellow of the Royal Geographical Society. The initial fee for membership was twenty pounds Sterling, as Zwemer remembered it. Though the amount nearly floored the prospective member and caused Cantine much mirth at his expense, still he raised the fee and sent it. At a later time he was elected an honorary member for life.

There were student conferences in Oklahoma and Colorado during May and June. Later in the summer the traveler went to Europe again for the Baslow Student Conference of 1908. The major portion of his work throughout the year was for the Student Volunteer Movement.

That his mind was still on the work for Mohammedans, however, is illustrated from an incident in the home at Mount Vernon. The boy, Raymund, who was six or seven years old, was playing with some papers on the floor. His mother called him several times but he did not answer. Finally the father, from the next room, said, "Raymund don't you hear your mother calling you?" The boy replied, "Tell her I'm busy. I'm making a map of the Moslem World."

Throughout the year 1909 Zwemer continued to work for the Reformed Board in raising funds, and for the S.V.M. in finding missionary recruits. The arrangement was that the Board continued to pay his salary and the Volunteer Movement his travel expenses. Throughout these years, as all his life, enough money was provided to meet the expenses of the family, but like the manna in the wilderness there was nothing left over. On various occasions in later life Zwemer made the remark, "I have always lived from hand to mouth, but it has been the Lord's hand and my mouth."

In addition to other responsibilities he took on, about this time, the solicitation of funds for the Nile Mission Press. Yet divided attention did not seem to make him less effective in any one of the directions taken by his effort. All of the work seemed to fit in together like a jig-saw puzzle and as he often said there was no way to account for the fact aside from the guiding hand of God in all of it.

Amy Ruth was very ill at home in Mount Vernon, New York, but was well enough so that the father could leave to attend the Laymen's Convention in Birmingham, Alabama, February 16, 1909. Then he returned directly for a week at the University of Wisconsin in the latter part of the same month. In April there was the Missionary Congress in Toronto. In all of these and many others Zwemer was one of the most powerful speakers.

In May he was again at the University of Virginia and shortly after at Johns Hopkins in Baltimore. As he raced across the Campus there from one meeting to another he was accompanied by a young medical student by the name of Paul W. Harrison. They talked as they ran, the student said that if Zwemer could prove that Arabia was the most difficult field in the world he would go there as a medical missionary. Gasping for breath as they ran the older man promised to prove that to him the next day if he would come around and talk to him. He did, the case was proved, Harrison went to Arabia and became one of the best known medical missionaries of the world.

Zwemer taught courses on Islam and the need of the Moslem World for the Christian Gospel at conferences in Ashville, North Carolina, Lake Geneva, Northfield and other places. He continued work in colleges and the churches throughout the year, his efforts being crowned with more than ordinary success. He began to be wearied, however, with the constant schedule of trains and he longed to be back in the heat and humidity of the Persian Gulf among his beloved Arabs.

One incident in raising funds would never be forgotten. Dr. John Timothy Stone had given the missionary the opportunity of speaking five minutes from his pulpit at the Sunday morning service. Following this Zwemer was invited to dinner with Mrs. Nettie McCormick. Without too much in the way of persuasion the good lady was constrained to make a donation toward the Nile Mission Press, which desired a new building in Cairo for this great work of spreading Christian Literature among Moslems.

Mrs. McCormick made out a check and handed it to the solicitor. He soon afterward politely excused himself and left. He wanted to see the amount of the check. It was for $10,000. He also noted it was made out to Arthur J. Brown, the Secretary of the Presbyterian Board of Foreign Missions, for the Nile Mission Press. Of course, another sales talk was required upon the return to New York to get Brown to endorse the check for this enterprise, but it was accomplished and the Nile Mission Press was assured of its building.

The young missionary was becoming more and more anxious to return to Arabia but was persuaded by Dr. John R. Mott to stay over for the Student Volunteer Convention held in Rochester in January, 1910, where he proved again to be a powerful influence. He was appointed a member of Committee No. I for the General Missionary Conference which was to be held in Edinburgh. This was the section on the Occupation of the Field. He began at once to center attention on the fields which were not as yet occupied and to gather information concerning them.

In the meantime visits to universities and colleges continued. The University of Chicago and Harvard were high points on this list, as was the World Sunday School Convention in Washington, D.C., in May of 1910. Later in the month he sailed for the remarkable conference in Edinburgh which was the most widely representative missionary gathering in the world, held up to that time.

A notable event which followed the Edinburgh meeting was the formation of a Committee on the publication of a quarterly magazine concerning the Moslem World. This was the inception of something which was to become a major interest over a period of nearly forty years. Before his return to

America, Zwemer attended a student conference in Denmark during late June and sailed to arrive in New York on the twelfth of July.

Preparations for the return to Arabia were now begun in earnest. Arrangements were made to leave Bessie and Raymund with friends in Chicago. The family sailed taking the two younger daughters. The steamer was the König Albert which left New York September tenth. There was a meeting en route concerning the possible establishment of a hospital in Jedda, the port of Mecca, under the auspices of the British C.M.S. This plan was frustrated but afterwards taken up again when Miss Jenny de Mayer made her prolonged visit to Jedda for Christian service.[3] A few days were spent in Egypt. On the twenty-fourth of October the family arrived in the old home at Bahrein. How different it was now from the first arrival to open the pioneer station! There stood the fine hospital with the windmill which Zwemer's mechanical ability had enabled him to assemble and erect with native help. There were also good homes for the new members of the station.

Preparation began at once, however, for the Lucknow Conference and it was not long before the missionary was off for Y.M.C.A. and Y.W. Conferences on the two sides of India, at Bombay and Calcutta. He also visited Benares, Allahabad, the college at Aligarh, Delhi, Lahore and other cities.

The year progressed with entire absorption in the Mission work, but early in September Mrs. Zwemer was forced to return to America with the two little girls because it was necessary for her to make other arrangements for Raymund and Bessie. After the departure of the family, annual meeting was held at Bahrein in November, and in December Zwemer visited Basrah and Baghdad on Mission business.

Mention should be made of the two books written while in America during the period covered. The first was *Islam A Challenge to Faith,* published in 1907; and following the Edinburgh Conference, *The Unoccupied Mission Fields of Africa and Asia.* Both were published by the Student Volunteer Movement and neither the author nor his Mission received any royalty from them. Both had a very wide circulation. The manuscript of a third book, *The Moslem Christ,* was completed at Bahrein in May 1911.

On the journey out from the United States to Arabia the editor was occupied in working on the first number of *The Moslem World.* What busy years these had been! The detention in America had meant much to the Kingdom of Christ in the recruiting of force and the raising of funds. There had been great accomplishments, but the immediate future held even wider horizons of service.

---

3. Cf. **Adventures with God**, by Jenny E. de Mayer. Evangelical Publishers, Toronto, 1948.

VII

In the Land of the Pyramids

"The Church must awake to her duty toward Islam. Who will wake her and keep her awake unless it be those who have heard the challenge of Islam, and who, going out against her, have found her armor decayed, her weapons antiquated and her children, though proud and reticent, still unhappy?"

—ROBERT E. SPEER
at the Cairo Conference

CHAPTER SEVEN

IN THE LAND OF THE PYRAMIDS

After the return to Bahrein, Zwemer was called away from Arabia for conferences and had a large part in planning these, so far as the Moslem world was concerned. From the very beginning his view had extended beyond Arabia and on to Mohammedans wherever they were found. It was not surprising, therefore, that in 1912 a definite call came to him to make headquarters in Cairo and become a general leader in missions to Moslems.

This would indeed be a far different task than the pioneer venture in Bahrein, a work which he had started and where much of his heart lay. Cairo was in a way the capital of Africa as well as of Egypt. It was the intellectual center of the Moslem world and a strategic point of vast influence for Christian missions.

The direct call came from the United Presbyterian Mission in Egypt, but was ably seconded by the British Church Missionary Society and especially by Canon W. H. T. Gairdner who was working for Moslems in Cairo at this time. The Nile Mission Press also joined instantly in the call. (He later became chairman of their publication committee.) He was also to work with the Egypt General Mission, the Y.M.C.A., the American University, and in the production of Arabic Christian literature. In addition he held the responsibility of following up the conferences on Moslem work held in Cairo in 1906 and in Lucknow in 1911.

Negotiations were opened with the Reformed Board under which Zwemer was working in Bahrein. This organization finally consented to the arrangement with the idea that he should still spend time when in America in the work for that Board and the Arabian Mission, which he was certainly more than prepared to do since he did not intend to desert his own church and mission merely because he was called to a field of wider service.

The question of salary did not enter in to so large an extent for by this time the subject of our biography was supported by a special sponsor, a lady of the Southern Presbyterian Church who was willing to underwrite his salary whether in Arabia or Cairo. Much of his travel would be cared for by friends in the American Christian Literature Society for Moslems, which he had founded and of which he was field representative.

There was a hope that such a leader in Cairo would draw the various missions and other Christian organizations together in closer comity. In fact when the proposal was made such enthusiastic response came from both America and Great Britain that the request could not be pushed aside. After careful thought and much searching of heart and prayer, Zwemer decided to accept the call, and thus the change of headquarters to Cairo became the "second milestone" in his missionary career, as the call to Arabia had been the first.

So it was that he left Arabia to return to New York, by way of London, to join his family in America and take them out with him to the Land of the Pyramids. They sailed on September 7th, 1912, on the steamship Princess Irene.

When the matter of the move to Cairo came before the authorities of the Arabia Mission the reasons were so weighty that the following action was taken under date of January 24th, 1912.

"In view of the growing conviction of the need of special inter-denominational activity, as expressed in the resolutions of the Lucknow Conference and of the Arabian Mission, along editorial and general literary lines, in connection with the work among Mohammedans, of which activity Cairo would seem to be the natural center; and in view of Dr. Zwemer's recognized fitness for large service in these directions, it is resolved by the Trustees of the Arabian Mission that if the way shall open to Dr. Zwemer for this special service, and if he shall feel himself divinely called to it, he shall be given by us leave of absence, till further action, from the field in Arabia, so far as may be necessary, in order that he may carry on this projected editorial and literary work, with residence at Cairo.

"In taking the above action, it is, however, the understanding and the desire of the Trustees of the Arabian Mission that Dr. Zwemer shall still retain his relationship to them, and to the Church in which he has already rendered such distinguished service, in order that he may spend if possible a portion of his time with the mission of which he was a pioneer, and that the Church in which he has such wide and valuable personal connection, may have the needed benefit of his counsels and his influence in its missionary responsibilities."

It should be of interest for the record to quote from the minutes of the Egyptian Mission of the United Presbyterian Church. Under their meeting of May 4th, 1912, we read:

"The following special arrangement has been prepared, after consultation with Dr. Zwemer, as a general statement of the relations which he shall sustain to the Mission and of the work which shall be committed to him.

"1. That Dr. Zwemer shall be admitted to full membership in the Association of the American Mission and that he work under the direction of the Egyptian Association. It is understood that this does not involve his severing his relations with his own Board or Church in America.

"2. That the general work assigned to Dr. Zwemer shall be (a) Teaching in the Theological Seminary of the American Mission or lecturing on problems relating to Islam, (b) Conducting special missionary work for Moslems in Cairo, (c) Participating in the English services of the mission at Cairo, (d) Co-operating in literary work connected with the Nile Mission Press.

"3. That two hours daily or twelve hours approximately each week be reserved for the special literary work done in connection with the Nile Mission Press at Cairo, and that four months in the year — preferably during the summer season — be set aside for special work for the Moslem World or for the interests of the Arabian Mission of the Reformed Church in America.

"4. That since Dr. Zwemer is at present supported by a friend in America, the American Mission furnish him with a suitable residence at Cairo and make financial provision for such work as the Mission shall assign to him from year to year. The Nile Mission Press will, it is hoped, meet the expenses of travel connected with the work of the press.

"5. That the American Mission communicate to the Board of Foreign Missions of the Reformed Church in America its judgment that the conditions of the work and the urgency of the opportunity make it advisable that Dr. Zwemer complete his arrangements for his transfer to Cairo before October 1st, 1912, so that he may begin work at that time or as soon after as possible."[1]

Before he sailed for Cairo with his family the Missionary was busy in America for his own Board, as we read in the September 1912 issue of *The Mission Field.*

"The Trustees have authorized Dr. Zwemer to raise funds for the Arabian Mission wherever he sees the opportunity. They have felt the commanding necessity of a Security Fund which can be used as collateral on which money may be borrowed to supply the Mission during that part of the year in which the church's contributions do not meet its needs, and they have authorized Dr. Zwemer to collect such gifts as he can for the purpose. Accordingly Dr. Zwemer has been at the task with his usual activity and earnestness. He has delivered a large number of addresses and has been able to secure a beginning for this Security Fund, besides a number of special gifts for the regular work of the Arabian Mission. Mrs. Zwemer will not be less missed from the number of our missionaries resident in Arabia than will her husband, but she too will put her life into this new work to the great joy and advantage of the people of Cairo and the larger circle which will be reached by the works of her pen. As they go to Egypt, charged with the responsibilities of this wider work, let us pray for them more regularly and more earnestly, that they may be blessed richly in their own lives and made a greater and greater power in this war of the King of Kings against the hosts of Islam."

On arrival in Cairo the family was scarcely located in their new home before the father had more irons in the fire than the ordinary man would dare to contemplate. Beside the wide variety of local enterprises with the various

---

1. Minutes of the Egypt Mission, pp. 6, 7.

Missions he continued to edit *The Moslem World*. He plunged also with renewed interest into work with and for the Nile Mission Press, as is shown by his first New Year letter from Cairo, from which we may quote a few paragraphs.

"To Friends and Fellow Workers in America
    Bulaq, Cairo, Egypt, Dec. 26, 1912.
"Dear Friends :—

"This letter carries my heartiest greetings for the New Year to all . . . and I wish to express my heartfelt gratitude and appreciation of all that the American Committee has already done, by prayer and sympathy and sacrifice, for the Nile Mission Press and its work.

"My three months' residence here in this great metropolis has already confirmed my judgment that it is the one strategic place in the Moslem world from which we can influence every Moslem land, persistently and irresistibly, through the printed page.

"Egypt has practically become a British protectorate. Both Mr. Upson and myself have had personal interviews with Lord Kitchener and he is in full sympathy with the work that the Press is trying to accomplish.

"Some of our special literature for Moslems has been translated during the year and printed in India, South Africa, Persia, and China. The Methodist Press at Lucknow has since the Conference printed 1,810,000 pages of our Khutbas in Urdu. We have received requests, to which we could not respond, from the missionaries in Persia and in India to cooperate in printing a Persian Bible dictionary, and an English translation of the Koran with Arabic text, for use among Moslems . . . ."

The letter continues with enthusiastic plans for the purchase of new buildings for the Nile Mission Press. Zwemer was not only working in the matter of financial promotion for the Press, but was busy on a series of Arabic tracts, many of which became famous in Cairo and over the Moslem world. One of these entitled "Do You Pray" became so well known that people began to use this as a title and he would be pointed out on the street with the words, "There goes 'Do You Pray.' "

At Christmas time in 1912 William Borden arrived in Cairo. He was a young missionary from America, a graduate of Yale University and Princeton Theological Seminary. While in Seminary he had inherited a large fortune. He was intent on doing mission work in the most difficult field he could find, and had determined to work among Moslems in China on the borders of Tibet. He intended to open evangelistic and medical work and would support the station himself.

He had made his decision for foreign service under Zwemer's inspiration at a Student Volunteer Convention in Nashville, Tennessee, several years earlier. Now he came to Cairo to learn Arabic before going on to his Mohammedan field in China. To better acquire the language he lived with an Egyptian family. He became a familiar figure riding about town on his bicycle, distributing tracts and doing such evangelistic work as he could. His mother and sister left America to visit him in Cairo. They were on the journey out when "Bill" came down with spinal meningitis. On April 9th, 1913, he passed on to higher service. Zwemer conducted the funeral. The young life had been given up before he ever reached the mission field of his choice. His sacrifice has been compared to the alabaster box of ointment, poured out at the feet of the Christ who seeks the Moslem world as His own crown lands, where he lived and died in the days of His flesh. The Borden Memorial Hospital in Lanchow, Kansu, China, and other Christian institutions exist today as living monuments to the devotion and generosity of this young Christian.

During March there was a trip to Jedda in company with Mr. Charles T. Hooper for the purpose of opening a Bible depot. They also visited Yembo, the port of Medina in Arabia. The trip was most successful. A colleague describes another side of the venture.

"Mr. Hooper, the agent for the British and Foreign Bible Society, was planning a trip to Jedda which is the principal port of disembarkation for the Mohammedan pilgrims. Mr. Hooper's plan was to open a small shop in this important town with the hope that Mohammedans coming and going would buy portions of Scripture. And so it was decided that Dr. Zwemer would accompany him on the trip.

"Anyone who has lived in close contact with Dr. Zwemer knows that his mind is never idle and he was constantly making notes concerning articles that would appear in *The Moslem World*. While these two men were sitting in a government office there was a call on the telephone from Mecca and Dr. Zwemer had a great thrill because he had actually heard the voice of someone speaking from this holy city of the Mohammedans.

"After the return to Egypt some of us were asking Mr. Hooper concerning the success of his project and also concerning the journey to Jedda and back. He gave the information and then added, But never again with Zwemer! . . . . When we asked what the trouble might be, he said that he could not stay in bed for more than half an hour at a time . . . . for then, on would go the light, Zwemer would get out of bed, get some paper and a pencil, write a few sentences and then again to bed. When my eye-lids would get heavy again, up would come Zwemer, on again the light, and another few notes . . . . then off to bed again."

At many times in his life our missionary was down with a wide category of diseases. One of his closest calls came when Dr. and Mrs. Zwemer were on a Y.M.C.A. picnic. He took part in various sports and extreme exertion resulted in a very serious strangulated hernia. When the picnic boat returned to its dock an ambulance rushed Dr. Zwemer to the Prussian hospital where a serious operation was performed. Missionary colleagues feared he might not recover, but he rallied strongly.

He was out of the hospital in three weeks and June 18th sailed with his wife for Naples and on to the Pan-Presbyterian Conference in Aberdeen and to the Zurich world conference of the Sunday School Association. Here Zwemer delivered an address on *Childhood in the Moslem World* which was later enlarged to be published in book form.

The husband and wife visited many university and mission centers in Europe. To list some of the more important: Copenhagen, Hamburg, Berlin, Halle, Stuttgart, Tübingen, Liebenzell, Weisbaden, Bethel and Wernigerode.

By the first of September the Zwemers were back in Cairo and took part in an important conference for converts from Islam held that autumn. On December 8th he sailed from Port Said for the United States. The primary objective was the Student Volunteer Convention in Kansas City which began on January first, 1914.

This was followed by travel for the building fund of the Nile Mission Press and work for the Sunday School Association as a followup of the Zurich Conference. There were also a number of visits to the colleges for the Student Volunteer Movement. On April 15th, 1914, he sailed on the steamer "Francis Joseph" for Naples on the way back to Cairo. An interesting midnight conference was held on the 24th with all the mission workers of Algiers. The trip from Naples to Alexandria was made on the steamer "Gascot" and there were many interesting conversations with a fellow traveler, the Bishop of Uganda.

Another bit of sunlight may be shed on Zwemer's life and work from a column by "The Wayfarer" in the Presbyterian Church paper *The Continent*.

"Say, I've got a bottle of Zem-Zem water!" cried Zwemer, with enthusiasm. Lest there should be any reader who does not know the difference between Zem-Zem water and Zu-Zu ginger snaps, the Wayfarer hastens to explain that Zem-Zem is the sacred well at Mecca, which the Moslems claim sprang up miraculously beside Ishmael when Hagar was cast out into the wilderness by Abraham. Everyone of the 200,000 Moslem pilgrims who visit Mecca yearly must drink of this sin-cleansing water; and to take a small quantity home is the desire of every pilgrim. Now for Zwemer's story:

"I was going up to Cairo from Jedda on the pilgrim ship, and there was a man aboard who had some casks of Zem-Zem water, which he was carrying home as a business venture. I asked this man's son, who was not a good Moslem, to get me a bottle, and I would give him a dollar. After some demurring and persuading, he did so; and I slipped the bottle into my inside pocket. However, nothing can be kept secret on a pilgrim ship, and the fact that a Christian unbeliever had secured some of the sacred water, set the crowd to buzzing.

"I knew what was coming, so I slipped into my cabin and ordered a bottle of soda water from the steward. As soon as he left the room, I emptied this

2. Issue of March 19, 1914.

into the washbasin and poured the Zem-Zem water into the soda water bottle. Then I refilled the Mecca bottle with ordinary water, and replaced it in my pocket, the Zem-Zem water remaining safe in my cabin. When I got on deck the racket had increased. A deputation took the matter up with the Moslem captain, who came and asked me to give up the bottle, to avoid a riot. We argued a while, and then I let him have the bottle of water from my pocket. He drank it himself, with great delight, saying that Zem-Zem water curses whatever is the matter with you. I took my specimen of this holy water to Cairo and had it analyzed, and found that this precious fluid, which pious Moslems carry to the ends of the earth, was of just about the same purity as sewer water.

"Zwemer loves any sort of jokes, and he does his share of laughing and laugh-making. There are two pictures of Samuel M. Zwemer in the Wayfarer's mind, and they are consistent. One shows him at the table in a Grand Rapids hotel, with a few fellow missionary campaigners. It is late at night, and the day has been a full, hard one, of the soul-sapping sort. Now the bow is unbent. Funny stories are going the rounds, but it is Zwemer who, out of an experience stretching from Michigan to Arabia, is setting the table agog. The fun becomes hilarious and riotous. The head waiter appears, to judge of this disorder, which plainly has no spirituous origin. That is one time when the Wayfarer thought there was a real chance of his being expelled from a hotel for disorderly conduct. No professional entertainer has ever made the Wayfarer laugh as did Samuel Marinus Zwemer. The fighter whose sword is sharpened on the grindstone of humor is a foe to fear.

"The other picture shows Zwemer as a platform crusader. He had spoken at three great meetings in one day. From the last address he was hastening to a sleeping car. For more than an hour he had poured out the wonderful riches of his stored mind and intense life upon this one subject of Christianity's summons to adventure in the Moslem world. It was not an address 'gotten up'; it was a full heart poured out. All the elements of great oratory were there. The call was the crusading cry of a Peter the Hermit. As he came down from the platform his face was pale and drawn. 'Now is my soul straitened,' leaped to the Wayfarer's mind. This man is pouring out his soul; the zeal of the cross is eating him up. But such as he, are at once the glory and hope of the church's world-wide conquests."

In *The Missionary Review of the World* Zwemer wrote an article under the title "The Tale of Three Cities." They were Mecca, the spiritual capital of Islam, Constantinople the political capital at that time, and Cairo, the intellectual capital. The article quoted from a telegram sent by Dr. Charles R. Watson after a visit to Moslem lands, the words which have since become classic in regard to the uses of Christian literature in the Islamic world. He said:

"No agency can penetrate Islam so deeply, abide so persistently, witness so daringly and influence so irresistibly as the printed page."

The article by Zwemer concluded:

"Mecca represents the unoccupied fields of Islam, and challenges faith and heroism. Constantinople, with its mosque of St. Sophia, appeals to our loyalty. We must win back what was lost to the Church of Christ. And Cairo is the city of opportunity, of the open door and the beckoning hand. Mecca represents Islam as the excluder, behind closed doors, defying the entrance of the Christ; Constantinople, Islam as the intruder into the domains of the King; Cairo reminds us that in Africa Islam is the great rival faith, and that here must be fought to the finish the struggle for a continent. The three cities voice the appeal of three continents, Asia, Europe and Africa, to be freed from the thraldom of Mohammed and welcomed into the glorious liberty of the children of God."

In 1914 William T. Ellis wrote an article which was published in *The Century Magazine,* under the title "American and Turk in Holy War." It was a first-hand study of the Sheik-ul-Islam as a representative of his religion and Samuel M. Zwemer as a representative of Christianity. The conclusion of the well-known writer was, that since the leaders of Islam had called for a Holy War and their followers would not respond, the weapons of the future would be those of peaceful argument and the printed page, such as Zwemer was using in behalf of the Christian cause.

Of his work in Cairo Dr. James G. Hunt, a colleague of the United Presbyterian Mission wrote:

"He taught in the Theological Seminary, preached frequently in Arabic and English, and was intensely zealous and active in various forms of work for the Moslems.

"He may be said to be a man of one idea. While his interests and knowledge were wide, I never talked with him ten minutes that the conversation did not veer to Islam. I am told that he set out one day to visit the famous tombs of the Kings in Luxor. On the way he met a Mohammedan funeral procession, and noting something in the customs that he had not encountered before, he turned aside and followed the procession, and never got to the tombs of the Kings. I asked him once for verification of this story and he admitted that it was substantially true.

"He had the most acquisitive mind that I ever met. He would go down a street in Cairo and observe customs and superstitions, reading matter and characters, that would escape the notice of most of us. He had an abundance of fresh illustrations for any theme on which he was speaking. This made him a fascinating teacher.

"He also had an inventive mind, fertile with fresh plans for the work. Almost too much so, in fact, for practical work. In a committee meeting, his mind would scintillate with new ideas that would commend themselves to the rest of us. But perhaps after we had decided on a plan that we would follow, we might meet again a little later, and he would seem to have quite forgotten the plan he had suggested and on which we had agreed, and would have a whole batch of new plans. I recall that he said once after leaving such a meeting that he could suggest plans but he needed someone else to carry them out.

"He was always a lovable character and had a keen sense of humor that made him a delightful companion. He was the center of any group in which he might be."

The first World War brought work among soldiers as well as the routine for the various missions and the Press. One story concerning the service for fighting men is typical. Zwemer was asked to speak at the Sunday service for a British contingent near Cairo. He went and found a large tent ready and many seats, nearly all empty. He went out in front of the tent and gave the Moslem call to prayer. Naturally, it could be heard over the whole section of the cantonment. Soldiers came running from every direction to see what the noise was about. He invited them all in to the service and had a fine congregation.

Of work in these years he writes in the magazine *Neglected Arabia:*

"All the missions working in Egypt have special cause for thanksgiving that in the midst of all the horrors of this world war and disturbances in the Near East all our work has gone on unhindered. From the very outbreak of hostilities until now, the strong and firm hand of the British Government has so protected Egypt that there have been no disturbances in the country and that no invasion from without has seriously threatened our peace. In fact the war has added to our opportunities rather than in any sense curtailed them. Schools, hospitals, the Mission Press and public meetings have been conducted as usual, and in addition we have had thousands of soldiers from Australia, New Zealand, India and South Africa. Among them the Y.M. C.A. and the various missions have carried on a ministry of friendship and a campaign of evangelism which has yielded large results. Under the able direction of men like Mr. Wm. Jessup and Mr. H. W. White, a special evangelistic campaign was conducted for two weeks and hundreds of men made decisions for Christ.

"My special work this year, as heretofore, has been along literary lines in connection with the Nile Mission Press, teaching in the Theological Seminary and also at the Cairo Study Center. In the Theological Seminary this year we have sixteen students in the regular classes and fourteen in the evangelists' class, who are taking a special course. It is a rare privilege to read Al-Ghazali with these graduates from Assiut College who are preparing themselves for the ministry, and to study Islam with the future leaders of the Church in Egypt in order that they themselves may plan for the speedy evangelization of their own country. Making Disciples that make disciples

"At the Cairo Study Center Canon W. H. T. Gairdner has charge of language study and by his new method, through the use of phonetics and the colloquial, remarkable progress is being made. Mr. R. F. McNeile, an-

other missionary of the Church Missionary Society, and I have given lectures
on Islam and methods of work. Twenty new missionaries of various
societies are taking these courses. In addition to the lectures every first day
of the month is a red letter day, for then parties are arranged under the leadership of the staff for the purpose of seeing various forms of Moslem life
and missionary work in this great city.

"Mr. and Mrs. Stephen R. Trowbridge and three other missionaries of
the American Board who are studying Arabic in Cairo live in the same apartment house with us near the heart of the city. In fact we might describe
this apartment house, of which the uppermost flat is our home, as that of
Titus Justus, 'whose house joined hard to the synagogue.' The chief synagogue of Cairo, one of the wealthiest Jewish congregations in the world is
less than a stone's throw from my study window. They have a large library
of ancient books and manuscripts and also a remarkable collection of Penta-
teuch manuscripts. In the study of Islam one is more and more impressed
how much Mohammed owed to Judaism and how much modern Jewish
ritual is like that of Islam.

"Most of the readers of your paper know that Mr. Trowbridge has come
to Cairo as the secretary of the World's Sunday-school Association for
Moslem lands, and that he is putting forth special efforts to arouse the interest of both missionaries and native pastors in the problem of Mohammedan
childhood. At the request of his committee it was my privilege recently on
their behalf to make a visit to the Sudan. I left Cairo on Saturday, March
4, and reached Assiut the same evening. That night and on the following
Sunday I had special meetings at the church and for the students of Assiut
College. On Monday I arrived at Luxor. Here I visited the American
Mission Girls' School as well as the Boys' School, and in both places spoke
to the children and distributed literature."

The trip in the Sudan was of special interest to Zwemer, as it was an area
that had been much upon his heart and mind. He was anxious to visit
Khartoum and see the place where the noted Christian General Gordon had
made his last stand and gave his life. The missions there also profited by his
addresses and advice.

He was in Europe and America on several occasions during the war years.
In 1915 he gave a series of lectures at Princeton Theological Seminary and
then returned to Cairo.

During 1916 there came what he described as the darkest days of all his
missionary life. That summer both of the parents and two children had
typhoid. There were days of great anxiety but finally prayers were answered and health returned to all. Even while he was ill the patient had
been working on his books on *Al Ghazali* and *Childhood in the Moslem
World.*

A number of missionaries from Egypt and other fields made the journey
home via the Pacific because of war conditions in the Atlantic Ocean. One
who was with him on the journey said:

"On the trip home wherever we landed Dr. Zwemer immediately made inquiry concerning Mohammedans that might be located in the cities and all the way from Port Said to Shanghai we found some in every port and of course Zwemer provided tracts and Scripture portions that could be given to these Mohammedan people. One of these visits was particularly interesting to us as we compared the customs of the Mohammedans in China with the stricter customs of the Moslems in Egypt. We gave the sheikh and his students in a little Mohammedan school a great surprise when we repeated for them the first sura of the Koran."

Since the subject of our narrative returned to America often, in addition to many visits to Europe and over the world of Islam, it may have made it a little more difficult psychologically for other missionaries who were forced to remain many years on the field between all too infrequent furloughs in the homeland. In spite of this there was generally thankfulness that his headquarters were in Cairo and that he could be there for at least part of the time. The visits over Africa, Europe and Asia became frequent and extended as Zwemer was more in demand for conference on Moslem work wherever it was carried on—or should be—by various missions from many countries.

In May of 1921 Dr. Zwemer went to Constantinople for a series of addresses. It is interesting to note that he spoke at Robert College at the same time that the famous historian Arnold Toynbee was delivering a series of lectures there on the relations of Eastern and Western civilizations. Zwemer also was one of the leaders at the "Paradise Student Conference" at International College in Smyrna.

A colleague in Egypt tells an interesting incident:

"In recent years we have had an organization in Cairo which was sponsored and promoted principally by our good friend Bishop Gwynne who was the Mission Bishop of the Church of England in Cairo. Bishop Gwynne was a great friend of all the missionaries and a very particular friend of Dr. Zwemer. The good Bishop was very zealous in promoting this organization but the fly in the sweet ointment of fellowship was the matter of ordination. This question was discussed frequently, not so much in the fellowship itself as in the more private meetings in conversations that we had together. To our dear Bishop the matter was very simple and one day as he was talking to Dr. Zwemer he said, 'There is no great difficulty; I could ordain you and then you in turn could ordain other missionaries and soon we would all have the Episcopal ordination and we could work together in our separate societies but we could have closer fellowship together under this arrangement.' A twinkle came into Dr. Zwemer's eye and he said, 'I'll tell you, Bishop; I have the final solution. If you will let me baptize you I will let you ordain me.' "

In June, 1923 Zwemer attended the General Synod of the Reformed Church in America held at Asbury Park, New Jersey. He was elected president of the Synod but sailed later in the month for England and the continent and was back in Egypt by September.

Of his work at the oldest and greatest of the Moslem universities the missionary wrote:

"The Azhar, always considered as a center of fanaticism and intolerance, has in recent years opened its doors not only to tourists and visitors willing to pay four piastres for a ticket and to don the yellow leather slippers, lest they defile the sanctuary; today they welcome missionaries. My earliest attempt to preach the gospel in the Azhar was some six years ago in company with a learned Egyptian convert, Mikhail Mansoor, who knew many of the professors, as a former student, and they were polite to us both, but it was a cold politeness with no response to our message, and with very little respect for Christianity. However, at a second and third visit we were able to place in the library of this great University a large Arabic reference Bible, together with a complete commentary, a concordance and Bible dictionary. This gift proved the entering wedge, and in succeding years I have made many friends. Scarcely a week goes by when I am in Cairo without visiting the Azhar, either alone or in company with tourists, missionaries and studdents of our theological seminary. To such a degree have I won the friendship of many of the teachers that they greet me warmly on arrival allowing me to sit and 'listen in' at their lectures, and in one case even made no objection when I interfered with a case of corporal punishment where a teacher was beating a pupil unmercifully. This man is now my warm friend.

"During the past few months I have found a responsiveness which is most encouraging. A number of teachers expressed a desire to possess copies of the Bible, and through the courtesy of the American Bible Society and their agent, we were able to place nearly a dozen copies in the hands of the professors, and over 150 copies of Matthew's Gospel in the hands of students attending the lectures.

"In the court of the blind I have many friends, and it is pathetic to watch how they eagerly approach me when I come to wish them greetings. No class in Egypt is more in need of the gospel than these blind or open-eyed blind leaders of the blind. Steeped in Mohammedan learning, but ignorant of any righteousness save that according to the law, the gospel is to them indeed a strange message. However, the isolation of this group of people is broken into by the daily press. One may see those who are not blind reading the newspapers even during lesson periods.

"In the book-selling quarter just outside of the Azhar, copies of French novels translated into Arabic, and scientific literature of the modern type is also on sale and finds eager purchasers. Some of these book shops even handle the Scriptures. Controversial works against Christianity, however, nearly all originate within the precincts of this University. It is therefore the more encouraging to find fanaticism decreasing and a friendly response to the presentation of the principles of Christianity and its teaching.

"The American University in Cairo has recently begun an extension course giving popular lectures on hygiene and other subjects. The result was a gathering of 400 Moslem sheikhs from the Azhar, in the Assembly Hall of the American University at Cairo, February 24, 1925. The occasion was the exhibition of an educational film on the origin of life and the sex problem, treated from a Christian standpoint. Surely when so large a number are willing to come to a Christian institution for an extra-curriculum lecture, when numbers of them attend the meetings at Y.M.C.A. and hundreds are reading the Scriptures, we are facing a new day of opportunity and a new responsibility of intercession."

It was in this great Mohammedan University that an incident occurred which occasioned no little publicity, misunderstanding and discussion. There have been so many versions of the story that we have asked Dr. H. E. Philips of the United Presbyterian Mission to recount the facts in the case and also a sequel which is not generally known. It should be remembered in the first place that there was a great deal of feeling in Cairo at this time as a reaction against the Jerusalem Conference of Christian forces.

"Throughout Dr. Zwemer's ministry in Egypt he was very diligent in the distribution of tracts and being a man with many friends he was a frequent visitor to the great University Al-Azhar. When he was in the University going and coming among the students and professors he frequently gave away tracts or portions of Scripture. The teachers finally protested against this and asked the government to forbid such distribution. Under these conditions it seemed better to Zwemer to stop giving out tracts in the University. However, one day when he was taking some friends through this great Mohammedan school one of the young men on his way to class spoke to Dr. Zwemer and asked him if he had any tracts with him. He felt in his pocket and found he had four and these he gave to the student who continued on his way to class and distributed the four tracts among his fellow students.

"It happened that the professor of this particular class was a very fanatical man and having seen what was done he sprang up from his seat on the floor and grabbed these tracts and tore them to pieces and gave the men a severe scolding for having anything to do with this man. The matter was reported to the officials and was taken up with the British government and Dr. Zwemer was called on the carpet. The result for the moment was that Dr. Zwemer was asked to leave the country for a season; which he proceeded to do by taking a boat from Port Said to Cyprus and by returning two weeks later on the same boat to Egypt. So far as I know that was the end of the matter for Dr. Zwemer.

"But there is a sequel that should not be missed and it is this: One night a Mohammedan Sudanese sheikh came to my house for discussion. He was a student in the university and his history in a word was this: His own father was a Mohammedan qadi (judge) in the Sudan and there were three boys in the family — two of whom were already graduates of Al Azhar

University and were at the time teaching in the Sudan. This young man studied in one of the important mosques in Khartoum. While he was in this city he one day found a Christian book-store and secured some Christian literature that was intended for Mohammedan readers. At the end of his first year he decided to go to Cairo and attend Al Azhar University.

"When he entered the School he was given a locker for his books and the following day he was called to the office of one of the professors and was severely rebuked for having this Christian literature in his locker. It happened that the young man had secured a copy of the New Testament and had been reading somewhat from it. He was present at the time when Dr. Zwemer gave the four tracts to one of the students and when the sheikh who was making such an uproar threw them on the floor he and another of the students gathered up the fragments which they put in their pockets and after they had returned to their rooms they very carefully pieced these portions together until they were able to read the whole tract.

"This young man seemed to be an honest seeker for the truth; his comment concerning the tract was that he was greatly impressed by all that Dr. Zwemer said. It was a pleasure to hear this man pray and he assured me that if he knew how he could be supported he would leave Islam and become a Christian. He was forbidden to leave the University without special permission and so careful was his class officer that he appointed a fellow student to keep guard over this man by day and another to watch him in the evening lest he should come to the American mission for discussions.

"Just before leaving Cairo this young man whom I had not seen for months appeared at my door. One of his guards had gone home on a visit; the other had fallen ill on that particular day and so he went to his class officer and asked permission to visit a friend who lived beyond our place. He visited a friend, but as he stated, 'In my permission there was nothing said about the road I had to travel as I came back.' We had a good talk together and prayer." The young man became a staunch Christian and was killed in a street accident some time later.

Note should be made of the fact that Zwemer was associated with Dr. Arthur Jeffery, head of the school of Oriental Studies in the American University at Cairo. This young man who had come to the Near East as a missionary from Australia was always admired by Zwemer as one of the finest of Islamic scholars. He later came to the United States to teach Arabic and Islamics in Columbia University and Union Seminary of New York City. Another close friend of these years was Dr. James K. Quay who came to Cairo with the United Presbyterian Mission and was later Secretary of the Y.M.C.A. in that city. Dr. Quay later went to Princeton Theological Seminary as Vice President.

Wilbert B. Smith, who was for many years Secretary of the Y.M.C.A. in Cairo writes in a recent letter:

"Zwemer was in Cairo when I arrived there in February, 1921, and introduced me to a good many people in the Christian community. He also took me to the Azhar for the first time.

"One of my problems was to find suitable premises in which to begin the Association work for Egyptians. We looked all over the city. One day Zwemer and two or three others and I were together in my car in this search, when he suddenly said, 'I know just the place. It is the palace of the former Prime Minister Nubar Pasha up on Sharia Nubar Pasha. Let's go and see it.' This we did immediately. As you may recall, it is the property of two acres with the old palace at the front. It was exactly what we needed. Before the year was out, the money was secured for its purchase and since 1922 it has served as the center for Cairo Central Y.M.C.A.; headquarters for the National Council of the Y.M.C.A. (three additional branches grew out of Cairo — Alexandria, Assiut and Minieh).[3] For many years, four American secretaries lived in apartments which were constructed on top of the main building.

"Through the years, Zwemer was very helpful to me, especially in making us keep our eyes on the Moslem community. There is no one who has done more for me in that particular matter than Zwemer, beginning back in 1907 when he and I were candidate secretaries of the Student Volunteer Movement in New York. Together we started a candidate department and when he went back to Egypt, I took over the job alone."

In one of his letters home our missionary gives a good idea of the scope covered by his general work in the land of the Pyramids.

"My dear friends:

"The circle of those who remember us daily in prayer may be interested to know of the daily round and common task that falls to our lot in this great city. Almost as soon as I arrived in September the course of lectures at the School of Oriental Studies for new missionaries began, and every week we have had a group or groups numbering all the way from thirty to fifty present. I have lectured on Methods of Evangelism, The Moslem Christ, Mohammedan Mysticism, and am just now beginning a new course on Christian Literature for Moslems. In the Theological Seminary and the Evangelists' School we have similar courses, though more suitable to the Coptic students who attend. I have preached every Sunday since coming to Egypt, both in English and in Arabic. In addition to the churches in Cairo, it has been my privilege to visit Port Said, Benha, Zagazig, Assiut and other centers for conferences of the native church. At these conferences, it will interest you to know, we are using a new study book in Arabic, entitled 'The Nearest Way to the Moslem Heart.' This little book was prepared last year by A. T. Upson and myself, and has been found quite useful.

"Because of efficient stenographic help, I was able to complete the manuscript of a new book to be entitled 'The Law of Apostasy.' It

---

3. It should be noted that several other centers have been opened by the Y.M.C.A. in additional cities and work has reached as many as 500 underprivileged boys in Cairo at a time.

deals with the difficulties Moslem converts have, and how they surmount them. I hope that it will be published some time this summer. You doubtless know of the *Orient and Occident,* a magazine published jointly by the Church Missionary Society and the other Missions. We are greatly encouraged because of its increased circulation and the eagerness with which the Christian message is welcomed everywhere.

"At present we are in the midst of busy preparations for the Conference of Missionaries to be held in Cairo. This is one of the series which is being held in the Near East on behalf of the International Missionary Council. As chairman of the Committee of Arrangements a great deal of the preparatory work falls to my lot, but we anticipate that the results of the Conference will be worth all the efforts of preparation in drawing closer together the workers of all these fields, and laying the burden upon the churches at home for the evangelization of Moslems.

"The annual meeting of our American Mission occurs early in February, and the Conference begins February 22nd. Mrs. Zwemer and I expect to attend the general conference at Jerusalem early in April, and then proceed to Baghdad at Dr. Mott's request to hold a regional conference there for the missionaries of Arabia and Persia. After that the Committee on Field Work desires me to visit India during the summer to hold conferences with groups of missionaries and to investigate the conditions of Moslem evangelism on similar lines to those we followed last year in Java, Sumatra and North Africa. Mrs. Zwemer will accompany me to India. We ask a special interest in your prayers."

After some seventeen years the time came to leave Cairo for other fields of service. The local press referred to Zwemer as "The leading authority on Islamics from the Christian standpoint."

Part Three
In Journeyings Often

VIII

Tale of Two Continents

"Yet another force that is aggressively our antagonist is Mohammedanism. We see it actively spreading over Africa, where Christianity is not progressive. It comes with the Arab-slaver and was identified with the slave traffic. It comes now with a certain racial pride and appeals to the African, because it seems to link him with a great world-empire."

DONALD FRAZER in
Students and the Modern Missionary Crusade, p. 207.

"Difficulties are not without their advantages. They are not to unnerve us. They are not to be regarded simply as subjects for discussion nor as grounds for scepticism and pessimism. They are not to cause inaction, but rather to intensify activity. They were made to be overcome. Above all they are to create profound distrust in human plans and energy, and to drive us to God."

JOHN R. MOTT in
The Evangelization of the World in This Generation, p. 50

CHAPTER EIGHT

A TALE OF TWO CONTINENTS

One of Zwemer's books bore the title "Across the World of Islam." He was certainly qualified to write such a volume from personal observation. A large part of his work was evangelistic itineration, not in a local field but on a world scale. He was the roving ambassador of good will in Christian work for Moslems.

With this chapter we begin a section of the biography like a travel book, which covers journeys to many parts of the world. In the following pages we consider his rather prodigious accomplishments in the two continents of Europe and Africa during the nineteen twenties. After attendance at a Workers' Conference in Jerusalem in April, 1922, he prepared for a trip through the Moslem lands south of the Mediterranean.

I. Mission to North Africa

A visit to the various mission stations of North Africa was planned for May and June, 1922, at the request of Dr. John R. Mott. The purpose of the visit was to make arrangements for subsequent conferences in the area and the general Jerusalem meeting to be held under the auspices of the International Missionary Council. The visitor was also to represent the World Sunday School Association and as field secretary for the American Christian Literature Society for Moslems would seek to stimulate the publication and distribution of the Christian message through the printed page. There was also the definite hope that conferences together might develop better feeling and more of comity among the various missionary organizations at work in the territory.

On April 27th the traveling missionary left Port Said for Marsailles and sailed from that city to reach Algiers on May 5th. After contact with several of the missionary leaders there he left by sleeping car for Tunis, where he arrived at 11:30 p.m. the next day.

On Sunday, May 7th, Zwemer preached in Tunis twice in Arabic and once through an interpreter in French. The following day there were visits to the Methodist Mission and the London Society for the Jews, where he spoke to 150 children in their orphanage school. He also saw the tomb in a cemetery at Tunis of John Howard Payne, author of "Home Sweet Home," whose final resting place thus seems to have been a long way from home.

That afternoon there was a conference with the workers of the various missions where he presented the matter of the Jerusalem meeting and discussed the local work for Moslems. The editor also notes that he secured a number of subscribers for *The Moslem World*. He also recorded that there was a very deep spirit of faith among the missionaries concerning efforts to reach Moslems. A convert was baptized at the time, and he retained the name of Mohammed, which surprised the visitor, as he was used to the custom of change to a definitely Christian name at the time of baptism. The bazaar was visited at night where there was a general feasting and celebration, since it was the month of *Ramadhan* and Moslems had fasted throughout the daylight hours.

On the following day there was a trip to Kairwan, a holy city in that part of Africa which few missionaries had visited. The party arrived in a rainstorm, but soon arranged to visit the Great Mosque with special permits from the local French authorities. This mosque is claimed to be the fourth in sanctity in the whole world of Islam. Another shrine dedicated to the barber of the prophet was also visited, and a third to a local saint who had been a blacksmith. His shrine was decorated with four anchors, said to have been taken from the ark of Noah!

The visitors proceeded by auto to Sus or Sousse, where they toured the extensive catacombs dating from the second Christian century, and known as the Catacombs of the Good Shepherd. They noted a carving, from which the catacomb was no doubt named, showing Christ with a lamb, as well as symbols of the dove, the anchor and the word PAX.

Sousse was the center of a great agricultural district or settlement. The city had a population of some 29,000, about half of them French and Italian. In the surrounding country there was said to be 300,000 acres planted to barley and several million olive trees. The party visited the Methodist Mission and Dr. Zwemer spoke on "Islam as a Missionary Problem". They returned to Tunis where an evening meeting was held for Moslems, the subject was "Arabia and Missions" and latern slides were used.

On the eleventh of May there was a meeting for children in the Methodist mission, followed by a trip of some ten miles to the ruins of ancient Carthage, and its museum with the large collection from Punic, Roman and Christian times. In his notes the visitor set down that he was thrilled to visit the place which had been the home of three great fathers of the church. He lists them as Cyprian — Churchman and Organizer, Tertullian — Controversialist and Dogmatist, Augustine — Mystic and Saint.

The visiting missionary asked people concerning Raymund Lull, but most had never heard of him. The Roman Catholic White Fathers had a strong work there, largely among French and Italians; however, a great many former Moslems have been baptized in their various North African stations.

The next day, Friday, May 12th, was spent on the train to Constantine. Quite contrary to most ideas concerning North Africa it was described as a marvelous country with olive gardens and vineyards, forests of cork trees and fields of barley. Gospels were given out to Arabs; and French police officers came to make sure what sort of literature was being distributed.

That night the traveler reached Constantine and was entertained at the home of Dr. and Mrs. Percy Smith, of the American Methodist Mission, who were soon to leave for Algiers to take charge of the study center and the training of new workers.

A conference was held the next day at which Zwemer led the devotions and presented the objects of his visit to all missionaries of the city. Sunday was a very busy day. Dr. Zwemer spoke to the French congregation in the morning, and to the Arabic groups in the afternoon. There were some eighty converts from Islam present. The Sunday school was also visited and he addressed another service, by interpretation, in the evening. Lantern slides on Islam in Arabia and China were used at this time. There were some 250 in attendance, many of them young Moslems.

Always on the lookout for anything connected with Islam, Zwemer spotted on the French paper money a text from the Koran and was not satisfied until he found out why it was there. The fact was that the French money had depreciated and the Arabs in Algeria didn't want to accept it. The reason given was that there were nude pictures in the design printed on the currency. An orientalist was consulted by the Government, who suggested that the money be stamped with the Koranic text in Arabic, "Woe to the debasers of coinage." The scheme worked and the French paper currency was restored to par.

Following the Conference there were the usual meetings for the public in general and for Moslems. At the latter meeting three converts from Islam added their testimony to that of the visiting missionary and he was led to thank God for the great opportunities in Algeria.

Dr. Percy Smith went on from Constantine as a traveling companion and guide. From May 15th to 21st they visited a large number of towns and met local missionaries. The visitor did not find either Roman Catholic or Protestant Christians who knew much about Raymund Lull, though he inquired of many in Bugia, or Bougie, as it is now known, the very place where Lull was stoned.

At Tazmalt the headquarters of the British mission of the Plymouth Brethren was visited and a conference was held. There was a meeting of some thirty or forty converts and inquirers. The visitor spoke on "Raymund Lull and his Gospel."

At Sidi Aich the Methodist mission plant was inspected. Plans were under way to make this a leading station for the agricultural work of the mission. It was the center of some twenty villages and situated in a rich country of olive orchards and vineyards. The party went on up the mountains by automobile. The languages were Kabyle and French. At one station forty missionaries and Christian workers had gathered and all took part together in a communion service.

On May 18th Zwemer was overjoyed by the invitation to attend a "Zikr" or meeting of the Omariyeh order of dervishes. There was a hall, about 25 by 14 feet lighted with electricity. At one end was a closet where they kept the properties for their ritual. At one corner sat the head of the order, who spoke with the visitor in Arabic, at the other corner were several musicians with tambourines and reed-pipes. The musicians and finally all members of the order began swaying with the rythmic thumping of the instruments. Finally all smote their breasts with their hands and fell to their knees. In this position they crept to the Sheikh who had them bend over to inhale smoking incense, and then put something like snuff in their nostrils. The powder is said to be made from a local plant known as "datura," which benumbs or hypnotizes.

The music grew louder and the devotees were siezed with violent shaking. One young man arose and danced over the sharp edge of a sword and struck himself with it several times without apparent injury. Then iron rods were stuck through the cheeks and arms of another youth and into the muscles of his breast. He danced around with these for some time and finally they were withdrawn with no sign of blood. One of the order explained to the guests that Allah made all of these things harmless to those who were utterly absorbed in his worship.

A visit was paid to a leading French Protestant of the region, M. Bouscasse, who had charge of a paper mill. He knew of Dr. John R. Mott and had read the life of Raymund Lull. He was also informed concerning the Edinburgh and Lucknow Conferences and promised to do all he possibly could to cooperate in local gatherings to be held at the time of Dr. Mott's contemplated visit.

The journey by car across the Kabyle mountains was over very good roads through forests of oak, ash and pine. The mountains rise to an altitude of 2,500 feet and there was some snow on their summits even in late May. At a mountain village there was a meeting of converts, some sixty were present. Zwemer spoke in English and Arabic and was interpreted in French and Kabyle. The people seemed to be prosperous and there were vineyards and olive groves, as well as many cork trees. The Kabyle country impressed the visitor as one of great natural resources.

As he traveled on from village to village of the territory he visited independent French missionaries who had made some converts, and stations of the Methodist and Brethren Missions. The journey was continued by Ford car to Viller-ville, where the traveler took a train, arriving the evening of May 21st, in Algiers. He remained there until May 28th. On the evening of the 23rd there was a large meeting of some 200 Moslems. Zwemer was introduced by Dr. Percy Smith and spoke for about an hour.

The Algiers Conference began on May 24th and lasted through the 26th. The meetings were at the American Methodist Church. Some eighty delegates from Algeria and Tunisia represented the Methodist Episcopal Mission, the North Africa Mission, the Algiers Mission Band, the Brethren Mission, and a number of independent organizations.

Dr. Zwemer led the daily devotional meetings with a series of addresses. The discussion began on the familiar theme of Christian Literature and since the visitor represented the American Christian Literature Society for Moslems, he could promise financial help in evangelistic publication if all missions in the field would cooperate, so that the production of literature might be a truly united effort to avoid duplication.

A Committee on Literature was appointed for the area. The same action was taken after discussion on a committee to cooperate with the World Sunday School Association. Before adjournment the Conference also elected a committee to arrange for the forthcoming visit of Dr. John R. Mott and the conferences to be held with him in Morocco, Algeria and Tunisia.

We quote the final few sentences of the Conference minutes, to show that great strides had been taken toward mission comity.

"The Conference closed with the Holy Communion Service, in which all the delegates participated. As we left it was with the realization that God had drawn near in these three days, and that we had been more closely linked together as missionaries and missions, and had gained a new vision of the needs and possibilities — the yet greater things which God is expecting from us for the Moslem World. The organization of three Inter-mission committees on important matters will doubtless result in a definite Inter-mission organization soon. Perfect harmony characterized all the discussions."

The few remaining days of the month were spent in Algiers. On Sunday Zwemer spoke at several services. At the evening meeting when lantern slides of Arabia were shown a Moslem who had been on the pilgrimage to Mecca helped to interpret the views. Though the Christian viewpoint was outspoken there was a fine reception of the lecture.

The meeting with Mr. J. H. Smelton who conducts a special work for the blind, under the auspices of the Algiers Mission Band, was noteworthy. He was 72 years old and had learned Arabic when past 60 and also spoke French and Kabyle. He was a deeply spiritual man and a shining light for the blind.[1]

Before he left Zwemer met with the new Committee on Literature and a budget of requests was prepared for presentation to the A.C.L.S.M.[2] to cover publication in French, Arabic and Kabyle.

On Wednesday, May 31st, the traveler left Algiers at 8:00 a.m. and arrived in Oran that evening about seven. He was accompanied on the journey by the Rev. J. Paul Cook, a French pastor at the time working with the Algiers Mission Band. He had made a great reputation as chaplain of the French Foreign Legion in the First World War and was a splendid guide and interpreter. There were stops at Oran and Tlemcen, where Zwemer spoke to the Young Algerian Club on *The Foundations of Ethics and Social Progress*. There were seventy young men present who evinced lively

---

1. It is interesting to note that Mr. Smelton after this visit produced one of Zwemer's Arabic tracts, "The Three Blind Men," in Braille.
2. See Chapter XIII.

interest in the address and the question period and accepted a number of Gospels and tracts.

The country is again described as beautiful with cherry and olive trees, vineyards and numerous waterfalls. It reminded the traveler of southern France. There was a stop at Oudja and from there the journey to Fez was made by automobile.

During two days in Fez the local missionaries were visited and there was a meeting of French Protestants where Zwemer spoke through an interpreter. He also gave out his French tract on "The Moslem Problem," which had just been printed in Algiers.

The bazaars and mosques of the city were visited and the notable water system was described in his journal. Built in the thirteenth century the water is provided for the city by an elaborate system of pipes and channels. Almost every mosque and public building has a constantly flowing water fountain in the courtyard. On June 6th the party left for Casablanca.

The first important engagement there was a conference with the noted Colonial administrator Marshal Lyautey, at that time Governor General of France in Morocco. Dr. Zwemer's companion, the Rev. J. Paul Cook, was a personal friend of long standing. The Marshal greeted him in his office; he was dressed in a light blue uniform with the gilt stars on the sleeves to denote his rank as a Marshal of France.

He dictated letters of introduction for Dr. Zwemer to other officials. He impressed the callers as a man who might easily lose his temper and yet one who could show mercy and kindness. In spite of his heavy eyebrows and moustache and his face wrinkled with care and age, the visitor remarks "he would not frighten a child because of the kindly eyes."

On Sunday the visiting missionary preached in the British Church at the morning service on John 1:14; his subject was "Heredity, Environment, or God." In the afternoon he spoke at the French Protestant Temple on the Moslem Problem to a large gathering of Christians. The French Protestant pastor offered his church for Dr. Mott's conference if one should be held in Casablanca.

A two-day conference was held in Marrakesh with the members of the South Morocco Mission which took up the matter of a literature committee and one to cooperate with the World Sunday School Association. It was decided that members from Morocco ought to be added to the Algerian Committee in these matters rather than forming separate committees. Casablanca was considered the best place for a conference under Dr. Mott and it was said that delegates would be sent from South Morocco. The Rev. J. Paul Cook took part in the discussions and as usual Dr. Zwemer gave the devotional addresses.

After the conference on June 14th the visitors returned to Casablanca and, with only a short stop there, went on to Rabat where they arrived about six o'clock in the evening. The next day they went to call on the Minister of

Education with a letter of introduction from Marshal Lyautey. In an hour's conference they were given a general view of education in Morocco and a number of pamphlets that described the whole program.

On the sixteenth of June two friends who had been together since Algiers parted company, Mr. Cook to return to his work in Algeria and Dr. Zwemer to start for Tangier. He arrived there in the afternoon and found welcome mail from home. The visitor was enthusiastically received by Mr. and Mrs. Stevens of the British and Foreign Bible Society, by Mr. H. P. Elson of Canada, who conducted the Raymund Lull Home, and by other missionaries.

As a climax Dr. Zwemer received an invitation to dinner with the Sultan of Tangier, which came through prominent Moslems he had met in the city. He was unable to accept, however, as his ship sailed before the time. He departed on the Steamship "Wilis" June 23rd, for Marsailles, and was then off for an extended visit to the Netherlands Indies.

The missionary had visited many of the cities which were to become famous during the North African campaigns of World War II. When the American invasion of North Africa finally came many soldiers and sailors were surprised to find the church and missionaries in occupation wherever they went in these Moslem lands.

The Zwemer visit had accomplished much to bring about a more cooperative spirit between various missions and had quickened an interest in the reaching of Mohammedans through the Gospel of the printed page. Plans were also made for the North Africa Missionary Conferences which preceded the general Jerusalem meeting. Finally, the visitor himself now had a far better understanding of the whole of Moslem North Africa, the "Land of the Vanished Church," for it was in this region that Islam probably made its greatest conquest of Christianity.

II Deputation in South Africa

In 1925 a united missionary campaign was planned for South Africa under the direction of Dr. Donald Frazer of the Free Church of Scotland. This was carried on in cooperation with the various churches represented in the area. Dr. Zwemer was asked to go with Dr. Frazer in the months of June and July on this mission.

In the four synods of the Cape, Natal, Transvaal and Orange Free State the Dutch Reformed Church counted more than a million adherents at the time. The next largest body in the Union was the Wesleyan Methodist Church with some 800,000 members and adherents and the Church of England counted about 700,000. The Presbyterians and other smaller groups united in the intensive missionary campaign.

Dr. Zwemer went on the special invitation of the Dutch Reformed Church and his function was to call attention to the need of work for Moslems and to find out something about Islam in this vast area as well as to inspire and instruct people by his messages and counsel. What he did ascertain came as something of a discovery, as mission leadership in the home lands had for most part failed, before his visit, to fully realize the proportions of the task of Mohammedan evangelism in the Union of South Africa.

With his ability to preach in Dutch or English to general congregations and in Arabic to Moslems, he seemed providentially fitted for a general missionary ministry in South Africa. There is no doubt that the campaign left a deep impression on the Union, and Zwemer was in no small degree responsible for its success. The arrangements for his journey were made by the Reverend A. C. Murray of the Dutch Reformed Church and all items were so well cared for that much more was accomplished than would seem possible in the space of two months. The visitor noted that the memory of the great Andrew Murray was still fragrant in the whole South Africa field and that many members of this family were still active in church and missionary work.

Aside from the leader of the campaign, Dr. Donald Frazer of Livingstonia, and Dr. Zwemer, the other principals were the Reverend Arnold G. Bryson of China, under the auspices of the London Missionary Society, and the Reverend A. J. Haile of South Africa. These were the main speakers, though many others took part in the special effort.

On May 15th, 1925, Dr. Zwemer left Southampton on the steamship "Saxon," which arrived in Capetown on the first of June. The visitor went at once to see the Mohammedan quarter and to begin the collection of data on Islam, which was to prove such a valuable part of his visit.

The next day a special conference was held of twenty-five missionaries representing five different societies. A list of eighteen questions concerning Moslems and work for them was discussed and passed upon to be sent out all over South Africa to gather a comprehensive picture of the situation in regard to missions and Islam.

The questionnaire was framed to draw out information concerning Moslems in every district and to find out what missionary effort was being carried on for them, as well as the extent of Christian literature for them in use. A number of factual interrogations were also made as to the number of mosques, the percentage of illiteracy, etc. There were also questions on the religious, economic and political status of the Mohammedans. These queries were sent out to forty districts and were also distributed at later conferences.

The gathering appointed a committee representing the various agencies to consider work for Moslems in the local field of Capetown. Cooperation was urged in the production of literature and the training of special workers for Islam.

Dr. Zwemer bore a letter of introduction from the Archbishop of Canterbury. The following day he had luncheon with the Coadjutor Bishop of Capetown. He also visited the Houses of Parliament and gave an address in the town hall before the annual meeting of the Sudan United Mission.

The leaders for the Missionary Campaign gathered at Stellenbosch from June 5th to 7th to perfect plans and lay the devotional foundation for the effort. Zwemer spoke to the students in the Theological Seminary. After the football game between Capetown and Stellenbosch on Saturday afternoon, he spoke to nine hundred people at a Saturday evening prayer service in *De Groote Kerke*. On Sunday he preached in Dutch and English. He had also looked up the Mohammedan population and made visits to the mosques.

On June 8th the Missionary Deputation had luncheon with the Earl of Athlone and Princess Alice at the Governor General's residence. In the afternoon the mayor tendered them a reception in the City Hall. There was a public meeting in University Hall in the evening.

On the 9th of June began the first series of meetings under the Missionary Campaign. Zwemer's first address was in the Cathedral on the subject of "Islam and the British Empire." From then on he took his full share of the speaking in churches, schools and in meetings for University students. The program often required three or four addresses a day. With all of these he did not for a moment neglect the special task of reaching Moslems. On the evening of June 11th there was a special meeting for them in the City Banqueting Hall, where beside the address something like a hundred portions of Scripture were received by the guests.

During the busy days that followed there were many public meetings. He spoke before the Women's Board of the Dutch Reformed Church on "The New World of Islam", in the oldest church at the Cape. He also addressed the students of the Diocesan College and a meeting of the Clergy of Capetown in the Lutheran Church.

During the rest of June there were successive meetings of the campaign in Worcester, Kimberley and Bloemfontein. At Kimberley the largest diamond mine in the world was visited. Then came the Natal Missionary Conference at Durban where over one hundred missionary delegates were present. The opening address was on the burning question of the race problem; it was felt that the key to this situation lay in the hands of the Christian missionary bodies and it could only be solved through their leadership.

The next important meeting was the General Missionary Conference of South Africa, held at Johannesburg, from June 30th to July 3rd. The meetings convened in the Baptist Centenary Hall. One session of the Conference was devoted to the need of work among Moslems. The list of questions concerning Islam in their locality was distributed to all delegates. Zwemer gave four addresses at the Conference. The following resolutions were adopted:

"The General Missionary Conference of South Africa wishes to place on record and to convey to the Committee which has the direction of Dr. Zwemer's work its hearty thanks that the committee has spared Dr. Zwemer from the manifold calls upon him to do for South Africa the magnificent work that he has done. He has drawn us very near the Master in his tender devotional messages. He has brought us information and stimulus in his challenging presentation of Islam and the duty of the Christian Church towards it. He has preached the Gospel of Human Brotherhood in such winsome fashion and with such eloquence that his message has reached far beyond conference halls and will, we are sure, have substantial results in the education of public opinion on the subject of Christian Race Relationships."

And concerning Islam, the following:

"1. The members of the Conference be urged to make all possible use of suitable literature in presenting to Moslems the Christian Message and to secure such literature from the Nile Mission Press, either direct or through a committee appointed by the Natal Missionary Conference.

"2. The Conference would welcome any effort of the Committee on work amongst Moslems to secure the appointment of a trained Missionary to work amongst the Moslems of South Africa, and would commend to the South African Churches the wisdom of sharing in the support of such a missionary.

"3. That the Executive endeavour to arrange for a thorough investigation by a competent investigator of the facts regarding the drawing of European girls into Islam and the preparation of a confidential report thereon."

The visitor also conducted a special meeting for Moslems, held in the Bantu Social Center of the American Board Mission. There was friendly discussion and tea, followed by a visit to the mosque. Tracts in Arabic and Gujerati were distributed. The following day the leader of the Moslem community gave a return tea which was widely publicized. The *Johannesburg Star* for July 4, 1925, had a leading article with pictures of Dr. Zwemer and his Moslem host Habib Motan, under the heading:

"A Moslem Love Feast
Cross and Crescent at Tea"

The article said in part: "It was the strangest gathering of Cross and Crescent that has ever been seen in Johannesburg. Turbaned Mussulmans, staunch followers of Islam, Christians of all denominations — all seated at a feast prepared by Habib Motan at his home near the mosque in lower Kirke Street."

"The guest of honor was Dr. S. M. Zwemer, D.D., F.R.G.S."

The article goes on to state that the guest spoke "with an American accent." Most of the language was Arabic, however. It was a very happy meeting and the Moslems expressed their joy at the visit of one who knew Islam so well and had sympathy with them, as they felt many Christians in South Africa neither had understanding of them nor sympathy toward them.

Another very interesting event in Johannesburg was a visit to the Ferreir Deep Gold mine, where he talked with Moslem miners 2,600 feet beneath the ground and later sent Arabic tracts to them!

Immediately following the General Conference in Johannesburg he took the train on July 4th for Pretoria, there to take part in the Twenty Second General Conference of the Student Association of South Africa. Some 240 student delegates were in attendance. For the first time in the history of the Association there were two negro leaders on the platform. The subject of the Conference was "Christianity a Universal Religion; no other Saviour; no race excluded and no human activity excepted." The program was printed in Dutch and English. Here again, as throughout the South African journey, it was a providential blessing that Zwemer was equally fluent in these two languages. He had major addresses each day and conducted a series of four studies with a special group on: 1. The Bible, a Missionary Book; 2. Prayer and Missions; 3. Islam as a Missionary Religion; 4. Every Christian a Missionary.

On Sunday, July 5th, he preached in the Anglican Church and also in the de Groote Kerke, in the Dutch language, on the race problem, to a gathering of 1,800 people.

On the eighth of July Zwemer began a long journey by train to Portuguese East Africa and Nyassaland. From Pretoria he traveled to Mefeking and the next day arrived at Bulawayo, where a meeting was held in the Wesleyan Church for missionaries and other Christian leaders. He proceeded to Salisbury and on to Beira on the coast. His schedule was delayed by two special trains for the party of The Prince of Wales and also by a wreck on the road.

Beira is one of the chief ports of Portuguese East Africa, through which trade passes for Rhodesia and Nyassaland. He was there for a day and visited the Moslem part of the town and the mosque. Here an Egyptian teacher was telling Negro boys to collect coppers and send them to the Caliphate Committee in Bombay to help the Riffs of Morroco in their holy war against the French, which certainly constitutes a perfect illustration of the solidarity of Islam!

July 13th he left on the *Trans-Zambezi, Central Africa and Shire Highlands Railway* for Blantyre. It was an interesting trip through East African forest and jungle. He noted that at Caia there was a large sugar factory which employed among its workers 150 Moslems from India. This explains *how* Islam spreads in Africa.

The mighty Zambezi River was crossed by a small steamer on which the passengers had dinner and spent the night. The total distance from Beira to Blantyre is 349 miles and the fare 190 shillings —"about sixpence a mile!" the traveler exclaims. Though the train was about three hours late and arrived at Blantyre at 9:30 p.m. he was met by the Reverend Alexander Hetherwick, senior member of the Church of Scotland Mission, who was a member of the International Missionary Council.

The next day they went on by motor lorry 124 miles to Fort Johnson and met members of the Universities' Mission. The party passed through

Zomba, capital of Nyassaland, and Likweno en route. About sunset they arrived at Mponda's village, of which Livingstone speaks in his journal as a center of the slave trade.

There were visits to the mosque in Fort Johnson and to Lake Nyassa and then began the Conference with Christian Workers in Mponda's village. The majority of those who took part were from the Universities' Mission, but the Dutch Reformed Church also was represented. An interested government official and his wife were present. The Conference adopted resolutions looking to a survey of Islam in Nyassaland, an advance in the use of Christian literature for Moslems, and the possible training of special workers in Cairo. Dr. Zwemer spoke to a native gathering and left by motor lorry for the return to Zomba. On the trip he visited a member of the Government Medical Service who was busy on a translation of the Koran into Yao, using the Arabic character.

In Zomba on July 19th he preached to an overflow native congregation of more than a thousand. The text was John 17:1-3 and the sermon was interpreted in the native language. In the afternoon the traveler visited a new Indian Mosque, built at a cost of two thousand pounds Sterling, on land given by the Government for the purpose.

That evening there was a special meeting for Europeans, at which the Governor, Sir Charles Bowring, was present. The next day a Moslem village named Ali Taipan was visited where Dr. Zwemer spoke to about 250 people near the mosque, the leader of the village, Ali himself, acted as interpreter from Arabic to Yao. The visiting missionary had dinner with Sir Charles and Lady Bowring. The Governor was a grandson of the author of the hymn "In the Cross of Christ I Glory."

In Blantyre a Conference was held on July 22nd with representatives of the Societies working in Southern Nayassaland and Portuguese East Africa. Those present were from the Church of Scotland Mission, the Dutch Reformed Church Mission, the Nyassaland Industrial Mission, and the Seventh Day Adventist Mission. Dr. Zwemer acted as chairman and a number of resolutions were adopted looking to a greater activity in Moslem work. Emphasis was placed on the training of native pastors in the understanding of Islam and work for those who had been touched by the Mohammedan missionary efforts. There was a round table conference with the native church leaders in the afternoon and a special meeting with the delegates of the Dutch Reformed Church in the evening.

The following day Zwemer was off by the mail train for Beira and on to Salisbury, across Rhodesia and Bechuanaland. A note in his journal tells that during this trip his overcoat was taken from his compartment. On August 2nd the Apostle to the Moslems sailed on the steamer "Windsor Castle" for Southampton, where he arrived August 17th, 1925. On board he had been busily engaged working with a stenographer on reports of his visit and articles for the International Review of Missions and The Moslem World.

The itinerary in South Africa had covered 6,245 miles by rail and motor car. The traveler remarked, "The great areas of the Union of Rhodesia, Portuguese East Africa and Nyassaland are only appreciated when you spend long days and nights in crossing the vast veldt and creeping up the steep grades that lead from the coast to plateaus of five or six thousand feet altitude."

One of the chief results of the visit was to awaken the United States and Europe to the extent of the Mohammedan missionary problem in South Africa. Zwemer issued a report on this, which we need not quote here at length, but merely say that from census figures and thoroughly informed estimates he found that there were something like 283,190 Moslems in South Africa. The Cape Province had nearly 25,000; there were approximately 150,000 in Portuguese East Africa. The census figures for Nyassaland were Pagans 1,123,918; Christians 103,110 and Moslems 73,915.

The missionary campaign had a marked influence upon the whole of the Union and even beyond. General Smuts wrote to the organizing secretary as follows:

"Deep down in the heart of white South Africa is the desire to be fair, and to do justice to our coloured and black fellow-men among whom Providence has cast our lot; to build up in Africa a stable ethical civilization, a civilization of the helping hand, and not of mere exploitation of the black man." Such an ideal "cannot be realized apart from the Sermon on the Mount, apart from the great human principles which underlie all true civilization of the spirit . . . I wish this mission the fullest measure of success."

The expenses of Dr. Zwemer throughout his whole trip were paid by the Dutch Reformed Church of South Africa, and concerning that body he wrote:

"Whether we judge by the voluminous contributions which Andrew Murray made to the spiritual life of the past century through his writings or by the influence the memory of his life still exerts in all South Africa; whether we visit the Huguenot Memorial Hall at Capetown or the Theological Seminary and University at Stellenbosch; whether we witness the permanence and power of the family altar in the home of the Boers or their place in national life — the impression remains that the Dutch Reformed Church of South Africa, true to the motto on the seal of its oldest congregation, 'De Hoop en Beschaamt Niet,' has 'Hope that maketh not ashamed' ".

As we take a bird's eye view of this visit in South Africa and in the following chapter read the narrative of his trip to the Netherlands Indies, we cannot help but marvel at the fact that God in His providence had prepared a man with such an understanding of Islam and such a mastery of the Dutch and English languages — as well as Arabic, to visit these fields as an apostle to arouse interest in missionary work for Moslems.

Nicely said, Wilson!

III. Hither and Yon in Europe

On invitation from the Missionary Societies in Great Britain Dr. Zwemer made a flying trip to England during April and May of 1925. During twenty-three days he spoke at the meetings of fourteen leading organizations. In churches and including other gatherings he gave a total of 36 addresses before approximately 37,200 people. It may be that few missionaries have addressed in so short a time so many people of great influence in the missionary enterprise.

We can here only list the schedule of the "Flying Dutchman" and let it speak for itself. He began on Wednesday, April 22nd, before a meeting of the Board of the London Missionary Society. They were contemplating special work for Moslems in India and China and desired expert advice from one who had visited the followers of Islam in these areas.

The next day there was a largely attended meeting of the Society for the Propagation of the Gospel. One of the most ancient of the sending missionary bodies, this organization is still full of power and drive. The Archbishop of Canterbury presided and introduced Dr. Zwemer. The address was printed in the magazine of the Society and the missionary to Moslems was invited to Lambeth Palace by the Archbishop, but was unable to accept the invitation due to the intensive speaking schedule of his time in Britain.

On Sunday he spoke at morning and evening services in Derby, for the Church Missionary Society, and the next day attended meetings arranged by the same official society of the Church of England. There was a luncheon for the clergy of the vicinity and a popular meeting in Temperance Hall.

Wednesday, April 29th, was a busy and memorable day. Zwemer and Dr. John R. Mott had breakfast together, after which the program included the morning meeting of the Wesleyan Missionary Society Board. There was a luncheon in honor of Dr. Mott and in the evening a meeting in Queen's Hall of the Baptist Missionary Society. Zwemer spoke on "God's Love for Mohammedans."

The following afternoon he gave an address before the Zenana Bible and Medical Society at their public meeting. That evening he spoke at a similar gathering of The Sudan United Mission. On the first of May there was a luncheon meeting with Methodist ministers from all over the London area, some forty were present at the Y.M.C.A. in Tottenham Court Road. In the evening he spoke to about sixty students at the Church Missionary Society Training Institute for Women.

The services on Sunday were arranged by the Wesleyan Methodist Missionary societies. He spoke three times, twice in prominent churches and in the afternoon to a mass meeting of about 2,000 working men. The next day the same Missionary Society had their great public meeting in the Westminster Central Hall in the morning. He spoke there and in the afternoon at the public meeting of the Nile Mission Press. Here he was on most familiar ground, his address was published and widely circulated in pamphlet form under the title, "The Arabic Language and Islam."

On the following evening he spoke before the largest gathering of the campaign, it was the Annual Church Missionary Society meeting in Albert Hall. There were some 8,000 present, his subject was, "The Old Gospel in the New World of Islam". The next morning he spoke at the meeting of the British and Foreign Bible Society and at public meetings for the Egypt General Mission both afternoon and evening. He met with the standing committee of the Society for the Propogation of the Gospel in a discussion of preparation for missionary service. Public meetings ensued for the Church of England Zenana Missionary Society and the Fellowship of Faith, the latter being in Eccleston Hall. On Sunday he went to Bristol where his appointments were arranged by the Wesleyan Methodist Missionary Society again. In the morning he spoke in Trinity Methodist Church and in the afternoon to a meeting of about one thousand men at Central Hall. On Monday there was a meeting for all the clergy in the same place, at three o'clock in the afternoon about 1,500 women of the laboring class came with their children to hear him speak on "Women of the World of Islam".

On Tuesday, May 12th, he was back in London for the great public meeting of the China Inland Mission in Queen's Hall. He spoke on "Islam in China" and brought out the past neglect and present opportunity. On the following two final days of the visit he spoke at the public meeting of the British Syria Mission, then the council meeting of the Jerusalem and the East Mission where he remarked that he "met many bishops". The final evening public meeting in Queen's Hall was under the auspices of the London Missionary Society. The next day he sailed for South Africa. He must have needed a sea trip after such a round of public meetings and other addresses for the great missionary societies of Britain. Certainly few men would have had the enormous energy and vitality to complete such a schedule!

Journey to Scandinavia

The Zwemers went to America for the marriage of their daughter Nellie Elizabeth to Rev. Claude L. Pickens, Jr., a young Episcopal clergyman of Alexandria, Virginia. The wedding took place at Mount Vernon, New York, on August 27th, 1925. Dr. and Mrs. Zwemer sailed for Europe on the "Mauretania" September first.

Following a short visit in England they arrived at the Hook of Holland on September 11th and took the train for Hamburg. From that point the journey was continued by sleeping car to Copenhagen, where they arrived the next morning. During the stay in Denmark they were entertained by Count Moltke in his ancient mansion. Soon after their arrival the couple visited the metropolitan church and saw those masterpieces in marble, Christ and the Apostles by Thorwaldsen.

On Sunday the visitors attended service in the Cathedral Church and in the afternoon had a meeting with missionary leaders. In the evening there was a popular address at the new Y.M.C.A. building, in Denmark this organization is known by the initials K.F.U.K. The hall was crowded with some 600 people. Zwemer spoke on God's Love for Moslems.

Monday afternoon representatives of the Danish Missionary Societies met with the visitors, again at the Y.M.C.A. Dr. Zwemer spoke on Cooperation in Work for Moslems. The subject was vital because of the great number of Danish Missionary Societies and the further multiplication of small organizations with no unified program and no general committee. For the good of the work the visitor urged upon them more unity in organization and planning. At an evening meeting in the University Zwemer spoke to 250 students on The New World of Islam.

The crossing to Sweden was made on September 15th. That same day in Stockholm Mrs. Zwemer conducted an afternoon meeting for women in the Y.W.C.A. where the wife of the local bishop presided. In the evening Dr. Zwemer addressed four hundred students of Lund University. A number of the faculty were present. Aside from the many meetings the editor was busy during this trip in preparing the material for the January 1926 number of *The Moslem World*. They went on from Stockholm to Gottenburg where an evening address was given in the high school auditorium. There were about two hundred present and admission was charged, which the speaker thought was rather unusual, but a good idea.

On Friday, September 15th, the Zwemers arrived in Olso, the capital of Norway. The name of the city had but recently been changed from Christiania. The visitors in this city and in other places stayed at the mission hotels which were found in connection with the training schools for missionaries. The societies in Norway had no direct missionary work for Mohammedans, though they were represented in areas where there were Moslems, like India and China. The Lutheran Church is predominant in Norway though there are some Baptists and other Protestant organizations. There are very few Roman Catholics in the Scandinavian countries.

A student conference was held at the University where Zwemer spoke twice in the general meetings and had many interviews. Saturday evening there was a banquet at a restaurant on an eminence overlooking the city. The location was a center for skiing and other winter sports and the visitor remembered a big open fire of fir logs in the dining hall. Those present represented the secretaries and leaders of most all the Norwegian missionary societies. Mrs. Zwemer gave a talk on mission life in Bahrein and he spoke concerning his call to missionary service.

On Sunday, September 20th, the visiting missionary spoke in the Trefoldighedskirken in Oslo, or Trinity Church. On Monday the couple returned to Stockholm and took the train for Upsala. There again they were entertained in the Missionary Training Home. There was a meeting for the University community under the auspices of the Student Christian Association. Zwemer spoke for nearly an hour, and remarks in his diary that only one lady fainted.

There was a supper meeting at the Y.M.C.A. where the missionary gave the Moslem call to prayer and a talk on mission service for Islam. It should be noted that the custom in these countries was to have dinner about three o'clock in the afternoon and supper at nine or ten o'clock at night, following an evening meeting.

The next day there was a visit to the Swedish Church Mission. They maintained at the time 134 missionaries at work in India, China and Natal. The visitor notes the fact that due to a government concession the mission pays no postage, but has the franking privilege for its mail. The Zwemers had a very interesting visit for tea with Archbishop L. O. J. Söderblom. He was the utmost in hospitality and spoke English, German and French fluently; the visitors also met a parish pastor, Tor Andrae, who was an authority on Islam, the author of several books, as well as articles in *The Moslem World*.

The next day the guests were entertained for luncheon ·by the Archbishop. He talked much of the recent conference on Faith and Life in which he had such an important part. He evinced a vital interest in all the movements toward church unity. The Zwemers returned to Stockholm for the main object of their visit, the General Nordish Missionary Conference which met from September 23rd to the 27th. There were more than 1,400 delegates present from Denmark, Norway, Sweden and Finland.

An interesting visit was paid to the offices of the Swedish Free Church Missionary Society. Their work in Abyssinia and other African missions had produced several hundred converts from Islam. The General Secretary, Pastor Dahlberg, asked for permission to translate and publish several of Zwemer's books in Swedish. It was granted in writing.

The Zwemers were entertained at the home of His Royal Highness, Prince O. Bernadotte, brother of the King of Sweden. The host was a friend of Robert Wilder, and is described by his guest as "a fine Christian democrat". The prince had a charming wife and a family of three daughters and two sons. Early in the Conference Archbishop Soderblom gave an eloquent speech on Christian Missions and Peace. Zwemer gave two addresses to the General Conference which met in the great auditorium near the center of Stockholm. He also preached on Sunday to a congregation of 1,600 in the Katarina Church. Among the speakers at the conference was also Pastor Alfred Nielsen of Denmark, whom the Zwemers knew well as a missionary in Damascus. There was a final evening meeting in one of the Free churches where several missionaries were on the program. Zwemer spoke on Missions in the Islamic World.

They said their farewells and left by sleeping car on the night of the 27th for Berlin. The party was four hours on a fine ferry-boat that carried the sleeping cars and through coaches. They arrived at 8:03 a.m. in Berlin and were there for a time visiting several of the German missionary societies and being entertained at a reception in the home of the prominent historian and Professor of Missions, Julius Richter.

On the morning of September 20th they left for Italy and were all day on the train passing through Bavaria. After a short stop in Munich they went to Trieste where on October 1st they sailed for Egypt.

If the reader has followed Zwemer through the rapid-fire series of meetings and addresses in Scandinavia it is hardly necessary to suggest why Canon Gairdner of Cairo called him "A steam engine in breeches"!

Eastern Europe and the Balkans

Zwemer visited Poland and the Balkan countries in 1927. Concerning this he wrote:

"It is not generally known that in Southern Europe there are still nearly three million followers of the Arabian Prophet, chiefly in Yugo-Slavia, Albania, Rumania and Bulgaria. These are living, as minority groups, in the midst of Christians. Their racial origin is in some places Tatar or Turkish, the descendants of the old Moslem conquerors. In other places Serbians, Bulgarians, (Pomaks), Albanians and Gypsies have been 'converted' to Islam many decades since, and cannot easily be distinguished from orthodox Turks.

"Eager to learn the needs of these people, and to know something at first hand of the missionary opportunity among them, we recently visited some of the great Moslem centers such as Rustchuk, Varna, Constanza, Sofia, Philopoppolis, Belgrade and Serajevo. We saw more, however, in the smaller towns, away from the usual routes, in places like Bazargic, Shumma, and Majidiya, where the old-fashioned life prevails, where men still mourn the abolition of the Caliphate, women go veiled, young men wear the fez, and old men smoke the waterpipe. We were reminded at Warsaw, on a visit to the mosque and the Moslem cemetery, that there are six thousand Moslems in Poland; and by the noble marble monument to Sobieski that it was a Polish king who hurled back the wave of Turkish invasion from the gates of Vienna in 1683, and saved Europe.

"In Budapest we visited the little mosque-shrine to the last saint of Islam in Hungary, but once across the border and into the great plain of the Danube in Rumania we saw the familiar dress that distinguishes Moslem men and women everywhere.

"After arrival in Bucharest, the Paris of the Balkans, our host, the Reverend J. H. Adeney of the London Jews Society, took us for a visit to the beautiful little mosque, built in Carol Park by the government to adorn the exposition grounds, and now used for Moslem worship. We had a delightful hour discussing religious matters with the Mufti, who spoke Arabic quite easily, and gave us a warm welcome. Literature from the Nile Mission Press and the Scriptures in Arabic, Turkish, etc., were here and everywhere on our journey eagerly accepted. In fact, our lack of faith was rebuked, for our supply ran out long before the demand was met. A converted Jewish soldier in the Rumanian army for example bought Testaments for his Moslem comrades at the barracks."

A high point of the visit was a conference in Rustchuk. After Zwemer's address the meeting adopted the following resolution:

"We are greatly impressed with our Christian obligation to bring the Christ to our 750,000 Mohammedan neighbors in Bulgaria, therefore we, the delegates to the 47th Convention of the Bulgarian Evangelical Society representing the united body of Evangelical Christians working in Bulgaria, do hereby pledge ourselves to every possible interest in the evangelization of our Mohammedan brothers, and will give loyal cooperation to every effort to reach with the Gospel the thousands of Mohammedans in this land and elsewhere."

Everywhere the Apostle to Moslems went, his burning zeal was contagious among missionaries of all societies, national workers, and the agents of the Bible Society. After the trip his conclusion was:

"With specially trained workers, the wide use of Christian literature, and the union of all the scattered groups, we believe the Bulgarian Church could speedily win the seven hundred thousand Moslems back to Christ. The Pomaks are really lapsed Christians, prodigals to be welcomed back home.

"Just across the borders of Rumania and Bulgaria, there are the eighteen million Mohammedans of Russia; westward there are nearly two million Mohammedans in Albania and Yugo-Slavia. What a challenge to the Church, and what a strategic advantage the present missionary forces in Bulgaria and Rumania would have if they arose to their opportunity!"[3]

Motivator for sure!

---

3. **Missionary Review of the World**, October, 1927.

IX

Strategic Moslem Areas

MY TIMES ARE IN THY HAND

"Our life is like the dial of a clock,
The hands are God's hands passing o'er and o'er,
The short hand is the Hand of Discipline,
The long, the Hand of Mercy evermore.

"Slowly and surely Discipline must pass,
And God speaks, at each stroke His word of grace,
But ever on the Hand of Mercy moves,
With blessings sixty fold the trials efface.

"Each moment counts a blessing from our God,
Each hour a lesson in His school of Love.
Both hands are fastened to a pivot sure,
The great unchanging Heart of God above."

—SAMUEL M. ZWEMER

CHAPTER NINE

STRATEGIC MOSLEM AREAS

This chapter gives a brief account of visits to the Netherlands East Indies, Iraq, Arabia, and Iran. China and India will be subsequently considered.

The year 1922 was spent very largely in travel. A journey to North Africa has been chronicled in the previous chapter. On his return to Marsailles he visited the French Colonial Exposition, then sailed for the Netherlands Indies. He stopped at Colombo on July 13th and arrived at Padang, Sumatra, on the 18th, and went on to Batavia, Java, where he arrived on Thursday, July 20th.

The conferences in Java and Sumatra occupied his time until mid-September. The traveler arrived at Singapore September 19th, was at Colombo again on September 28th and reached Port Said on his return October 11th. A general conference on the Survey of Moslem Literature was held in Cairo November 7th to 13th. He was in Marseilles again on November 4th and sailed for the United States on the "Olympic," from Cherbourg on November 22nd, 1922.

In the North Africa and East Indian visits Zwemer had traveled more than 19,000 miles. He held fifteen major conferences and gave ninety-nine public addresses. Twenty-seven were in English and seventeen in Arabic, ten were in French by interpretation. He spoke in Dutch twenty-eight times in the East Indies, and addresses were given through interpreters ten times in Batak, five in Javanese and two in Malay. He visited twenty-three mission stations in Africa and twenty-five in Asia.

The reader will pardon all these details, but they must be set down to show the high pressure under which Zwemer worked. In all of this time there was not a single delay of consequence, not a day of illness, and not a break in the program which had been outlined months beforehand. Zwemer remarked, "Only prayer on the part of those who had planned and remembered this journey can account for the way it went through." To anyone who might be sceptical in this regard we should suggest that he endeavor to duplicate the record.

The missionary was impressed by the tropical verdure and magnificent mountain scenery of the islands. On Java there are some 125 volcanoes, fourteen of which were active at the time. His main interest, however, centered in the fact that the vast majority of the population in Java was Mohammedan. There are more converts from Islam to Christianity there than anywhere else in the world. In Java 37,526 former Moslems were members of the Christian churches, on the other islands there were some 8,000 additional, making a total of over 45,000. There are whole villages of Christian converts and many congregations all of whose members have been won from Islam.

A Moslem paper in an article on Zwemer's visit challenged his figures, claiming there were far more Christian converts than his compilation; but went on to question, "After all what are these among thirty million Moslems on Java alone?"

More than one hundred Moslem journals were published in the Dutch East Indies. A notable trophy of the visit is a special edition of the magazine "Medan-Moeslimin" in Samatra, given over to Dr. Zwemer's visit — such was the emphatic effect of his journey. The tone of the articles in the vernacular and in Dutch are very friendly, the missionary was respected because he could speak Arabic and knew Islam so well.

That the Netherlands Indies are a very vital section of Islam is attested by the fact that year after year there are far more pilgrims to Mecca from this region than from any other section of the Moslem World.

At the time of his visit there were sixteen Protestant missions at work in Java, with a total of 456 missionaries in all the islands of the Dutch East Indies. The invitation for this visit had come from the Dutch Reformed Churches of the Netherlands and his schedule and entertainment were arranged by their missions, with official approval of the Dutch Missionary Consul. The main objects of the visit were two: 1) to acquaint the societies at work in Java and Sumatra with literature for Moslems, especially that produced in Arabic at Cairo and Beirut, and to stimulate the use of literature; 2) to secure greater comity between various organizations and general cooperation in conferences on Moslem work.

Something of the strenuous character of Zwemer's schedule is indicated by the following itinerary:

JULY 20 Arrived Batavia, Java
    21 Batavia
    22-23 Methodist Mission, Weltevreden
    24 Djokjakarta
    25 Solo
    26 Djokjakarta — Mission Reformed Churches
    27-29 Modjowarno. N.S.G.
    31-2 Aug. Margaradja — Dutch Baptist Mission

AUG. 2-3 Blora Salatiga Mission
    7-8 General Conference Solo
    9-10 Bandoeng and West Java
    11-12 Return to Weltevreden
    13 Methodist Mission, Buitenzorg
    14-19 Weltevreden — Conferences, Correspondence, Interviews
    20 Leave Batavia for Padang
    23 Arrive Padang, Sumatra. Rhenish Missions
    24 Leave Padang for Sibolga by auto

25 Arrive Sibolga (Rhenish Mission)
26 Simatorkis
27-28 Fargareetan — Java Comite Mission
29 Sipirok
30 Return to Sibolga

SEPT. 1 Simatorkis
3 Back to Sibolga
4 Pearadja — Dr. Warneck. Rhenish Mission
5-7 Toba and the Batak Mission — Penang Siantar
8-10 By auto and train to Medan
11 Leave Medan (Belawan) for Penang
13 Kualla Lampur
14-20 Malacca and Singapore
22 Leave Singapore on S. S. "Koning der Nederlanden" for Port Said

The schedule was very closely knit and left little time for relaxation, rest or possible delay. Such a plan might be expected to work out in Western countries, but to do it in the East — that is another matter.

The next day after arrival in Batavia there was a conference with members of the Methodist Mission at Weltevreden. Questions of unity in the production of literature, Dr. Mott's general conferences on work for Moslems, and missionary cooperation were discussed.

The visitor then went on for preliminary visits and local conferences at several stations in Western and Central Java. In a number of conferences the lady missionaries were present with their husbands as equals in counsel and voting for the first time. They had been considered "missionary wives" or helpers, but the actual mission business had formerly been left largely to the male members of the organization.

On the last two days of July the journey extended to Soerabaija in Eastern Java. This city is the commercial capital of that portion of the island and also a leading Islamic center. Dr. Zwemer preached there before a congregation of some 600. Practically every Sunday on the trip he spoke at one or more church services. In the visit to Eastern Java he was with Dr. Hendrick Kraemer, who was many years later to write for the Madras Conference the great missionary volume, "The Christian Message in a Non-Christian World." As the two were visiting a Moslem cemetery Zwemer spoke in Arabic to a woman who was sweeping the paths. She thought immediately that he was a learned Moslem dignitary and fell down to kiss his feet. Dr. Kraemer was also a companion on other portions of the trip in Java.

In a public meeting at a large church in Djokjakarta, Zwemer spoke for a full sixty minutes on *The Strength and Weakness of Islam.* The attention was very good and at the close a Moslem leader who had been on the pilgrimage to Mecca arose and said he wished to thank the speaker for pointing out the weakness of Islam and stated that he would like to have a similar meeting to point out the weakness of Christianity! On many occasions the friendly spirit of Moslems in the East Indies was quite in contrast to conditions in Arabia, Egypt, and other predominently Moslem areas.

Dr. Zwemer had a set of slides on *Islam in China and Arabia* which he used for a stereopticon lecture in several cities. In one place a *Hajji* cut in to explain certain things about pictures of Mecca, as he had been there and the lecturer had not.

The traveler was constantly noting Moslem customs and gathering information from every possible source. He made a drawing in his journal of a long cylindrical drum like those of Africa, used in Java to call Mohammedans to prayer in the Mosque. In Solo he visited a Roman Catholic Mission and found that their church had about eighty workers in Java.

For the Conference at Solo on August 7th and 8th delegates came from twelve stations and represented missions of various denominations and societies. The meagerness of existing books and tracts was emphasized by its display on a single table of all that existed in the four main languages! These were Javanese, Madurese, Sundanese and Maly. This one table contained samples of all Christian literature, aside from the Bible, that had been produced in eighty years of missionary effort.

Two things, however, gave a basis for future hope. There was general agreement on the fact that literature should be a joint effort and there was a single hymn book in Javanese which had gained general acceptance over the island. Following the conferences both production and distribution of Christian literature increased rapidly.

In Java, as in most of the world of Islam, the great obstacle to the Gospel of the printed page was illiteracy. Only about six per cent of the population was literate though the government had in progress an educational campaign of extensive proportions, but still very small in scope considering the millions of the population. The Government also produced quite a large amount of literature in the native languages and conducted lending libraries for this and Dutch books. This secular literature did not, of course, meet the needs of the missions.

It was found that not one of the missionaries present from Java knew Arabic and most of them were not very deeply aware of the real nature of Islam. However, a strong paper was read with plans for a common literature committee and a central bureau.

There was a discussion of distribution by colporteurs, by mail, through shops and reading rooms, and by individual gift or sale. The church and the mission were to cooperate in this, and did so, resulting in a great advance in work for Mohammedans through the printed page. An advisory committee was appointed to act with the American Christian Literature Society for Moslems, which would cooperate by furnishing funds for evangelistic literature, as they did in other parts of the Moslem world.

A prominent Moslem invited Dr. Zwemer to conduct a meeting in his home. There were 150 invited guests present and a fine spirit. The missionary spoke squarely from his own point of view and closed his address with prayer. It seems that Moslems in most parts of the world have deeper respect for a man of another religious faith who speaks straight from the shoulder, as they would about their own religion.

On visiting the marvelous ancient temple of "A Thousand Buddhas" the missionary made the comment, "This temple is at once a witness of the strength and weakness of Islam. It destroyed Buddhism and Hinduism but has not raised a single building of great architectural beauty like this in 800 years. It cast down the idols but today Moslems still offer incense and bring flowers to the Buddhas, and sacred trees and rocks in all Java."

On his return to western Java, Zwemer was impressed with work in Bandoeng, the great center for tea culture and quinine.

He discovered here that two versions of the Koran had been printed in Dutch, a fact of which he was not aware, though conversant with much of the literature in that language. He also visited the fine headquarters of the Salvation Army in Bandoeng, which is the center for their work in all the East Indies. Here he also saw a colony for lepers and heard an orchestra of players, many without fingers and some whose hands were gone and yet were able to play the drums or other instruments with their feet. The official publication of the Salvation Army had the full approval of the government and indeed heavy subsidies were contributed from official sources.

After visits and conferences in a number of other West-Java stations the traveler returned to Batavia. Here there were visits with many officials and an evening lecture before one of the learned societies, known as the Batavian Literary Society. There were 240 present, many of them Moslems. A lecture was also given by invitation at the Government Military School, with about 150 officers and their wives and cadets present. This was considered a rare opportunity. A visit was made to the oldest mosque in the city and Arabic gospels were received by those in charge of the edifice.

There were several days of conferences at Weltevreden and a second visit to the Methodist work there. On August 20th Zwemer preached in the large Dutch church, then after meeting a group of the clergy and other friends who came to say farewell, he sailed for Sumatra.

On the twenty-third of August the traveler reached Padang, Sumatra. Here he found many Arabic speaking Moslems and discovered that Egyptian newspapers were widely read. There were also matches for sale in the bazaar, made in Sweden but bearing the portrait of Abdul Hamid, the Moslem Khalif on the cover. Zwemer was invited to speak in a Moslem school attended by 800 boys and girls. Hajji Abdullah Ahmad, the leading Moslem of the city, returned the missionary in his private automobile to the steamer. That afternoon he sailed for Sibolga.

There the visitor was the guest of the Rhenish Mission. An incident took place the first evening in Sibolga which Zwemer never forgot. He was given a beautifully clean guest-room in one of the mission homes. His eye at once lighted upon a little verse in German by Maria Schwallenbach. He translated it into English and passed it on to many missionary friends over the world. It was:

> "Light of Eternity, Light divine
> Into my darkness shine,
> That the small may appear small
> And the great, greatest of all.
> Light of Eternity shine."

As he went to bed that night he heard a great steamer loading with tin and rubber not far away, but in the Light of Eternity he realized that the service of this little mission station was of greater consequence than all the commerce of the Indies. The little verse and the vision of that night remained an inspiration and incentive over the years.

There were conferences with the missionaries and then a visit into the interior. The trip by auto to Sipirok took from 8:00 a.m. until 5:30 in the afternoon. The road went up to an altitude of a thousand meters, through magnificent scenery, the journal of the traveler notes the great rubber plantations and also says: "Passed many villages, each with a church steeple and also a mosque."

At a village near Sipirok there was a great meeting of Batak tribesmen who had become Christians. Dr. Zwemer spoke twice through an interpreter, before a large congregation on Sunday, August 27th. On Monday there was another trip out from Sipirok to visit the leper asylum where a warm sulphur-spring provided mineral baths for the patients. There were visits to many stations and churches. Most of the travel was made by government car or truck.

On September first the party was off over steep mountains and valleys for Pearadja where a conference was held. Near the latter place they saw the monument to the early American pioneers who were martyred there.[1] The inscription was in German and reads, as translated by Zwemer:

Here Rest the Bones
of the two American Missionaries
Munson and Lyman
Killed and Eaten in the Year, 1834.
John 16:1-3
"The blood of the martyrs is the seed of the church of Jesus."

At the time our missionary paid his visit the first Batak convert, named Jacobus—baptized in 1861—was still alive. There were at that time some 210,000 Batak Christians in this area where the early missionaries were martyred. The traveler exclaims in his journal, "What hath God wrought!"

---

1. Samuel Munson and Henry Lyman, missionaries under The American Board of Commissioners for Foreign Missions, arrived in Batavia in 1833. The next year while on a journey to interior Sumatra they were martyred by Batak tribesmen.

On Sunday, September third, Zwemer was giving an address in the Theological School at Sipohoan. He continued past noon and about 12.20 there was an earthquake, but the people seemed quite used to tremors and asked the speaker to continue. However, he often used the illustration in after years to point the moral that an earthquake is needed in some theological schools.

The same evening he preached for an hour in Dutch to a congregation of 1500 in the large church. There were some of the first converts in the region present. At the close the women went out of the service first, followed by the men and all continued to sing hymns as they left the building.

The work of the Rhenish Mission was most impressive. Dr. Johannes Warneck accompanied Zwemer much of the time. They continued on the journey across Sumatra together until they parted on September 6th. Zwemer took the train for the great city of Medan, near the East Coast.

On September 13th, farewells were said and the traveler sailed for Penang. There a telegram was received from Dr. Ferguson-Davies, Bishop of Singapore, asking Zwemer to visit him at Kuala Kangsar, which invitation was accepted. There were happy days of visiting missionaries and their institutions in Penang, Taiping, at Kuala Kangsar with the Bishop and his chaplain and then to Kuala Lumpur, where there are other missions; then on to Malacca where he was met by American missionaries. After two busy days he went on to Singapore, where he arrived Tuesday, September 19th. He spoke at the Methodist Church and visited various missions urging them to work for Moslems. On the 22nd he sailed on the "Koning der Nederlanden" for Port Said.

The journey had inspired a great increase in the production and use of Christian literature, as well as greater cooperation between missions at work in Java and Sumatra. The work on the thickly populated island of Java and the relatively large number of converts from Islam was a great revelation and inspiration. He wrote in *The Missionary Review of the World:*

"Missions in Java are remarkable; (1) In the large results secured among an almost wholly Moslem population, and these results were secured not by superficial methods, but by a most thorough requirement for baptism. (2) In the preparation of Christian literature, including Bible translations, where the psychology of the people was taken into consideration, as perhaps on no other field. The Javanese mind was thoroughly understood in presenting the message, and therefore it received acceptance. (3) In spite of the many societies engaged in the work in one single field, the laws of comity have been strictly observed, and there is an increasing spirit of cooperation between the missions, especially in the production and distribution of Christian literature."

I I

We now turn to a visit which Dr. and Mrs. Zwemer made to Iraq in 1924. A series of conferences had been held under the leadership of John R. Mott in North Africa and the Near East, culminating in a conference on Work among Moslems in Jerusalem.

The Zwemers left Cairo on the last day of March and were at the General Conference for Workers in Moslem Lands, at Jerusalem, from April third to the seventh. Dr. Mott asked the Zwemers to hold a regional conference in Baghdad to pass on to workers in Iraq, Iran and Arabia the results of the Jerusalem meeting.

They left the Holy City on the morning of April eighth, and stopping at Nazareth and Nablus enroute, were in Haifa for the night. The next day they went up the coast past Tyre and Sidon to Beirut, where the American Press and the University were described as "Twin dynamos whose energy of light and power radiates in ever widening circles."

They drove over the Lebanons to Damascus and on the tenth of April left for the journey across the desert with the Nairn Transport Company. There were two Cadillac and two Buick cars, which carried some twenty passengers. The transport company furnished box lunches with hot tea and fruit at stops on the desert. For some 400 miles there was water in only one place, at Rutba Wells. Though there was no constructed road, the convoy sped on at forty to fifty miles an hour across the desert. The drivers knew their way across the flat plains as sailors know the sea.

Early on April 12th the party reached the Euphrates River at Ramadi, and the Zwemers must have sensed that they were coming home—they were in Mesopotamia again, where they had first met and were married. The bridge at Faluji had been washed away and it took them until afternoon to get across on a raft which could hardly be dignified by the term "ferry-boat," even on the Euphrates. Then on across the level plains again to Baghdad and the Tigris.

Who should await them at the Maude bridge but James Cantine, the co-founder with Zwemer of the Arabian Mission. Our traveler has described Baghdad as "A clash of color and civilizations, a complex of hotels, cinemas, tombs, mosques, churches, barracks, beer-halls, and business blocks—the minaret and the muezzin's call and the tall masts of the radio."

On Sunday, April 13th, Zwemer spoke at the English service and at a refugee gathering for Assyrians, who had been driven out of their mountain homes in the Urumia region of Iran and Kurdistan, now for several years settled at Baghdad. There was also an address to a cosmopolitan congregation of more than 150 at the famous Baghdad Y.M.C.A.

The conference began the same afternoon with an opening devotional service. There were twenty-six missionary delegates present from Arabia, Iraq and Iran. The sessions were held in the Y.M.C.A. which was a part of what had been the British Residency, where the Zwemers had their civil marriage service some twenty-eight years before.

The discussions of the Conference were taken up under five sections:
1. Occupation and Accessibility of the Field
2. Literature and Cooperation
3. Medical and Social Work
4. Evangelization and the Church
5. Education for Leadership.

The Zwemers could bring to their old colleagues and to delegates from other missions the findings of the Jerusalem Conference and latest reports on work for Moslems in other parts of the vast field. New enthusiasm was engendered and resolves made to create Christian literature that would be more effective in reaching Moslem hearts.

A new parliament was in session even as the Conference was meeting and the new flags of Iraq were everywhere in evidence. Between meetings many of the mission workers visited the palace of King Faisal and the Government University but lately established. Since the country was a British mandate there was new hope in the Conference for greater freedom of action in work among Moslems.

Late on the sixteenth of April the Zwemers took the "accommodation" train which had boxcars and also passenger coaches, sixteen in all, and started the journey down to Basrah, which they had made on a number of occasions in former years by river boat.

What they had seen of new buildings and institutions and new streets in Baghdad, the railroad restaurant near Ur of the Chaldees, the modern wharves and airfield at Basrah and the great oil city of Abadan all caused them to exclaim, "The old things have passed away. Mesopotamia faces a new day."

It was a wonderful Good Friday and Easter weekend in Basrah—where the Zwemers had first met. Now there was fellowship with a number of missionaries in the station and a growing church membership. What joy to see such progress and blessing for the work which had seemed all but impossible at its inception.

There were visits to the book depot and the schools, one for girls now and the famous high school for boys under Dr. John Van Ess. Reports were given on the conference at Jerusalem. They would have loved to stay on, but the mail steamer left only once every two weeks, so they were off for travel down the Persian Gulf, with stops at Kuwait—where they were allowed to go ashore and greet the missionaries in spite of quarantine—and also a stop at Bushire on the Persian side of the Gulf.

Then there was the real homecoming to Bahrein, the island station which Zwemer had opened. Things were different now. In the house they formerly occupied there was a Moslem school. A larger school for Persian boys was under construction. The Mission bookshop was still there, but across the street was an Arabic printing press and library. The Mission now had a school for girls, an answer to prayer and an outgrowth of the daily devoted work of Mrs. Zwemer with the girls and women during the early days in Bahrein.

On the skyline among the palm trees there were a number of windmills, made in Chicago. Zwemer had himself erected the first one for the Mission hospital, and there were stories of drilling for oil on the island, which were soon to become fact. Some years before on a picnic party the Zwemers and others had found indications on the surface of petroleum or bitumen on the Island and had reported their observation.

The Mission hospital was now receiving patients from a wide area and tours had been made to various inland cities of Arabia by the mission doctors at the request of the governors.

Of the city residents those who had been foes many years before now vied with other friends to show honor to the visitors. There were daily meetings and an impressive communion service before they left. Little wonder they were deeply affected, for nearby were the graves of the two little girls they had buried there when the work was new with the inscription on their tombstone, "Worthy is the Lamb to receive riches."

The journey was continued on the steamship "Barpeta" and wherever the boat stopped along the pirate coast the disembarking passeengers were loaded with tracts and Gospels for the villages.

At Muscat they met the two women who were bravely holding the station in spite of the awful heat and "heavens of brass and earth of iron." The results to outward appearances seemed so small: Zwemer asked himself whether after all it was worth while. He found the answer when he took a boat and visited the little cove where he prayed beside the graves of Bishop Thomas Valpy French, George Stone, and Dr. Sharon J. Thoms. Then he said, "No one can read the records of these lives without being convinced that where such seed has been sown the harvest must come."

The visit to their early mission field was over and they went on to India. The Sultan of Muscat was also a passenger on the same boat and you may be sure he received plenty of Christian literature to read.

Deputation to Persia

Some missionaries from Persia had been present at the Zwemer conference in Baghdad in 1924. Even before this time the Missions in Iran[2] had extended a cordial invitation that he visit that country and share his insight and enthusiasm for work among Moslems. In 1926 this became possible.

Dr. and Mrs. Zwemer came to Tabriz where the writer and his family were then located. The visit was a great blessing, both in a station conference, which reviewed the work for Moslems going on in that part of the field, and

_____

2. Iran is the name of the country used by its own people. The name Persia came through the Greeks who took it from Parsa, the southern province of the land.

in public addresses and private gatherings. The general addresses were interpreted in Azerbaijan Turkish, which is understood by most all of the races in that cosmopolitan field. At the time of his address on "The Greatest Character in History" the church was crowded with people of Armenian, Assyrian and Moslem background, the latter being in the majority. His address made a profound impression. It was afterward published by the mission.

Government officials and other prominent people gave teas for our visitors. We remember that all members of the Station and leaders of the church were invited to a dinner in honor of the Zwemers at the home of our Persian pastor, Stephan Khoobyar. When Mrs. Zwemer took the small cup of strong Turkish coffee after dinner one of the missionaries inquired, "Why, Mrs. Zwemer, do you drink coffee at night with impunity?" "No," she replied, "I take it with sugar."

As usual Dr. Zwemer visited Moslem book stores and printing presses in the great city of Tabriz, which has more than 200 mosques and one small Protestant church. Everywhere he distributed tracts and Gospels and his enthusiasm took hold of missionaries and national Christian workers alike. From that time on began the really wide use of Christian literature for Moslems in the province of Azerbaijan.

It was our joy and privilege to accompany the Zwemers on their trip to Urumia, or Rezaieh as it is now known, on the other side of the great salt lake by the same name. On the train and on the boat we heard a great many of the humorous stories which both of the Zwemers possessed. It was a trip long to be remembered, as was the visit to Urumia.

This local governor having heard of Dr. Zwemer had the military band out to meet him and he was received with great hospitality by all sections of the population. People came in from the villages of the surrounding plain for the public meetings. The members of the mission station received a great blessing in the conferences with the visitors and many Moslems came to attest the high value they placed on the mission schools and hospital.

One public address was on "Fishers of Men," It so happened that the Seventh Day Adventists had recently come into the district. During the question period Dr. Zwemer was asked what he thought of them and their work. Quick as a flash and in line with the address he had just finished, he replied: "Ah, they are zealous fishermen, but sometimes they cast their nets inside the nets of other people."

We can hardly do better than to give his own impressions of the Persian journey in a portion of an article he wrote for *The Missionary Review of the World*.[3]

After telling of the political and cultural renaissance which was even then in progress under Reza Shah Pahlavi, he continued:

"It is not, however, for these political and economic signs of promise that we call attention to the Persian horizon. There are more significant

3. Issue of January, 1927.

tokens of a new day. Persia faces a future, bright as the promise of God. This ancient Bible land, whose history holds so large a place in the Scriptures, and where one may still visit the graves of Esther and Mordecai, or read the inscriptions of Darius, is today an ideal Christian mission field — a door of hope in the world of Islam. Here we see an unrivaled example of comity and cooperation and Christian unity on the part of all the missions. Like other Moslem lands Persia is a difficult field, one that appeals to the heroic and that tests men's souls. But today, one hundred years after the first Protestant Christian mission was opened at Urmia, the whole land seems white unto harvest. Others have labored and the present small force of one hundred and sixty-two missionaries have entered into their labors.

"During our recent visit to Persia last summer it was our rare privilege to witness the joy of harvest and to see marvellous evidence of the power of the Gospel in winning Moslems to Christ.

"Public meetings were arranged by the missionaries for Moslems, Parsees, Christians, for students at the colleges in Teheran and Isfahan, and, best of all, those inimitable Persian garden parties where one could meet converts individually and see the new joy of Christ shining in their faces. In some places we witnessed public baptisms as at Kermanshah, at Teheran and at Isfahan. Never shall we forget that memorable Sunday, July 4th, when twenty-two adults bravely uttered their Declaration of Independence from Islam and all its bondage. One by one these Moslems, twelve men and ten women, were solemnly baptised. They took their vows in St. Luke's Church, before a large audience, of which the greater part were themselves Moslem converts. The native pastor who interrogated each candidate was himself a former Moslem and is today an apostle of Christ.

"In our long and difficult itinerary was rare adventure indeed; mile after mile we travelled over roads that can only be described as atrocious. An Indian Chauffeur drove us in a Buick car most of the way, but his conduct could not always have been truthfully described as Christian. The car, after many mishaps, got safely back in good repair to the Church Missionary Society College in Isfahan and the chauffeur, after a grievous fall and two attempts at suicide, returned to His Father's house, by the long road of repentance.

"One quotation from Mrs. Zwemer's diary must suffice as a description of our many varied experiences:

" 'May 21st, we left Hamaden for Tabriz — 428 miles. It used to take seventeen days, but we did it in two long days of fifteen hours each. We spent the night at Zenjan, a very fanatical town where many Bahais were cruelly put to death in years past. It also has skilled silversmiths who make wonderful filigree bags, rings, candlesticks and other articles. It seems a pity that such a large town with a population of kindly (although religiously fanatical) people should not be occupied by any mission. Zenjan is 5,546 feet above sea level. On the road we passed many fields with the opium poppy in full bloom, looking sweet and beautiful — flowers of white and pale lavender. What a parable! Such beauty, usefulness and destruction in these lovely blooms!'

"It was in Persia that we learned a new version of an old proverb: 'Late to bed and early to rise makes a missionary healthy, and wealthy and wise.' One medical missionary in charge of a large hospital spends two and a half hours daily in prayer and Bible study — no wonder that his paper on 'Spiritual Cooperation' read at the Teheran Conference deeply moved us all.

"What are some of our impressions and why do we believe that Persia faces a new future?

"1. Occupation. The Cross of Christ is in the field. No one doubts it and no one is ashamed of it. The work of evangelization has the right of way in mission policy. Education without evangelism is not dreamed of by any one in Persia. The field is in some parts well occupied and the forces are well distributed. On the other hand, the missions are convinced that 'Large sections of this field remain absolutely untouched as yet or are reached only by occasional itineration or colportage work... And beyond the eastern border lies Afghanistan with an estimated population of 4,000,000 as yet waiting for the spread of the Gospel. Yet, this country is more closely related to Persia than to any other, through the wide use of the Persian language and will ultimately be occupied, at least in part, from Persia.

"To evangelize the whole country — that is the practical issue. The whole country, now open and responsive should be evangelized before new and sinister forces exert greater power.

"II. Cooperation. Over the platform in the college hall at Teheran, where our conference met, was a large map of Persia showing the mission stations as 'little candles burning in the night' and over it were the words 'All One in Christ Jesus'. The old line drawn on the map was still there to mark the division of the Church Missionary Society field from that of the American Presbyterians in north and northwest Persia. But this line became only a historic landmark when in the fervor of love and perfect understanding, the slogan was adopted: 'There is no 34th parallel.' There is none on the map of the new Christian Church and none in the hearts of the missionaries. Bishop Linton is large-hearted enough to open his bishopric to Presbyterians and his horizon includes all Persia. The American 'bishops' are eager for close cooperation through organization, exchange of information, and close spiritual fellowship. It was a creative hour when the finding was adopted:

" 'We rejoice in and return thanks to God for the fine spirit of unity and harmony that now exists among the Christian forces in Persia, and it is our conviction that we should use every endeavor to keep the unity of the Spirit. We believe that there should be one undivided Church of Christ in Persia, and that it is a paramount privilege and duty of us all to work for the founding and growth of such a Persian Church.'

"III. Literature. Persian missions are still backward in providing suitable literature and have much to learn from other fields. In the presentation of the Message the appeal through 'eye-gate' has been unaccountably neglected. No one can over-estimate the work done by Persian pioneers in this task — Pfander, Tisdall, Potter, Rice and others, but their books have been more widely used outside of Persia than within. Both in the preparation and the distribution of Christian literature (except the Bible, which has been widely circulated) the missions are not keeping pace with the Moslem or Bahai, or Bolshevist press. We collected over eighty different Moslem newspapers and magazines now in circulation. Some of these are well illustrated and come from a large native Persian press at Berlin. Tabriz and Teheran have scores of Moslem bookshops where every kind of literature is on sale — in Arabic and Persian and French, even such as is anti-Christian. There is no Persian Christian paper, except a small monthly magazine for women published at Teheran.

"IV. Liberty. We found few restrictions in Persia and many evidences of a liberal spirit and a love for freedom. Those who have tasted of the new education refuse the old fodder of ignorant fanaticism and childish superstition. While at Semnan, where our car broke down, on the way to Meshed, we had opportunity to converse with Moslems of every type. This is the city where the late Dr. Esselstyn preached in the mosque and his life and words are still remembered. In a gathering of big-turbaned leaders they themselves suggested that we discuss the question 'Why Mohammed is not the apostle of God.' Such freedom of speech was typical of other occasions.

"Dissatisfaction with the old Islam, especially its low ethical standards and ideals, is not only increasing but is freely, sometimes loudly, expressed. Cartoons and caricatures in the comic press make fun of the *mullahs* and their ways. Many of those who have received secondary education have inwardly broken with Islam, and have broken finally, although they have not yet accepted the Christ. One of them said that real progress is impossible for Persia until the religion of Arabia has ceased to be the religion of the State. Another declared: 'Our country has had three things imposed on us from without by the Arabs: a foreign government, a foreign language, and a foreign religion. We have long been rid of the first, we are ridding ourselves of the second by purifying our language, but we have not yet got rid of the third.' "

The American Presbyterian Mission in the north of Iran and the British Church Missionary Society in the south had made elaborate preparations for the general conference held in Teheran. In many ways it was a milestone for mission work in Persia.[4] A number of the hopes and plans for further occupation of the field have not been realized. Perhaps the greatest single accomplishment was a tremendous upsurge in the production, publication and distribution of Christian literature for Moslems.

Previously the tracts and books, aside from the Bible, distributed over all Iran during the course of a year could be numbered by a few hundred. The very next year circulation had skyrocketed to more than a hundred thousand copies!

---

4. Papers prepared for the conference together with the findings were published by the Missions in a volume entitled **Mission Problems in New Persia**, American Press, Beirut, 1926. Board of Foreign Missions Presbyterian Church, U.S.A., 156 Fifth Avenue, New York.

Dr. William N. Wysham was chosen to head the Inter-Mission Literature Committee that was appointed, and under his able leadership the Christian literature soon presented more than 125 items, all the way from a Bible dictionary of a thousand pages, and a Church History and commentaries, on down to single page tracts and picture cards.

Bishop J. H. Linton of the C.M.S. took on new zeal for literature also and led his mission in a great advance. Certainly in this respect at least the visit was a turning point in mission work in Iran.

X

Ventures in India

"So if the Muslims are 'Indians,' it would seem that the Hindus are not. And if the Hindus are 'Indians,' it would seem that the Muslims are not. These vast bodies of men are so acutely conscious of their differences that they not only refuse to eat together or think together or pray together, they refuse even to live in the same unit of territory. They want their own geography as well as their own history; they want their own earth as well as their own heaven."

> — BEVERLEY NICHOLS
> *Verdict on India,*
> Page 7

"The history of Indian Missions from the beginning has shown that God intended India to be evangelized."

> — HELEN HOLCOMB
> *Men of Might in Indian Missions*

CHAPTER TEN

VENTURES IN INDIA

Though Samuel Zwemer was never stationed in India it may be said that few men of his generation had a closer knowledge of the missionary work of all denominations and in all parts of the sub-continent than he. The Apostle to Islam visited India and what is now Pakistan many times. He was first there with his family on a vacation from Bahrein in November of the year 1900. Again in October of 1902 they escaped the heat of Arabia for a rest at Landour in the North and then went on to give addresses at Calcutta and Madras in November. While in south India he also visited the Arcot mission of the Reformed Church in America.

Then in December of 1902 he had a part in the Decennial Conference for Missions of all India. It was there that he met missionaries from many parts of the country who were vitally interested in work for Moslems and plans emerged for a general conference on Islam to be held in Cairo at some future date.

In December of 1910 and January 1911 Zwemer attended YMCA and YWCA conferences in Bombay and Calcutta. At this time he visited Bankipur, Benares, Allahabad, Aligarh and Delhi. He had a chief part in the organization and conduct of the Lucknow Conference from January 23rd to 28th, 1911, which will be considered in detail in a later chapter. Again in 1917 he visited missions of North India on his way to China.

The two major visitations to India, however, were accomplished in 1924 and 1927-28. These journeys were made on the basis of long and careful prayer and planning and with definite objects in view. They covered nearly every part of the vast sub-continent.

The visit in 1924 was made in response to an invitation from the National Christian Council of India. Zwemer went as representative of the American Christian Literature Society for Moslems. There was also the request of Dr. John R. Mott, that following the series of conferences in North Africa and the Near East and the general meeting at Jerusalem, he should carry both the greetings and the findings of these gatherings to the Missions of India. At the outset it would be well to quote the Jerusalem finding on India:

"It is astonishing that Moslem India also is in a very real sense an unoccupied field. Little special work for Moslems is carried on although there are 69,000,000 of them. There are large cities like Bombay, Lucknow, Delhi and Lahore, where formerly there was special effort to win Moslems, but where now there are no missionaries wholly devoted to this task.

"While there are more than 5,000 missionaries in India, the number of these who are specially prepared and set apart for the evangelization of Moslems is pitifully small. Only a few centers like Dacca, Rawalpindi, Peshawar, and Quetta can be said to have missionaries devoting their whole time to Moslem work.

"Though on the other hand it may be said that there are many places where missionaries are giving part of their time to Moslems yet even when one considers all this, it is still clear that there is such a serious lack of attention being given to the Moslem problem in proportion to its importance that its adequate consideration by all missions in India is urgently required."

Mrs. Zwemer accompanied her husband on this journey, taking part in the various meetings and sharing her experiences of missionary work in Arabia and Cairo. The time covered was May 20th to August 7th, 1924. On the former date they arrived in Bombay, where mail had accumulated and was answered. On the following day they took the train for Lucknow. He mentions in his journal that even for dwellers in Arabia it was hot on the train, one hundred and eight degrees to be exact! They arrived in Lucknow on the 22nd where they were met by Dr. Murray T. Titus of the Methodist Church Mission who was secretary of the Literature Committee for Moslems. They managed to get in visits to the Mission Press and educational institutions, the ancient palaces of the kings, and the Shiah training college for leaders of that division of Islam.

On the 24th the Zwemers went on to Aligarh where they visited the Moslem university; then to Delhi on the 25th where they were entertained at the Cambridge Mission. Two days later the travelers were in Lahore where there was a four-hour meeting of the Christian Literature Committee. Several prominent missionaries were members and four leading converts from Islam were also on the committee. Various plans for publication were considered; some 70,000 tracts for Mohammedans had recently been printed. It was decided to request $2,500 from the A.C.L.S.M. for new publications.

Next there was a visit to Qadian, the center of the Ahmadiya movement, where Zwemer put a number of questions to the head of that modernistic sect and found that they were considered heretics by the orthodox Sunni Moslems. There was a visit at Gurdaspur, a station of the United Presbyterian Mission, where the party slept out under the stars with the beautiful snow-capped Himalayas in the distance. The journey continued to the hill stations of Landour and Mussourie.

In Landour there was a reception on May 31st in Kellog Memorial Church with some 350 present. The visitors were the guests of Dr. W. R. Cummings and Dr. J. J. Lucas. On Sunday, June 1st, Zwemer preached morning and evening. On Monday he spoke at the annual meeting of the British and Foreign Bible Society in Mussourie. On Tuesday the meetings of the Missionary Institute began. The total number of missionaries present was about two hundred, representing some twenty societies and including a large number of students from the language school.

From June 3rd through the 6th there were daily sessions from 10:30 to 1:30 with half an hour for questions. He also gave a brief course in Islamics under four topics; Islam as a World Problem, an Indian Problem, Modern Movements, and Missionary Methods.

The daily devotional talks were at five in the afternoon. On Friday evening there was a special meeting for Moslems with about 250 present where there were numerous questions at the end of his address.

On Sunday, June 8th, there were two services at the Methodist and Union Churches in Mussourie; then a return to Landour. The next day there was a final meeting wth the members of the language school and then the party was off down the mountains and on to Dehra Dun by five o'clock in the afternoon. It had been truly a remarkable "Convention for the Deepening of the Spiritual Life," as it was termed at Mussourie.

After an address to Moslems and Hindus in Dehra Dun the journey was continued to the beautiful hill station of Naini Tal. There another conference was held from June 11th to 17th. Some 120 missionaries were present, largely from the Methodist and C.M.S. missions, with a few from the London Missionary Society and other organizations. The program was similar to that given at Mussourie.

On the 18th of June they left for Calcutta where they arrived on the 20th. During the next four days there was a meeting of the Committee on Christian Literature, a missionary conference, and on Sunday services in the morning at the Methodist Church and in the evening at the Scotch Presbyterian Church. There was also a lunch with the Oxford Fathers at their Brotherhood house and meetings with members of the India Christian Council and other missionaries.

The next move was to Bogra in central Bengal where a conference was held June 26th to 29th. It was found that there was a remarkable opportunity for work with Moslems in Bengal and there were many converts in the church. A questionnaire was circulated at this and other conferences to gather data on Islam in the district. The answers formed a basis for discussion in subsequent meetings. The queries also sought to establish the reasons why Moslem work was relatively neglected and what methods might be effectively used.

The resolutions of the Bogra conference are an example of those passed at subsequent meetings:

"The delegates assembled in this Conference express sincere appreciation of the valuable and intensely practical series of discourses given by Dr. and Mrs. Zwemer.

"1. Notwithstanding the limited number of workers in N. E. Bengal it is fully recognized that work among Moslems has been conducted assiduously, and therefore definite results have been obtained. The future is full of promise. These results have been largely due to a knowledge of the Moslem mind, and a sympathetic approach to it, coupled with a liberal and discriminate use of specially prepared literature;

"2. Recognizing that this work demands a special training, and that without this we cannot hope for the best results, the Conference asks that Mission Home Boards and Field Committee definitely accept the policy of setting apart workers, Indian and European, and training them for this service. The revival of Arabic studies and the marked increase in the output of the Moslem press, make it advisable that workers among Moslems, especially Indian workers, should acquire at least an elementary knowledge of Arabic;

"3. The Conference urges that pastors endeavor to cultivate in their congregations a keen sense of brotherhood and unity in the church, regardless of the previous racial, social or religious distinctions of converts, and also impress on them the necessity of offering inquirers a hospitable reception;

"4. The conference urges the need of strong reinforcements in view of the following facts:

(a) Bengal is one of the three most densely populated Moslem areas in the world:

(b) The total number of Moslems in Bengal equals the combined populations of Arabia, Persia and Egypt;

(c) The Moslems of Bengal are more accessible and responsible than those of the aforementioned countries;·

(d) The encouraging results of the past demand far greater efforts and larger forces on this field;

(e) The rapidly changing conditions of the Mohammedan world and the steadily increasing demand for the education of both sexes, constitute both an opportunity and a challenge to the Christian Church.

"5. As education is spreading rapidly, not only in towns but in villages and zenanas, there is urgent need for simple books in the Mussulman-Bengali dialect. The ready reception accorded to those already published proves conclusively that there is a demand for this class of literature.

On June 30th the Zwemers were back again in Calcutta and he gave an address at the Missionary Conference in the Thoburn Memorial Church. At night there was a second meeting in another Methodist Church where a number of Moslems were present.

The schedule then called for a journey across India to Bombay for a week of conferences and meetings. Dr. Zwemer gave addresses to different groups at the Y.M.C.A. and spoke before the meeting of the Bombay branch of the Royal Asiatic Society on The New World of Islam. On Sunday he preached at the Wesleyan Church in the morning and to a large audience in Wilson Hall in the evening. He also spoke through interpretation to a morning service in Hindustani and at an afternoon gathering in Marathi.

On Monday he addressed the meeting of the Inter-Collegiate Christian Students Association, and that evening spoke before the opening meeting of the Bombay Missionary Conference. The next day he lectured before the Bombay Indian Christian Association. It may be noted that in the findings of the Bombay Missionary Conference there is, among others, the following statement:

> "This joint meeting of members of the Bombay Missionary Conference and the Bombay Indian Christian Association is of the opinion:
> 1. That the 'finding on India' of the Jerusalem Conference is fully justified, so far as the Bombay Province is concerned;
> 2. That the members of the Bombay Missionary Conference are deeply impressed with the importance of the Moslem problem;
> 3. That steps should be taken to see whether provision could not be made for the appointment of a missionary in Bombay city who would devote his whole time to work among Moslems."

There followed missionary conferences in Poona and in Hyderabad, the capital of the Nizam's dominions. In Poona the Zwemers visited the headquarters of the Ismailia sect, made famous in Europe by their leader the Agha Khan. In Hyderabad there were four public addresses in St. George's Hall. At one of the meetings the Nizam of Hyderabad, known at that time as the richest man in the world, appeared with a retinue and a number of princes, members of the royal household. The lecture was on "The New World of Islam." The Nizam shook hands with the speaker and later wrote a friendly letter, preserved as a souvenir by the visitors. After a few words of a complimentary nature on the address, the Nizam wrote:

> "In case you are staying longer in Hyderabad, would you care to come to the dinner and dance which is fixed on July 24th (7:30) in order to give me more opportunity of making acquaintance with a man, who is a thorough scholar of Arabic as well as a good lecturer."

Dr. and Mrs. Zwemer attended the dinner but not the dance; even though the invitation came from royalty. At the dinner His Highness presented Mrs. Zwemer with a gold brooch and her husband with a silver cigarette case! The Nizam is a liberal educated Moslem. A year later than this visit he wrote a poem in Persian on the Prince of Peace, published in the *Star of India*. The last stanza reads:

> "What was Jesus' mission, Osman?
> Ask them whom he came to guide.
> Gave his life for their redemption,
> For his flock he gladly died."[1]

In Madras for four days there were conferences with missionaries and National Christians. At a garden party especially for Moslems, the speaker noted several policemen present; they had come at the request of those in charge of the services and the guest was told this was the usual procedure in such cases. There were a number of leading questions but no trouble.

1. **The Cross Above the Crescent,** p. 109.

Zwemer spoke on the "Authenticity and the Necessity of the Death of Christ."
He also preached at the general Sunday service of the Y.M.C.A. and, as he
did in every city, made visits to Moslem publishing houses and book shops.

On July 22nd he was at Veniyambadi where he visited the schools and held
a conference with the Lutheran missionaries. Here at last he found a missionary who was a thorough Arabic scholar, Dr. A. E. Brux. He had recently been appointed to spend his full time in work for Moslems.

From the 23rd to the 28th the Zwemers visited the Arcot Mission of their
own denomination, the Reformed Church in America. After stops of various
lengths at other stations they reached Vellore where a conference was held
with missionaries and Indian workers. There were more than one hundred
present, representing five different societies. There was interest in work for
Moslems but scarcely any knowledge of Islam among the missionaries. An
evening public meeting in a theatre, where Zwemer's topic was "Christianity
the Final Religion," drew an audience of about four hundred. It must have
attracted considerable attention, for a Brahman scattered handbills announc-
ing that he would give a lecture on "Christ — a Myth." The following evening the theatre was crowded for Zwemer's lecture by a larger audience
than the previous night.

The Vellore Conference began their findings with the following paragraph:
> "This Conference desires to place on record its high sense of obliga-
> tion to the Reverend Dr. Zwemer of Cairo, for the inspiring and valu-
> able services rendered by him to Christians in general and Christian
> Missions in particular of this part of the Presidency by his very learned
> and instructive lectures on 'Mohammedanism' and 'Work Among Mos-
> lems.' In deep appreciation of their valuable services the Conference
> desires to convey its grateful thanks to Dr. and Mrs. Zwemer. It is
> hoped that the impulse which Dr. and Mrs. Zwemer have now given to
> the work among Mohammedans may be followed up by future visits."

The next place of call was Bangalore where there was an address in the
Union Theological Seminary in the morning and one for Moslems at the
Y.M.C.A. at four in the afternoon. That evening there was a conference of
about twenty missionaries and forty national workers. Resolutions were
adopted on the need of more aggressive work for Moslems and concerning the
need of Christian literature. On their return to Madras it was discovered
that floods had disrupted railroad travel from Madura southward, so they
left for Colombo, the city of their final conference, by steamer, and on August 7th departed on the S. S. "President Adams."

The conference in Colombo may be epitomized by one of their resolutions:
> "This conference of Christian workers called together by the Chris-
> tian Council in Ceylon and meeting at the Y.M.C.A., Colombo, on the 6th
> and 7th of August, 1924, for consultation with Dr. Zwemer records its
> regret that no organized missions exist for the Mohammedans in Cey-

lon. The approach to them has been (1) through women workers who labor specially but not solely among them as evangelists, (2) through medical missions for women in out-stations, (3) through open air meetings attended freely by Mohammedans, (4) through colporteurs and (5) through schools, elementary and secondary.

"1. It recommends the Christian Council in Ceylon to direct its Propaganda Committee to consider the possibility of procuring qualified workers who shall devote all their time to Moslems, whether through one Society or by cooperative methods. Such persons to be specially trained. If even one were procured on a cooperative basis, he might· be a helper to all others concerned in such work."

A printed report on *Islam in India Today* was published, a summary from which we quote:

"Moslem India is in a very real sense an unoccupied field. The visit has confirmed beyond doubt this statement from the Jerusalem Conference. A crying need exists for specially trained workers. The activity of the Moslem Press challenges the churches to make a far wider use of Christian literature. New light was thrown on the aggressive missionary activities of Moslems in India. Special workers must be set apart and proper training for them provided. The treatment of converts and inquirers should be studied by the church. The present attitude of the educated Moslem to the Gospel is sympathetic. The Moslems of India are a backward class and need the social help Christian Missions can give."

The report of the Zwemer visit was considered at the autumn meeting in 1924 of the National Christian Council, as well as the recommendations passed by the eleven local conferences. In introducing the subject to the Council Dr. Murray T. Titus called to their attention that it was of imperative concern, because one-third of all the Moslems of the world lived in India. The following action was taken:

> "In view of his recent visit to India which has at once awakened us to the existence of the great need for work among the neglected Moslems of this land, and which has aroused the Christian forces to new and determined lines of action, we would welcome another and longer visit from Dr. Zwemer for the purpose of continuing the work he has so well begun among us as soon as his Society can make the necessary arrangements."

II

The visit requested was made from the latter part of September, 1927, to the end of February, 1928. Three men largely responsible for the arrangements in India were Dr. N. MacNicol, secretary of the National Christian Council, Dr. M. T. Titus, who had helped so much in the earlier visit, and Dr. L. Bevan Jones, who had by this time taken a leading place in scholarship and understanding of the Moslem problem. Zwemer expresses his appreciation of these three in the introduction to his report of the visitation.

The plan and purpose of the visit was outlined as follows:

"Our plan is a course of nine or ten days in each of several places; the course to be attended by missionaries and Indian Christian workers who desire definitely to devote themselves, if not for whole, at least for part of their time to work among Moslems, and who would wish to study Islam in its more recent developments and the methods of presenting Christianity to Moslems and the problems inherent in their presentation.

"In addition to these intensive courses we should hope that Dr. Zwemer would both be available for devotional meetings of a general kind and for evangelistic and apologetic work among Moslems, and we should also, of course, secure extra opportunities for extended conference between him and leading missionaries and Christian workers connected with the Provincial and National Christian Council."[2]

It was possible for Mrs. Zwemer to accompany her husband on this trip also. The schedule was about as arduous as that of the former visit and the time was much longer, being more than four months as compared to about two months and a half spent on the 1924 itineration. The expressed wish of the Committee that he might visit fewer places and spend longer periods of time did not work out, for the reason that so many places were insistent in their desire to have the Zwemers for one of the conferences. The period of the meetings was therefore, of necessity, shortened to about a week for each conference, with five days of instruction.

Thorough preparation had been made for this India-wide effort to train missionaries and inspire them for work among Moslems. For a period of two years a Committee had been at work on a survey which was published for the Conferences. It was entitled, "The Muslims of India, Burma and Ceylon, and the Extent of the Christian Missionary Enterprise Among Them." With this careful study of the area, concerning Islam and Christian Missions it was not necessary to circulate a questionnaire at each conference as had been done on the former visit.

A survey of this extended tour is given in the following itinerary covered by Dr. and Mrs. Zwemer:

Arrived in Bombay	September 23rd	Study of the Moslem press
Ahmadabad	October 3rd-7th	Group Conference
Bombay	October 8th-15th	Group Conference
Karachi	October 17th-23rd	Group Conference
Ludhiana	October 26th-27th	Meeting of Presbyterian Mission
Rawal Pindi	October 29th-Nov. 1st	Group Conference
Peshawar	November 2nd	Visit to Khyber-pass and station meeting
Lahore	November 3rd-9th	Group Conference
Delhi	November 10th-15th	Group Conference
Cawnpore	November 13th	Mrs. Zwemer's special meeting
Lucknow	November 16th-21st	Group Conference
Bareilly	November 22nd-25th	M. E. Conference
Jubbulpore	November 26th-Dec. 2nd	Group Conference

2. From the report of the Committee on Moslem Work of the National Christian Council.

Calcutta ....December 4th-10th ....Group Conference
Dacca ....December 12th-18th ....Group Conference
Dacca ....December 19th-29th ....Christmas Holidays
Allahabad ....December 31st-Jan. 3rd ....Meeting of Committee on
Literature for Moslems
Calcutta ....January 4th ....
Hyderabad ....January 6th-12th ....Group Conference
Bangalore ....January 14th-21st ....Group Conference
Madras ....January 22nd-27th ....Group Conference
Vellore ....January 28th-29th ....Reformed Church (Arcot) Mission
Vanyambadi and Calicut ..January 29th-Feb. 3rd ....Conference with Lutheran and
Basel Missions
Madura ....February 4th-9th ....Group Conference
Kodikanal ....February 10th-11th ....Visit to School
Kandy ....February 13th-20th ....Group Conference
Colombo ....February 20th-25th ....Group Conference
Sailed for Port Said
(S.S. d'Artagnan)............February 28th ....

Allowing for some changes in accordance with the local conditions the same general plan for the program was followed at each of the study conferences. There were in most cases ten lectures on the subject of "Mohammedan Apologetics or How to Carry the Gospel Message to the Moslem Heart." The lectures of one hour each were usually

I. Introductory: Importance of the subject. Its literature. II. The Message. What is Christianity? III. The Moslem Mind. IV. The Genuineness of the Bible. V. The Authority of the Bible. VI. Mohammedan objections to the teaching of the Bible in general. VII. The Trinty. VIII. The Death of Christ: the Atonement. IX. What place does Christianity give Mohammed? X. Dealing with Inquirers, Converts and Backsliders.

There were also five lectures on a series of topics which varied according to locality. They were on such subjects as: Islam in India, New Aspects of Islam, Islam and Animism, The Preparation and Use of Literature, Methods of Work, and Women in Islam, the last topic being given by Mrs. Zwemer.

There were also a series of public lectures in each place where a conference was held as well as preaching in churches. Schools and colleges were visited and lectures given to students and faculty. The program in each place also provided time for the bazaars, places of interest, mosques and Islamic book shops. In addition, there was a display of Christian literature and books on Islam. Tracts and Gospels were widely distributed and subscriptions were taken for *The Moslem World*. During the visit a hundred copies of the general survey volume, "Christian Literature in Moslem Lands" were sold. The volume was put out by a committee and published by the Doubleday Doran Company in America, but editorial work was done by Dr. Zwemer and other missionaries in Cairo. In each language area there would also be an exhibit of Christian literature in the local vernacular, which was often an object lesson, as missionaries realized how little had actually been printed in many of the languages used largely by Moslems.

Mrs. Amy E. Zwemer wrote a long letter to a few friends at home giving her account of this tour in India, from which we quote since it gives a special point of view and brings to us the reactions concerning work for women. We omit the account of the opening conferences and most of the visit in South India, but include enough to give a view of the journey from Mrs. Zwemer's keen and sympathetic pen:

"From Karachi we travelled through the Sind desert, a dry and dusty ride, we were literally covered with sand. We arrived in Lahore after a night and a day of heat and dust and were very thankful to be in a home once again. We stayed only one night and next afternoon left for Ludhiana to attend the annual meeting of the Presbyterian Punjab Mission. We were the guests of Dr. Edith Brown, who has done much heroic work in establishing the Women's Christian Medical College and Hospital—it has grown in twenty-five years from eight students to eighty; and fifty nurses and a large number of compounders and nurses' aids and other workers, and buildings in proportion. Dr. Zwemer led devotions for the members of the Mission and gave a lecture on Islam to the Indian Christians and Missionaries. I led devotions for the students and nurses in the Medical School. Next morning in the small hours we left for Rawalpindi. It took about twelve hours, and the train crossed several rivers, one or two had very long bridges and the trains passed over slowly because the bridges were being repaired. Our friends of the United Presbyterian Mission are in command of the work in 'Pindi.' Dr. and Mrs. Porter of Gordon College welcomed us to their comfortable home. The meetings began the same evening in one of the lecture rooms of the College. Delegates had come from long distances to this conference from some of the outposts scattered along the Northwest Frontier.

"In addition to the usual lectures to workers, there were evangelistic addresses on the street corners and also for the students of the Gordon College each day. The attention of the students was excellent. On Sunday two services were held for Indian Congregations through interpretation, and one for an English congregation. The weather was quite cold in Rawalpindi and pleasant after the great heat of the plains. The lectures were finished on Nov. 1st and at 4:50 p.m. we left for Peshawar. We stayed for 24 hours and were the guests of Rev. and Mrs. Wigram of the C.M.S. This mission has a college and large hospital in addition to other lines of work. Next morning Dr. Cox of the hospital very kindly drove us to the Khyber Pass and at the top we looked over into Afghanistan, that long closed land. We left again at eleven p.m. and arrived in Rawalpindi at 6:30 a.m. There was time between trains to go to the home of Dr. and Mrs. Porter. We had breakfast and returned to the train. We arrived in Lahore about 4:30 p.m. and were the guests of Dr. and Mrs. Rice of the Forman Christian College. The meetings were held in the Y.M.C.A. Evening lectures for the public were also held in their large hall and the place was crowded each night; a few belligerent Moslems wished to answer the speaker after the lecture and tried to do so by quoting passages from the Bible and the Koran, the audience listened quietly and then were dismissed without disturbance. One young Moslem said that he was conscious of being a better man than Jesus. It took a lot of self control to keep calm when he talked in this way. We were royally entertained in many of the charmng homes of the college faculty, including that of the president, Dr. and Mrs. Lucas—also the secretaries of the Y.M.C.A. and our friends Mr. and Mrs. Hume and others.

"Service was held on Sunday morning in the American Presbyterian Church, and in the evening Dr. Zwemer also preached in the Cathedral, this beautiful Christian building in the midst of a non-Christian city was built many years ago by Bishop Valpy French. On Nov. 9th we left at 9:30 for Delhi. We were the guests of the Cambridge Mission during our stay. The attendance was rather smaller than in other places but the lectures on popular Islam brought together a larger number. I was asked to take some meetings in Cawnpore so I left Delhi after two days. Cawnpore is famous because of the terrible tragedy of the Mutiny in 1857. There are large cotton mills here, and the owners of the mills have done a splendid piece of welfare work in building up two model villages for the factory hands.

"In Cawnpore I spoke five times to the workers and twice in the schools. From Cawnpore I went to Lucknow and Dr. Zwemer went from Delhi to Lucknow.

"The regular lecture course began next morning. In the afternoon we were invited to meet some of the prominent families of the city, Christian, Hindu, and Moslem. It was a great gathering on the lawn of the Reid Christian College; refreshments were served to about 150 people. After the garden party all adjourned to the assembly hall for a public address. In Lucknow at the close of the regular conference, a day and a half was given for the consideration of 'Giving the Christian message to Purdah Nashin Women.' Papers and addresses were read, followed by discussion, problems were worked out for the more efficient preparation and presentation of our message. In Lucknow we were the guests of Dr. and Mrs. Pickett of the Methodist Episcopal Mission."

After describing meetings and conferences in several other places, Mrs. Zwemer continues, "Indian villages and custom and scenery have been almost overdescribed so I refrain and continue our journey. In Calcutta I stayed in Bishop's House by the kind invitation of the Metropolitan. Dr. Zwemer left for Allahabad to attend a Committee meeting and he preached in the Cathedral and addressed the students of the Ewing Christian College. He returned to Calcutta early on January 4th. We visited the scene of Carey's work in Serampore, saw the library and museum, which testify to the marvellous record of his achievements. Serampore is fifteen miles from Calcutta, so our visit was rather a hurried one.

"We then visited the Nizam's dominions in Hyderabad where splendid work is being done by all, though the field is difficult. The Conference lasted for five days and, as usual, the interest grew as the lectures proceeded, and many expressed the wish that the lectures might go on much longer. After the lectures, one morning Mr. and Mrs. Coan of the Y.M.C.A., Secunderabad, drove us to Medak, a remarkable station of the Wesleyans where there are sixty-thousand Christians who have been brought in by the mass movements. The church for these people is a most beautiful building in Gothic style with a tower 146 feet high and can be seen for miles around. Two thousand people can be seated. The interior is beautiful and should inspire the worshippers. There is also a good hospital, boys and girls schools and a theological college. It was a drive of 140 miles there so we had only fifty minutes to have tea and view the wonders of this great work."

Although many examples might be given of friendliness and affection from Moslems throughout this visit, we should not get a proper picture unless the other side were also shown. Though it is admittedly blasphemous, we quote from a front page editorial in "The Light," Moslem journal of Lahore, edition of November 10th, 1927:

"The task of the Christian missionary in the House of Islam is at best an unenviable one for he fights in the East a losing battle for a cause which has been lost in the West whence he comes. While Dr. Zwemer lectures in Lahore on Christianity and endeavours with almost pathetic futility to encourage belief in the ancient, barbaric conception of an angry God to be mollified by human and divine sacrifices, Bishop Barnes of Birmingham denies that there can be any virtue in 'God-eating.' Freud and Frazer have shown that the Christian sacrament idea is merely a survival of the superstitious, remorse and fear of a parricide who in remote ages slew the Old Man of the Tribe in order to possess himself of the women; yet so loath is this ancient obsession to die that even as I write Dr. Zwemer declares in Lahore his belief that Jesus Christ made a vicarious sacrifice of his life to remove the wrath of God from mankind. If Dr. Zwemer and men of his way of thinking were content to cherish their quaint beliefs in silence we Muslims would be content to pity them in silence; but when such men go out of their way to urge others to adopt ancient, anthropomorphic superstitions, it becomes necessary for us to dispute with them—to show them that mankind has progressed beyond the narrow and dark beliefs of Christianity and is drawing ever nearer to Islam as the only rational, natural and scientific conception of the Creator and the scheme of creation."

The same journal also taunted Dr. Zwemer in another issue, saying that since he had been unsuccessful in trying to convert Moslems in various lands he had sent his daughter and son-in-law to China in the hope that Moslems there might be easier to reach. At the time of this visit an association was organized known as *The Brotherhood of St. Andrew* which has done a great deal in subsequent years both in leading Mohammedans to Christ and making for them a welcome to the Christian church from those of other backgrounds. The brotherhood was made up of both converts from Islam and others who desired to join its membership and in the spirit of the Apostle Andrew, to bring their brothers to Christ. The declared objects of the Brotherhood are as follows:

"(1) To endeavour to bring the Moslems to the feet of Christ. (2) To promote feelings of love and sympathy between the converts from Islam. (3) To help them out of their troubles and difficulties. (4) To provide scholarships for the deserving and needy Moslem converts for higher education. (5) To establish a Convert's Home for Moslems and an extensive library and reading room. (6) To start a weekly paper in Urdu on the lines of the 'Epiphany' of Calcutta. (7) The circulation of a Quarterly Prayer Cycle amongst members and sympathizers. (8) Production and distribution of adequate and suitable Christian literature for and among Moslems."

In commenting on the accomplishments of Zwemer in India Dr. Murray T. Titus mentions especially his long and close cooperation with The Christian Literature Committee for Moslems and his aid in the establishment of the Henry Martyn School for Islamic studies.

Mrs. Zwemer has mentioned the fact that her husband doubled back from Calcutta to attend a meeting of the All-India Committee on Christian Literature for Moslems, which met in Allahabad from December 31st to January 3rd. Nearly all the members of the Committee were present, including Rev. L. Bevan Jones, Rev. Murray T. Titus, Professor Mohammed Ismail, Professor Sirajud-Din, Rev. M. S. Pitt and Mr. (later Bishop) J. A. Subhan. After a survey of the needs in the various language areas the following cable was sent to the American Christian Literature Society in New York:

"Hearty New Year Greetings, I Thess. 1:2, 3. A splendid opportunity presents itself if funds are provided by you. Thirty-nine books not yet published in six languages, total expense $3500. The need is urgent, communicate this to all friends. Join us in prayer for funds. Do not disappoint us. Christian Literature Committee Meeting. Titus. Zwemer."

The society at home did its part and literature for Moslems received a mighty impetus from this visit.

In January the Conferences in Hyderabad in Bangalore and Madras were all eminently successful. During the last week of the month there was a Conference with members of the Reformed Mission at Vellore followed by another with members of the Lutheran and Basel missions at Venyambadi and Calicut. In the former place a Lutheran missionary, the Rev. A. E. Brux, Ph.D., met on a former visit, was still making progress in his special work for Moslems and beginnings had been made in Christian literature for them in Tamil. At Calicut and other cities of Malabar the Moslem group known as the Mappillas was visited. They are increasing rapidly by propaganda and social pressure. Many low caste women are said to come over to Islam to become wives of Moslem men. There were twenty-three Moslem presses in Malabar.

At Madura there was a good conference and a summary of the lectures on Islam was prepared by Rev. Martin Taylor and published in Tamil in the

magazine of the United Church of South India, and reprinted in pamphlet
form. From Madura they went to Kodikanal to visit the school for the
children of missionaries. Then they were off for Ceylon and the final conferences of the journey. Two courses of lectures were given on this occasion, one at Kandy where interpretation in Tamil was necessary, the
other course in the Y.M.C.A. at Colombo.

The total journey from Egypt and return covered 15,362 miles of which
8,815 miles of travel were in India.

On April 21st, 1928, after the Zwemers had come and gone the Committee
on Work Among Moslems met in Lahore. We might quote the names of
those who were present, as they comprise a roster of the leaders at the time
for India in this phase of work. Then we shall end this chapter with their
resolution concerning the Zwemer visit.

The Committee on Work Among Moslems:

H. C. Velte, Convener, A. P. Mission, Saharanpur
F. J. Western, S. P. G. Cambridge Mission, Delhi
L. Bevan Jones, Baptist Mission Dacca, Bengal
M. M. Ismail, A. P. Mission, F. C. College, Lahore
R. Siraj-ud-Din, F. C. College, Lahore
J. A. Subhan, M. E. Mission, Bareilly
M. S. Pitt, M. E. Mission, Jubbulpore, G. P.
H. J. Lane Smith, C. M. S., Clare Road, Byculla, Bombay
M. T. Titus, Sec'y., M. E. Mission, Hardoi, U. P.
A. I. Revnell, Wesleyan Mission, St. Mark's, Simla
F. H. Russell, Un. Ch. of Canada, Dhar, G. I.
M. E. Wigram, C. M. S., 32 Mozang Rd., Lahore
William Sutherland, United Pres. Mission, Campbellpur., Punj.
N. MacNicol, Sec'y., N. C. C., 1, Stavely Rd., Poona.

"*Resolution re. Dr. Zwemer's Visit.* This Committee desires to express
its sincere appreciation of the very valuable services rendered to the cause of
Missions to Muslims in this country by Dr. and Mrs. Zwemer during their
recent visit. By the series of conferences which he conducted, he has
awakened a new concern throughout the land, shown the way to more effective effort, and induced a greater number to engage in this enterprise.

"The influence of his personal example as a student of Islam, an earnest
evangelist and a lover of Muslims will abide, and will go far to help remove
the reproach that Christian Missions in India have, in the past, neglected
these people.

"To Mrs. Zwemer, who accompanied her husband and held meetings for
women workers, to Dr. Zwemer for the cheerful way in which he carried out
his heavy programme, and to his Society and others who made it possible for
him to make this visit we accord our heartfelt thanks."

XI

The Fourth Religion of China

"One of the treasures in my library is a bound volume of *Friends of Moslems*, Vol. I-X. In 1927 I became a member of the Society of Friends of the Moslems in China. How much has been accomplished during the past twenty years in their work of faith and labor of love and patience of hope only the day of Judgment and Reward will reveal.

"The Apostle Paul disputed in the synagogues, raised a tumult in Ephesus among the worshippers of Diana, was shamefully persecuted, scourged and imprisoned; but he was without doubt and whole-heartedly the friend of Jew and Gentile and for their sakes he suffered the loss of all things. What a glorious list of friends he had in Rome itself before he went there as prisoner! Read the sixteenth chapter of Romans for an index to the greatness of his loving heart. It is that same apostolic spirit which led the group of fifty missionaries meeting in Room 305 of the Mission's Building, Shanghai, on May 10, 1927, to found this Society. Isaac Mason and others of the early leaders have entered their reward but the work goes on and this Quarterly News Letter is everywhere welcomed. It is a silver trumpet that has never sounded retreat. God bless its message for China and the world of Islam! It is needed today."

SAMUEL M. ZWEMER,
in *Friends of Moslems*,
Vol. XX, No. 1.

CHAPTER ELEVEN

THE FOURTH RELIGION OF CHINA

The three great historic religions of China are Confucianism, Taoism and Buddhism. Islam is the fourth non-Christian religion. As in most of the mission fields, so in China, Moslems have been relatively neglected. In fact, there were many areas where missionaries did not distinguish the followers of the Arabian prophet from other Chinese. Because of his general interest in Mohammedans, wherever they might be located, Zwemer had long cherished the hope that he might at some time visit China.

Certain missionary societies in Great Britain and friends in America became interested in such a tour, and the matter was taken up with the China Continuation Committee of the National Missionary Conference of 1913 in Shanghai. This body was the forerunner of later Christian Councils. After correspondence with Dr. A. L. Warnshius and the Rev. E. C. Lobenstine of the C.C.C., that body took the following action in April, 1916:

"With reference to the letter received from Mr. Marshall Broomhall of the China Inland Mission,

"VOTED to instruct the Foreign Secretary to reply to Mr. Broomhall and to Dr. Zwemer in substance as follows:-

"That the Committee has heard with much pleasure of the proposed visit of Dr. Zwemer to China, and although present conditions in the country make it impossible at this time to plan definitely for such a visit, it hopes such a visit may be made within the near future, and also that its opinion is, that Dr. Zwemer's visit should be for a considerably longer period than is suggested in his letter, in order that besides visiting Yunnan he might also reach places on the Yangtze perhaps as far as Ichang and possibly other places as far northwest as Sianfu as well as Nanking, Peking and other cities more easily accessible. The committee thinks that the aim of the visit should be (a) to help the Missions and Chinese Churches to recognize the possibility of fruitful evangelism among Moslems, and to learn how best to present the gospel to them, and to plan for a larger use of effective literature specially prepared for Chinese Moslems and (b) to endeavour to arrange for special evangelistic campaigns in some of the larger Moslem centers."

Correspondence was continued as to plans for the journey and Zwemer left Cairo May 18th, 1917, and arrived in Shanghai July 7th. Members of the China Continuation Committee and other missionaries and nationals who were especially interested in work for Moslems joined in the preliminary correspondence and arrangements for the journey. Among the deeply interested was the Rev. Charles L. Ogilvie, a Presbyterian missionary of Peking, who accompanied the visitor for a portion of his journey as interpreter and guide.

There was first an extensive visit to the province of Honan in central China, which has a considerable Moslem population. Dr. Zwemer visited four of the largest cities and held public meetings as well as conferences with the missionaries and national workers. The public meetings, some of them held in the mosques by invitation of Chinese Mohammedan leaders, were a practical demonstration of the fact that such direct work was possible. It was also found that much more was accomplished by making a separate attempt to win Moslems than by merely addressing them together with Chinese of other religious faith. Plans and methods of work for Islam in other lands were discussed with members of the various stations in Honan and proposals were made for the inauguration of special work for Mohammedans.

Since at this season of the year so many of the missionaries were gathered at the four great summer resorts of Chefoo, Kuling, Chikungshan and Feitaiho, Zwemer visited each of these places for a general conference on Evangelization of the Moslem population of China. It was evident from the resolutions adopted at each of these conferences that the mission body had come to see more clearly than ever before the necessity of special work for the followers of the Arabian prophet.

Considerable quantities of Christian literature were distributed throughout the tour. In Peking a general exhibit of Chinese Mohammedan literature was arranged, which was far more comprehensive than anything which had been previously gathered in one place. Leaders of the extensive Moslem population in Peking were visited and some of these gave Dr. Zwemer a petition to President Woodrow Wilson asking him to stop World War I, which was in progress at the time.

On September 13th, 1917, Dr. Zwemer left Shanghai to return to Cairo. Among the many results of the visit was a special "Moslem number" of *The Chinese Recorder,* published in October, 1917. The leading editorial was on the Zwemer visit and all the articles had to do with a new spirit in work for the Mohammedans of China. One of the principal articles was by the visitor and another, which we shall quote at length, gives us one of the best reviews of the general effects on missionary work in this most populous of all lands.

The Rev. R. A. Jaffray, of the Christian and Missionary Alliance, wrote under the title, "The Significance to the Missionary of Dr. Zwemer's Visit":

"It is an interesting and instructive study to observe how God in His wise and gracious providence has placed His chosen workers in the most neglected parts of the world to witness His Message to all people. Not only is it true that geographically He has thus distributed His workers, but He has also taken account of the peculiar religious tendencies of the peoples of the earth and has called and specially qualified missionaries for these peculiar conditions.

"Of all the non-Christian religions of the world none is perhaps more distinctive than that of Mohammedanism, and in the whole missionary body in all parts of the world no man is perhaps more definitely called to a specific work than is Doctor Samuel M. Zwemer, of Arabia and Egypt.

"Doctor Zwemer has been known to most of the missionaries of China by name for many years as the author of many books on the Moslem problem, as the editor of THE MOSLEM WORLD, and as a prominent speaker at large missionary conventions in both America and Europe, but it was a special treat for those who this summer were privileged to attend the Conferences held at Kuling, Chikungshan, Peitaiho, and Chefoo and hear his direct and inspiring messages.

"Besides bringing his hearers a great deal of new light on the subject so near his heart, that of Moslemism and the work of Christ in Moslem lands, Doctor Zwemer also brought to us strong and stirring messages from the Word of God. Many China missionaries who may read these lines will recall with real spiritual profit and blessing some precious truth of Scripture made clear and applied to the heart, some impression of the Holy Spirit through Doctor Zwemer's Bible talks. Some of us will never forget the searching words on 'Limiting the Holy One of Israel' and 'The Scars of the Saviour' and on 'Blindness' to all earthly things that is consequent to the brightness of the vision of the Glorious One. (Acts 22:11).

"But the primary purpose of Doctor Zwemer's visit to China was not to entertain or even edify the missionary body with Bible messages, helpful, instructive and necessary as this ministry is in connection with visits from men of God during the summer months. Nor was his object merely to bring us information and helpful suggestion about working among Moslems, though there is no man living better qualified to do this; but the main object of his visit was to gain information regarding Moslems in China and seek to stir our hearts to more prayer and definite effort for the salvation of these neglected millions.

"During each of the four Conferences held a representative committee was appointed to draw up the 'Findings' of the Conference. The following is a condensed summary of the findings of the four Conferences held at Kuling, Chikungshan, Peitaiho, and Chefoo

1. Each Conference records its hearty thanks to God for sending Doctor Zwemer to China and for the blessing and help obtained through his addresses.

2. Each Conference further records its purpose to pray increasingly for the Moslem lands, the workers and their most difficult problems. It is suggested to all who find help in regulated plans of prayer, the desirability of remembering work among Mohammedans on Friday, the Moslem Sabbath.

3. It was generally agreed at these Conferences that nothing like the serious and special attention the Moslem population in China deserves has been given it in the past and that from now on some concerted effort should be made to reach and intelligently deal with these people.

4. It is suggested that in order to effectually deal with the problem of Chinese Moslems it is essential that fuller and more accurate information should be obtained than is at present available, on the subject, and

that it be recommended to the China Continuation Committee, that the Committee on Survey and Occupation be asked to include this in the purview of that Committee, as an object of great and urgent importance. It is generally agreed that, roughly speaking, the Mohammedan population in China is found largely in the five provinces of Honan, Shensi, Kansu, Yunnan, and Chihli.

5. Inasmuch as in these provinces the leaders of Moslemism read Arabic, it is suggested that the Home Boards be recommended to send out men with a knowledge of Arabic for special work among the Mohammedans of China.

6. At each of the Conferences it was strongly urged that the much needed literature for work among Moslems be prepared and published without delay.

"The Sunday offerings at the Conventions were voted to be used toward supplying this needed literature. Much more money is needed, however, for this purpose, and special prayer is asked that this shall be supplied.

"All the Conferences unite in the suggestion that some kind of permanent organization for the carrying on of work in China among Moslems should be effected.

"The concensus of these opinions was that the matter of reaching the Chinese Moslems with the Gospel should be considered of such importance as to necessitate the immediate appointment of a strong permanent Committee under the China Continuation Committee. It was generally agreed that there is urgent need for some one to be set free to give his whole time to the work and the Chefoo Conference was of the opinion that three secretaries for Moslem work are needed.

"In closing, the writer would again refer to the all-important ministry of prayer and urge upon us all that we take the needs of the Chinese Moslems, as well as Moslems all over the world, upon our hearts more than ever in the past. To many of us it may be more or less a new subject for prayer; but with light upon it our responsibility is increased and we dare not be careless in the matter of intercession. All the plans and organizations suggested will be of no avail and will not result in the conversion of one soul to Christ unless it be accompanied by our prayers in the all-prevailing Name of Jesus Christ our Lord."

II

After his first visit in 1917 Zwemer was in China for a short time on his way home to America in 1918. As has been mentioned in a previous chapter he was with a number of other missionaries from Egypt and various fields. The journey to the homeland was made by the Pacific because of Atlantic crossings being limited by conditions of World War I. There was some opportunity to meet Moslems and missionary friends, but these were only brief contacts.

Following the marriage of Nellie Elizabeth Zwemer to the Reverend Claude L. Pickens Jr. of the Protestant Episcopal Church, the young couple were appointed missionaries to China. From the first they exhibited a vital and hereditary interest in Moslem work and were soon largely engaged in this type of service. The daughter and son-in-law were, therefore, actively engaged in the plans for the most extensive visit which Dr. Zwemer made to China, in 1933.

Missions for Moslems had made much progress since the former tour, and a quarterly newsletter under the title *Friends of Moslems* was in its Seventh volume in 1933. This visit, like the former one was made in answer to repeated requests from the field. It is notable that the expenses of the journey to Western China on which the Reverend Claude L. Pickens accompanied him, were met by gifts in China itself donated through the Society of Friends of Moslems.

Dr. Zwemer had passed through a serious illness in America early in the year and there was doubt for a time that his physicians would agree to the journey. They would no doubt have raised their hands in holy horror had they known that he was to make a trip by horse, mule-litter and other conveyance up to the borders of Tibet!

The objects of the journey were a response to the invitations received, to study once more Islam in China and give both devotional and inspirational addresses at the summer gatherings, as well as the holding of local conferences with missionaries and leading them in discussion of problems in work for Islam. Meetings for Moslems were also planned in a number of places and Christian literature was distributed and its further production in China considered.

The itinerary of the journey was as follows:

	Approx. miles
May 26 — Left San Francisco on S.S. President Harrison	
June 19 — Arrived Shanghai via Honolulu and Kobe	6,597
June 20 — Train for Tungkuan via Nanking, Pukow, Hauchow, Kaifeng, and Chengchow (meetings were held in the last two cities named)	750
June 24 — Motor car to Sian, the ancient capital of all China	90
June 28 — Airplane from Sian to Lanchow in Kansu	400
June 29 - July 16 — Lanchow to Sining, Shunhwa, in Tsinghai (Kokonor) Province, and Hochow, Kansu, by mule-litter or on horse-back, crossing the Yellow, the Sining, and the Tao Rivers by ferry boat	450
July 17 — arrived Lanchow. Conference	
July 20 — Airplane from Lanchow to Sian (3½ hours)	400
July 21 — Sian to railway terminus, Tungkuan by motor-bus	90
July 22-25 — Tungkuan to Hankow (and Kuling)	350
July 31-August 4 — Kuling Conference	
August 10 — Hankow to Shanghai (river steamer)	600
August 14-18 — Shanghai to Mokanshan and return	300

August 19 — Shanghai to San Francisco on
    S.S. President Coolidge   6,597
September 4 — Arrived San Francisco
September 9 — Arrived Princeton, New Jersey

                               Total   16,824

As Zwemer stated afterward, "No journey by magic carpet in The Arabian Nights could be more strangely fascinating than to travel by airplane from Sian, the old capital of China to Lanchow in Kansu, a distance of over four hundred miles in three and a half hours. Formerly the journey took three weeks. Traveling afterwards by mule litter eight hours a day toward the borders of Tibet and back across the great sparsely occupied areas of north-western China where brave men and heroic women are facing loneliness and hardship with first century joy—such was our experience."

But the sequel to the journey by plane was startling. On the plane Zwemer and Pickens sat on packing cases over the rough stretch of mountainous terrain. When they arrived they found the cases contained munitions and dynamite for the Chinese army!

After arrival in Shanghai on June 20th no time was lost in starting by rail for the West. They reached Kaifeng in Central China on the evening of June 21st (notice the time schedule!). Dr. Zwemer addressed the assembled missionaries representing the China Inland Mission, the Church of England in Canada, the American Free Methodist Mission and the Southern Baptist Convention. The visitors gave a graphic survey of Christian work in the Mohammedan world, there was a discussion period and again the great power of this man to bring people of different backgrounds together in co-operation was illustrated. As one has expressed it, "In a Zwemer Conference all mission workers feel very near to each other because all are very near to Christ."

Then a meeting was held in the church where some eight hundred Chinese heard the guest from America speak on "Follow me, and I will make you fishers of men." One of the Chinese pastors was interpreter at this meeting. The Rev. Claude L. Pickens acted as guide and counselor, and also kept a diary of the trip and took more than a hundred photographs.

The next day Miss Murray of the American Free Methodist Mission, and seven Chinese Christians went on with the party to Chengchow. There again there was a conference with workers of the Lutheran United, Free Methodist and Southern Baptist missions. In the afternoon the leader spoke to a gathering of three or four hundred Chinese Christians, and in the evening to some eight hundred Moslems, on "The Five Pillars" of the Christian Religion. This address was described by one present as "a practical demonstraton of how it should be done."

From Chengchow the visiting leaders went on by rail to Tungkuan, which was then the end of the railway. From there to Sian the ninety miles over roads that were "almost impossible because of blinding dust or deep mud and floods." The party met a heavy wind and driving rain storm, then had a number of flat tires and a real blowout, so that the trip of less than a hundred miles took the whole of two days. Those of us who have had similar experiences on the roads of almost any part of Asia before modern highways were built can testify what a cruel way this is to learn the virtue of patience.

In Sian there was a conference which brought together the mission workers of even more divergent groups. Here the Scandanavian Alliance Mission, the English Baptists, the Chung Heva Sheng Kung Hui[1], the Seventh Day Adventists and the Y.M.C.A. sent representatives.

The following morning more than a hundred Chinese workers for the Swedish Alliance Mission were gathered for a talk on work among Moslems. The party also visited the supposed site of the old Nestorian church in the western outskirts of the city. The foundations and some few columns of the church remain. The famous "Nestorian Tablet" describing the Christian Mission which labored here in the seventh century of our era is not now in the place where it was found, but in the Chinese Archaeological Museum of Sian. It was a thrill for the visitor to see these remains of very early Christian missionaries to China. The Imperial mosque of Sian, one of the largest in China was also visited.

On June 28th the journey to Lanchow was made by plane, as described above. Then on to Sining along the Yellow and Sining Rivers. The traveler remarked the extensive and beautiful fields of the deadly opium poppy in full bloom, and the fact that the drug would pay about fourteen times as much as any other crop. There were the huge wooden water wheels, forty to sixty feet high, for irrigation, driven by the current of the river and lifting up the water in buckets to be spilled into irrigation ditches at the top. The party was on horse and mule-litter, and at various stages along the way they were accompanied or met by missionaries who rode considerable distances to express their hospitality and friendship. This, it may be said, is a common custom among missionaries not only in China, but other parts of Asia, to ride out to meet visitors and often take a picnic lunch or tea along to eat by the roadside at the place of meeting.

On June 29th the Yellow River was crossed in a small ferry-boat which carried some twenty horses and mules in addition to more travelers than animals and a large amount of baggage. A dangerous diversion was created by one of the horses that tried to jump overboard into the river. Two days after the crossing the party was met by representatives of the China Inland Mission from Sining. There the visitors were the guests of Mr. and Mrs. George K. Harris, where they had a real bath after a week in Chinese Inns, and were entertained with what Dr. Zwemer called "lavish hospitality." Mr. Harris of the China Inland Mission was, moreover, a specialist on Moslem work and had even then written a number of articles which eventually came

---

1. "Chinese Holy Catholic Church," Anglican and Episcopalian.

to be published as the manual entitled "How to lead Moslems to Christ." He knew Arabic well.

The conference at Sining was one of remarkable interest. The workers were largely from the China Inland Mission. The secretary, S. H. Knight, writes in the minutes of the meeting:

"Arriving on the afternoon of July 3rd, by mule litter from Lanchow, the Doctor took his first meeting which was of a devotional character, that same evening. He brought with him in all his messages an up-to-date-ness and a freshness that was like a breeze in summer to us here, this being particularly noticeable in his first talk on "Re-thinking Missions." Dr. Zwemer was able to give us first hand some of the latest information of the strong opposition being offered to the Report[2] by eminent men such as Robert E. Speer, and of the definite evangelical stand which many hitherto hesitating had been led to take as they saw the trend of modernistic thought in Mission activity. He thought, however, that we would do well to re-think Missions. He then enumerated some of the problems known to us all in Missionary, especially Moslem, work. The sparseness of the results, prevalence of rice-Christians, the failure of some apparent earnest seekers after truth to believe in Christ, and the number of Christians who go back and walk no more with Him. Facing these 'mysteries of missionary work' squarely, he declared with conviction that there were none which were not fully answered in the Parables of the 'mysteries of the Kingdom' in Matt. 13. Elaborating further on this thought, the Doctor then went on to say that, in re-thinking Missions, it was not the want of new methods that should give us most anxiety. The modern missionary needed to listen more to the 'voice behind thee saying, this is the way walk ye in it.' We none of us like to listen to 'back-seat driving,' but it was what we needed most. We should, he affirmed, listen in these days to the voice of those days, to the voice of those in the back seat—the early missionary pioneers, the apostles who succeeded where we have failed. An analysis of the lives of these great men who first opened the various countries to the Gospel, revealed that they possessed several qualities sometimes absent from the modern missionary. Notable amongst these qualities were:— Vision; Knowledge (of the language and the people); Persistence; Passion for souls and Ability to Endure Loneliness. It was a 'new man' rather than a new method that was wanted. Given these same qualities in the missionary of today, unoccupied fields would soon be opened, and the problems which new methods have left unaltered, solved."

Full notes on the conference were published in the October number of *Friends for Moslems.* The gathering ended in a fitting climax when Dr. Zwemer led in the Communion meditation and gave the elements of the blessed sacrament to those hardy and lonely pioneers who serve so faithfully on the frontiers of the Kingdom.

A further two-day trip across the mountains brought the party to Payang-jung (Hualung) and another day to Hsünhua in both of which the China

2. Re-Thinking Missions, a Laymen's Inquiry, Harper and Brothers, New York, 1932.

Inland Mission, and stations were visited. The trip continued over a mountain pass at an altitude of more than 13,000 feet. On this stage a portion of the newly-made road gave way because of recent rainstorms and Zwemer's mule-litter went over the side. The mule rolled down, the baggage also, but the traveler was uninjured! And we should remember that a few short months before this adventurer, who was scaling thirteen thousand foot passes in the far reaches of western China and narrowly escaping plunges down into deep gorges and spending long days by mule and nights in Chinese inns, had been critically ill in Princeton!

On July 12th they arrived safely at Hochow in Kansu province. This city is called "The Mecca of China." Together with its surrounding villages there is a population of some 400,000. In the rebellion of 1928 there were terrible massacres of revenge taken in the district and destroyed villages could still be seen. The Moslems were the dominant group at the time of the visit and in one mosque some 2000 would gather on Friday. This is a station of the Christian and Missionary Alliance. In the conference at Hochow there were also members of the Pentecostal Mission and the China Inland Mission. On the twelfth Zwemer gave two addresses and led in the discussion. The next day he was a bit indisposed but provided a paper he had written on "The Six Cardinal Virtues" to be read, and by evening he was ready to give another address! Visits were made to the Moslem quarters of the town, and a school where 400 students were being taught Chinese, Arabic and English was operated under the "Moslem Forward Movement."

The farthest west had been the meeting at Sining and now from Howchow the journey was made back to Lanchow, which was reached on July 17th. The following two days there was an impressive conference the resolutions of which we shall quote, since they are similar to those adopted in Sining and Hochow and were later endorsed by the larger Missionary Conference at Kuling, with appropriate changes in the name of provinces. The findings were adopted as follows:

"That there should be a sufficient proportion of qualified full-time Moslem workers in Kansu, Ningsia and Tsinghai Provinces to present the Gospel adequately to all classes of the Moslems, not forgetting the women and girls in scattered villages.

"That these full-time workers should give special attention to the preparation of literature in Arabic and Chinese to meet all classes of the people.

"That in districts where there are Moslems residing, all missionaries should have some general knowledge of how to meet this special people, and that concise helps should be provided for giving such workers the necessary information.

"That mission councils in designating workers to areas where Moslems reside should take into consideration the appointment of those who, interested in the Moslems, are prepared to devote at least a proportion of their time to the work.

"That a manual for workers among Moslems should be compiled, giving concisely all elementary information necessary and advisable for new workers to have, including sources of further information.

"That in all tracts for Moslems in Chinese, the basic truths of our Christian faith, such as—the inspiration of the Bible, the Deity of Christ, the Virgin Birth, Crucifixion, Death, and Resurrection of our Lord, while presented to the Moslems in a spirit of love, should never be toned down to avoid giving offense to them."

It is quite natural that Dr. Zwemer should have a special interest in visiting the Borden Memorial Hospital in Lanchow since William Borden had become a Student Volunteer under his leadership and Zwemer had conducted the funeral services when Borden gave his life in Cairo while learning Arabic as a preparation for work in this station among the Moslems of Western China. Dr. Zwemer after the visit wrote, "The Borden Memorial Hospital is a very fine institution and one of two Christian hospitals in Kansu for five million people."

After the trip to visit the missionaries and the Moslems of the far west in China Zwemer set down five indelible impressions he had gained from the visit. They were:

1. The call of unoccupied areas and the sadly undermanned stations.
2. The ability and heroism of the rank and file of the mission workers.
3. The new China in the making.
4. Islam in China is not moribund but challenges attention through its program of education and publication.
5. The spiritually-minded Chinese Christians we met were increasingly conscious of their responsibility.

The return was again made by air to Sian, and by motor to the railhead, then on to Hankow, which was reached on July 23rd. The next engagements were the Conferences with large groups of missionaries at Kuling and Mokanshan. There had also been an invitation to a third conference at Peitaiho, but this plan had to be abandoned because of disturbed war conditions.

At Kuling, reached by sedan chair, there were some eight hundred present for a week. We could hardly do better in reflecting the impression made upon this tremendous gathering of Christian workers in China than to set down the statements of two leading missionaries as published in the *Kuling Echo* of August 5th, 1933.

"Impressions from the Kuling Convention

Dr. Samuel M. Zwemer, F.R.G.S., the main convention speaker, impresses one as being a rugged rock against which the waves of persecution, and hostile criticism and tribulation have dashed, without making any lasting mark. To the Islamic world in all its solidarity, he has thrown out the challenge: 'What think ye of Christ, whose son is He?' And to the Christian church, so often indifferent and indolent: 'The Christianizing of the Moslem world, whose task is it?'

"In delivering his forceful message, Dr. Zwemer enters invariably by the door of wholesome wit. The burden on his heart is the salvation of 250 million Mohammedans of the Moslem world, extending from Sudan to Kansu, and from Sumatra to Albania. In a graphic way he gave an airplane view of present-day conditions in Turkey, Egypt. Arabia, Persia, India, and China, as they affect the followers of Mohammed, and the cross-currents of modern civilization as they come into conflict with the ancient civilization of Islam. Nor did he underestimate the stupendous problems confronting the new missionaries that in our day set out to present Christ Jesus as Saviour to these people, and the necessity of a more adequate training of those who enter the joys of this service.

"While conceding that the Layman's Report rightly emphasized 're-thinking missions,' Dr. Zwemer stressed the solidarity of the Christian enterprise from the days of the apostles, and the necessity of our remaining in the main current of missionary activity and purpose, and of building on the foundations already laid, as did our missionary predecessors, the giants of former days.

"The Convention went on record as approving the plan of missions setting aside missionaries for full-time or part-time work among Chinese Moslems, and urging co-operative efforts along this line in the Central China area.

R. Mortenson"

Another missionary wrote:

"Words fail to describe the impression Dr. Zwemer left on the minds and hearts of his hearers, in regard to the great question of the presentation of the Gospel of Christ to the Moslem world. Dr. Zwemer has a heart full to overflowing with love and good will—and, I must add, with a most delightful sense of humor—but he did not mince matters. He showed us the greatness of the difficulties and made us realize with penitence and self-reproach, our past negligence and indifference toward this most challenging task." — Robert E. Wood.

At Kuling Dr. Zwemer was invited to the home of Chiang Kai-shek and his wife who asked for the prayers of the missionaries in the crisis and need of China at the time.

From Hankow the return to Shanghai was made by river boat, which just about completed the gamut of Chinese transportation for the trip, by mule-litter, sedan chair and by cart, by air and rail and auto, and now by river boat. There was a wonderful Chinese dinner in Shanghai with leaders of the Church of Christ in China and Dr. Zwemer and his daughter left for the final conference of the trip.

The meetings at Mokanshan were well attended and many missionaries and Chinese workers purchased literature, as they had at the other gatherings. The time in Mokanshan was limited, as Dr. Zwemer was sailing on August 19th for America. In less than three days he delivered six lectures on "The Searchlight of God," "Re-thinking Missions," "The New World of Islam," "Our God is a Consuming Fire," and "Islam in China."

One high point of the Kuling conference was a lecture to Chinese Christians. Mr. Richard C. S. Hu, of Hankow, was so affected that he expressed a desire to give his life to work for Chinese Moslems.

A comment which the visitor appreciated more than most others was a Moslem appreciation which appeared in Chinese Daily paper of Sian, Shensi on June 26th 1933. It read:

"Yesterday Dr. Samuel M. Zwemer, an American, visited the large mosque of this city. He had a long conversation with the head teacher of the Mosque. He is a thorough student of the Mohammedan Religion. A great religious leader and Doctor of Divinity, Mr. Zwemer is now over 60 years of age. He has traveled in the East and through the countries of England, France, Germany and Italy and has studied the conditions of various religions. He has in all spent about forty years in the countries of Afghanistan, Persia, Turkey, Egypt, etc., and has especially given himself to the study of Islam (The Hui Religion), which has made his knowledge and understanding of the same very deep.

"Yesterday forenoon at ten o'clock, Dr. Zwemer accompanied by Messrs. Pickens and Englund visited the Mosque on Hua Chiao Lane here in the city and had a talk with the head teacher, Mr. Ma Shoucheng and his assistant, Mr. An Chi-chieh in the school room. In conversation with Dr. Zwemer we conversed in the Arabic language. Regarding the Mohammedan religious doctrine and the inner meaning of the Koran, he had made a thorough study, resulting in an attitude of greatest friendliness."

The journey resulted in a great impetus to the cause of Christian literature for Moslems. Dr. Zwemer made out a *Minimum Literature* Program, which contained suggestions for fourteen basic publications with a view to reaching Moslems with the Gospel and instructing them in the Christian faith. The work for Mohammedans was undertaken with new spirit in central and northwest China and the cause of this work was brought to the attention of many missionaries and Chinese Christian workers who had scarcely considered it before. A circular letter to graduates of Princeton Theological Seminary among the missionaries in China brought a number of interesting objects for the missionary Museum which Dr. Zwemer was founding at Princeton, which will be described in a later chapter.

Data gathered on the journey was used in writing the article on the Moslems of China for the Atlas of Missions, and a map which was prepared for that volume and widely published in other connections giving the approximate number of Moslems in each province of China, was made up from facts ascertained on this trip.

Concerning the entire adventure Dr. Zwemer wrote, "Our safety on the journey was an answer to prayer and it is with thanksgiving to God that we record the memory of His great goodness, and express our firm faith in the coming of His Kingdom in spite of sword and flood and famine."

Part Four

The Harvest of the Years

XII

Missionary Conferences

"I have never got out of my memory the speech of Dr. Zwemer at one of the earlier conventions of this Movement, when he hung a great map of Islam before us, and with a sweep of his hand across all those darkened areas said: 'Thou O Christ art all I want; and Thou O Christ art all *they* want.' What Christ can do for any man He can do for every man."

— ROBERT E. SPEER.
Rochester Convention 1910,
Page 11.

CHAPTER TWELVE

MISSIONARY CONFERENCES

Zeal in the heart and mind of Samuel Zwemer for participation in and organization of Christian conferences began in the days when he was in Seminary and gained momentum across the years.

There were times during the visits to America and Great Britain, as well as in the Continental Countries of Europe and in the Moslem mission fields when he went from one conference to another in rapid succession. Mention has been made in our narrative of many such gatherings. In this chapter we review a few of the general conferences because of some special contribution by the one concerning whom we write.

I

At the momentous Student Volunteer Convention in Nashville, Tennessee, in 1906, the subject of his main address was: *Unprecedented Opportunities for Evangelizing the Mohammedan World.* He began:

"Sir William Muir, an acknowledged authority, has said, 'The sword of Mohammed and the Koran are the most stubborn enemies of civilization, liberty, and truth which the world has yet known.' To the unprejudiced mind his statement is a historical commonplace. While other religions and systems of error have fallen before the advance of truth, as Dagon before the ark of Jehovah, Islam, like mighty Goliath, defies the armies of the living God and the progress of Christ's Kingdom! In three continents it presents an unbroken front and is armed with a proud and aggressive spirit."[1]

He went on: "The hour is ripe. The situation, despite long neglect and almost universal apathy in many Christian circles, so far from being discouraging, is full of hope and pregnant with unprecedented opportunities."

He then enumerated and enlarged upon a sevenfold call to work for the world of Islam and ended: "The inspiration of the heroic leaders of the past is ours. Raymund Lull's prayers and tears are receiving answer now in Tunis and Algiers. He was the first, but not the last, missionary to the Moslems of Africa. Henry Martyn's life did not 'burn out for God'; it became a shining light for all Persia. The graves of Bishop French, and Keith-Falconer, and Peter Zwemer will rivet attention to Arabia until it is won for Christ.

"Pfander's books touch the Moslem conscience in a dozen lands today. Mirza Ibrahim's martyrdom is a rich heritage for the native Church in Persia; Maxwell Gordon's death will not be forgotten when Afghan-

---

1. **Students and the Modern Missionary Crusade,** Nashville Conference Report, 1906, p. 220.

istan opens its gates to Jesus Christ. As we look over these pioneer fields we cry out our Te Deum:

'The glorious company of the apostles praise Thee,
The noble army of martyrs praise Thee,'

and we here and now call upon the Holy Church throughout the world to rise to a new crusade and win back the Mohammedan world to Christ in this generation. God wills it. 'Father, the hour has come; glorify thy Son!' Amen."

Zwemer was also one of the leaders at the Student Volunteer Convention in Rochester in 1910 and Kansas City in 1914. At Rochester he spoke on *The Impending Struggle in Western Asia.* It was in this address that he used the words, "To His Kingdom there are no frontiers" which has been used again and again in many permutations and combinations.

The last paragraph of his address at Rochester was thrilling:

"Above all, think of the inspiration of Jesus' life in Western Asia. If God so loved the world, He loved it as a unit; but if Jesus Christ is the Son of Man, He loves Western Asia. His manger and His Cross stood there. In Western Asia His blood was spilled. In Western Asia He walked the hills. There His tears fell for Jerusalem. There His eye still rests. Thither He will come again. It was in Western Asia that He said, 'All authority is given unto Me;' and although for thirteen centuries His royal rights have been disputed by a usurper, they have never been abrogated. Shall we give Western Asia to Him, or shall Western Asia remain the Empire of Mohammed? Shall Bethlehem hear five times a day 'There is no god but God, and Mohammed is God's apostle', and shall not a single one of us dare go, if God will, in this year of our Lord nineteen hundred and ten unto Mecca itself, the very stronghold of Islam, and preach the Gospel of the great King?"[2]

Wherever he happened to be in the world, it seemed, John R. Mott would call Zwemer home for the great Student Volunteer Conventions. In 1914 he spent 113 days in the United States and during that time he made 151 addresses. Ten of them were at the Student Volunteer Convention in Kansas City. The titles of several will show what a wide range they covered. Among them were, *"The Fullness of Time for the Moslem World," "The Destiny of a Continent"* (Africa), *"The Contributions Theological Schools Should be Making to the Evangelization of the World". "The Power of Sacrifice", "The Present Situation in Arabia", "The Will of God for the Individual",* etc. At this gathering Zwemer no doubt made one of his greatest contributions to the movement, though he had been a power since its early days. He had been the first candidate secretary and, according to John R. Mott, was largely responsible for the greatly increased number of student volunteers who actually started for the mission field during the years of the Conferences mentioned above.[3]

<hr/>

2. Students and the Present Missionary Crisis, pp. 71-82.
3. Addresses and Papers, John R. Mott, Vol. I, p. 123.

As Sherwood Eddy has stated: "If he had never set foot in Arabia or Egypt, if his service had been confined to the colleges and Churches of America . . . his work would have been monumental. Zwemer was the blazing prophet of every platform summoning the Church to its most difficult task."[4]

II

The young men who founded the Arabian Mission thought long thoughts and their vision reached out to the whole of the Moslem World. Cantine very early sent Zwemer to India with the idea of a general Conference of those who were working for Moslems. This was proposed and the young man from Arabia was invited to return to the Decennial Conference in Madras in December 1902. There plans were laid on which Zwemer, together with Dr. H. U. Weitbracht of the C.M.S. Mission in Lahore, continued to carry on the correspondence.

By 1904 a Program Committee had been selected which decided to accept a cordial invitation from the American Mission to meet in Cairo. The date was set for April 4 to 8, 1906, and one more day was later added, so that the dates on which the first General Conference for work among Moslems finally met were April 4 to 9, 1906.

The unusual organizing talent of the young missionary from Arabia soon became evident. The Committee drew up a tentative program, an advisory committee was appointed in America. Boards and Societies with work in the Moslem World were asked to appoint delegates and those who were considered best able to do so were asked to write papers and addresses for the conference. All was not smooth sailing. There were many missionaries in different lands who had forebodings of the trouble that such a conference might cause. Even the president of a large university in the Near East cabled Dr. John R. Mott asking him to prevent the gathering.

In spite of the undercurrent of fearfulness on the part of some there was such a united response from the missions at work in Moslem lands that it was taken by those in charge as a divine assurance that the meetings should be held.

When they finally gathered, sixty-two appointed delegates representing twenty-nine missionary societies were present. In addition there were about sixty official visitors, the conference was not open to the public and admission was by ticket only. Dr. Samuel M. Zwemer was chosen as chairman at the first meeting and Dr. George Alexander of the First Presbyterian Church, New York, as vice-chairman.

On the evening before the opening there was a prayer meeting which really invoked the divine blessing and set the deep religious tone of all the meetings. Constant intercession for the different fields was continued as they respectively came up for review before the conference.

---

4. **Pathfinders of the World Missionary Crusade, p. 245.**

The program was divided into three main sections. I. The Scope of Missions to Moslems. II. Methods of Work among Moslems. III. The need for Prayer and Sacrifice in this Work. Under the first heading notable papers were read describing Islam in the various fields, many of them were contributed by names now famous as pioneers in the Islamic mission field. The papers on the second theme were no less noteworthy as to content or in the names of those who wrote the addresses. The spiritual need of the Mohammedan world and actual means of training workers and converts was finally considered.

The Conference led to the publication of two main volumes by Fleming H. Revell of New York. The one for general circulation *The Mohammedan World of Today*, edited by S. M. Zwemer, E. M. Wherry and James L. Barton. The second volume was for private circulation only. The title was *Methods of Mission Work among Moslems*. It contained the papers read on this subject and a review of the Conference discussion on them.

These were the first volumes ever issued to give a general review of the whole Moslem World and a discussion on the methods of work. Both were published before the end of the year 1906. This prompt printing was made possible by a gift of one hundred pounds Sterling from the Bible Lands Missions Aid Society of Great Britain.

It should be noted that women's work occupied a special place in the Conference and this phase led to the publication of a third volume, *Our Moslem Sisters*, by Annie Van Sommer and S. M. Zwemer. The book appeared in 1907.

The Cairo Conference undoubtedly resulted in a more comprehensive knowledge of the Moslem world than had been gathered before. It was the first bird's eye view of the whole task. The vast extent and the problems as well as the hopefulness of work for Moslems were for the first time brought into focus.

The general meeting also made possible a review of serious mistakes which had been made and laid the foundation for greater uniformity in the evangelistic approach to the followers of Islam

For the first time the strategic place that Christian literature should have in the Moslem work was realized and plans began to be made accordingly.

The Conference also did much to arouse the church to the great contest that was going on in areas of primitive Africa and Asia for the allegiance of these peoples, the two rivals being Islam and Christianity. The meetings and publications also did much to awaken the church to the fact that the world of Islam had long been a neglected field in the missionary strategy.

New hope and courage and a sense of unity in the tremendous task was produced among the delegates and reflected through them to the Missions which they represented. *It may be said that the Cairo Conference marked the beginning of a new era in the Christian Mission to Moslems.* From the standpoint of this biography it also launched Zwemer on his zeal for gathering facts concerning the whole world of Islam. In this connection the words of his long-time friend and colleague Charles R. Watson, president of the university of Cairo may be quoted:

"Dr. Zwemer's mind moves along dramatic lines. He is therefore at his best when surveying world movements such as those that are taking place in Islam. His facility for gathering facts is amazing."[5]

Scarcely was the Cairo Conference ended before plans were being made for a larger gathering on the same subject. This took place at Lucknow, India, some five years later.

The publications of the gathering at Cairo were as seed for a crop of literature concerning work for Moslems. The Central Committee on the United Study of Missions took up the subject. They published a mission study textbook on *The Nearer and Farther East* which sold more than 45,000 copies. The Student Volunteer Movement published Zwemer's book *Islam, A Challenge to Faith* which had large sale in several editions in the United States and Great Britain and was translated and published in German, Danish and French. The Young People's Missionary Movement of America sold more than 50,000 copies of their abridged text "The Moslem World." There were also many volumes written by missionaries in most of the great Moslem fields. It may be said that the Protestant churches gained a new conception of their duty to the world of Islam through the literary flood which followed the Cairo Conference.

III

Turning now to the Lucknow Conference which met January 23 to 28, 1911. On the Saturday previous there was a reception of delegates and introductions in the main college hall, which had been especially decorated for the occasion. Before the formal opening of the conference there was a sermon, concerning which we may quote Miss Jeanne L. Rollier in *Lutheran Woman's Work* for May, 1911:

"On Sunday evening, the 22nd, we were privileged to hear Dr. S. M. Zwemer of Arabia preach on the duties of the Church as elder brother, to the prodigal son, as Islam. The thought was new and startling to many of us, but we were soon convinced and condemned after hearing the preacher's heart and soul-piercing message, that the Church must, in order to reach the heart of this prodigal son, be like the Father, watching for his return and ready to embrace him and welcome him to the Father's home. This Sunday evening service was as the key to the Conference, for again and again the thought came home to our hearts during the solemn hours of the following week that Islam is our brother who can only be won by the love of the Church-love which needs to be like that of the Father in the touching parable of the prodigal son."

5. **The Moslem World,** January, 1917, p. 104.

There were two printed programs for the meeting, the one a very attractive souvenir booklet of 27 pages with cover picture and other illustrations, as well as blank pages for notes. The second was the ordinary printed Conference program. The prayer-room was open 24 hours a day and seasons of intercession followed the consideration of each general topic on the program.

At the opening session of the Conference Zwemer was elected Chairman and gave the opening address, which was a survey of the whole Moslem World. The subject was treated under the heading of 1. Statistics, 2. Political, 3. Social and Intellectual Movements, 4. The Changed Attitude of the Home Churches to the Moslem World.

Zwemer spoke for an hour and fifteen minutes and had the Conference in wrapt attention for the whole period. The address concluded:

"As our eyes sweep the horizon of all these lands dominated or imperilled by this great rival faith, each seems to stand out as typical of one of the factors in the great problem. Morocco is typical of the degradation of Islam; Persia of its disintegration; Arabia of its stagnation; Egypt of its attempted reformation; China shows the neglect of Islam; Java the conversion of Islam; India the opportunity to reach Islam; Equatorial Africa its peril. Each of these typical conditions is in itself an appeal. The supreme need of the Moslem world is Jesus Christ. He alone can give light to Morocco, unity to Persia, life to Arabia, re-birth to Egypt, reach the neglected in China, win Malaysia, meet the opportunity in India, and stop the agressive peril in Africa."

Writing on the conference in the April 1911 number of *The Missionary Review of the World*, Dr. Stephan Van R. Trowbridge of Turkey said: Dr. Zwemer's opening address 'Survey of the Moslem World' was remarkable for its force and for its wide vision. The address closed with an appeal to God to accomplish the task which 'with all there is of encouragement to our faith, remains big and baffling."

After the opening day the gathering considered a series of themes which were planned to bring out the problems and focus the needs of missions for Moslems everywhere. The matters considered were:

1. The Pan-Islamic Movement
2. Political Changes in the Moslem World
3. Government attitudes toward missions to Islam
4. Islam among Pagan races and measures to meet the Moslem advance
5. The Training of Missionaries for work among Moslems
6. Literature of Workers and Moslem needs
7. Reform Movements: Doctrinal and Social.

Work among women also had a prominent place on the program. Miss Lilias Trotter of Algiers and many other prominent women delegates were there, including Miss Annie Van Sommer of Egypt, founder of the Nile Mission Press and the co-author with Zwemer of the volume which appeared giving the papers on women's work. The title of the volume was *Daylight in the Harem*.

At the close of the Conference the Rt. Rev. G. A. Lefroy, D.D., Bishop of Lahore, speaking for about forty minutes without notes summarized the work of the meeting under five headings: 1. The Relation of Missions to Governments. 2. The Attitude of Christianity toward Islam. 3. Workers. 4. The Greatness of the Opportunity. 5. The need for a Deeper Life of Prayer.

An article in *The Indian Bookman* placed special stress upon the daily devotional periods of the whole gathering. "Another highly important fact which played a great part in the Conference was the period set apart during the noon hours daily for devotional exercises. Some member of the Conference was selected by the Chairman to conduct it, and the selection of leaders for this purpose indicated how considerable was Dr. Zwemer's knowledge of men he had to deal with. It was a time of genuine waiting upon God every day."

The article from which the above is quoted also gave the only criticisms of the Conference we have seen in reading a number of accounts from Indian, British and American papers and magazines. These were "1. The members of the Conference were too numerous. 2. A still weaker point was that all the papers which had been prepared for it were read in the Conference."

The papers were published after the Conference in the volume *Islam and Missions*, edited by Dr. E. M. Wherry, Dr. S. M. Zwemer and the Rev. C. G. Mylrea. This was a book of some 300 pages and was issued by Revell in New York.

The Resolutions of the Conference were published separately and marked *Confidential*. A Continuation Committee was appointed, made up of many famous missionaries from different parts of the Moslem World.

Following the Lucknow gathering the leading French Review on Islam, *Revue du Monde Musulman*, devoted the entire Volume XVI, 1911, to Protestant Missions in Moslem lands, under the title *The Conquest of the Moslem World*. The material was gathered and much of the writing was done by the editor himself, Professor A. Le Chatelier. The issue contained some 320 pages and although written with a Roman Catholic slant gave a most sympathetic account of the Lucknow Conference. Its origin, plans, program for advance are treated and there is an index of all Protestant missionary societies at work among Moslems, giving also a list of their periodicals. The volume is illustrated and has maps. There was also a review of the Edinburgh Conference and an article on Islam in China, but the focus was on Lucknow.

It is little wonder that the Moslem press of Cairo as well as in other centers where French is widely used should have become disturbed. A number of articles appeared against the French editor, to which he replied in his review by a long article entitled *"Il est Conquis"* (It is Conquered) in which he went on to show that politically and socially much of the world of Islam was under the governments of Christian lands and that social progress in the Moslem countries and advances in education had largely come through Christian missions.

There is no doubt that Lucknow 1911 had very far-reaching results. From its impetus there eventuated the Newman School of Missions in Jerusalem, the Henry Martyn School for the training of Missionaries to Moslems in India, the School of Oriental Studies of the American University at Cairo, and The Missionaries to Moslems League, a fellowship of prayer and encouragement for the work of Christian missions to Islam. It should also be remembered that 1911 was the first year of publication of *The Moslem World*.

Concerning the organization of the Fellowship of Faith for Moslems, we quote:

"The year 1915 was also an epochal year in Missionary effort, for it was then that the Christian Church in Britain was stirred to face up to the too long neglected task of the evangelization of the Moslem World. Dr. S. M. Zwemer was attending the Keswick Convention of that year and the great congregation gathered in the tent listened to his moving address on 'The Fullness of Time in the Moslem World', when he took as his text the words of Scripture — 'Master, we have toiled all night and have taken nothing; nevertheless at thy word we will let down the net'.

'Miss Annie Van Sommer, who had already been instrumental under God in praying into being the Egypt Mission Band, felt that now was the time for action, and she gathered around her a small company of like-minded fellow missionaries who formed the Fellowship of Faith for the Moslems, with Dr. Zwemer as its leader.

"The young tree then established has spread its branches far and wide, until now the Fellowship has an active membership of upwards of 850 in all parts of the world, and acts as a vital unifying force of all those who love the Moslems for Christ's sake, and seek to bring them to the Saviour by faith in Him and His power to save, through individual effort and prevailing prayer.

"Much could be written of the quiet undermining work that has been going on, and it is a matter for deep thanksgiving that the subject of this biography until his death at the advanced age of 84 was still Leader of the Fellowship and had seen much of the fruit of his sacrificial labour of love throughout the Moslem World."[6]

Samuel Zwemer had been one of the leading figures in the section which considered the Islamic world at the missionary conference of 1910 in Edinburgh. He was also prominent in the Jerusalem Conferences of 1924 and 1928, but they were organized and led by John R. Mott. Zwemer continued his zeal and support for Conferences on Moslem Missions up to and including the Princeton Conference of 1946, but Lucknow, 1911, was no doubt the zenith of his great conference career and together with Cairo, 1906, must remain as one of the major accomplishments of his life.

---

6. From the Fellowship of Faith for the Moslems News Letter of April 7, 1951.

XIII

The Moslem World and Literature

"Dr. Johnson once remarked that 'there are two objects of curiosity — the Christian world and the Mohammedan world. The subject is worthy of a careful examination, both for its own sake as one of the enigmas of religious history, and also to prepare our minds for an intelligent understanding of the amazing task to which God is leading the Church; viz. the conversion of the Moslem world to Christianity. The duty of Christianity to Mohammedanism, the enormous difficulties in the way of discharging it, the historic grandeur of the conflict, the way in which the honor of Christ is involved in the result, and the brilliant issues of victory all combine to make this problem of the true relation of Christian missions to Islam one of the most fascinating and momentous themes which the great missionary movement of the present century has brought to the attention of the Christian church."

REV. JAMES S. DENNIS, D.D.,
"Introduction to Arabia Cradle of Islam."

Chapter Thirteen

THE MOSLEM WORLD AND LITERATURE

Recalling the story about the wounded soldier of Napoleon who had no anaesthetic and as they probed for the bullet remarked, "Be careful, because a little deeper and you will strike my heart, and the Emperor is there." So Samuel Zwemer might have said if his heart were opened, *"The Moslem World* is there."

From the first number the magazine was entitled "A Quarterly Review of current events, literature and thought among Mohammedans, and the progress of Christian Missions in Moslem lands." It was the child of the editor and he not only gave his time with no remuneration across the years, but also carried the financial subsidy of the magazine largely on his own shoulders. While professor at Princeton Seminary he did not own a car, and Mrs. Zwemer had only part-time household help. What was saved in this way largely went to hospitality to the students and to the support of the Quarterly.

The first number appeared in January, 1911. As to the plan and policy of the periodical we quote from the opening editorial:

> "The question may well be asked, is there a place for a new quarterly concerning the Moslem World? Surely there is no lack of recent literature on Islam. Witness the enormous bibliography on the subject, both historical and philosophical, in all the principal languages of Europe and the Levant, not to speak of the attention given to the Moslem problem politically, the spread and disintegration of Islam as a religion, its cultural value or weakness and the marked unrest of all Moslem people, by the secular and religious press today. There are even publications exclusively devoted to the scientific study of Mohammedanism, two of which deserve special mention."

These two were the *Revue du Monde Musulman* in French and *Der Islam* in German. After mentioning them the editor continues:

> "The existence of all this literature, however, and the revival of interest in the great problem of Islam shown by the publication of these reviews, and the issue of a new 'Encyclopedia of Islam' simultaneously in three languages, only emphasize the opportunity and the place for an English quarterly review of current events, literature, and thought among Mohammedans as they affect the Church of Christ and its missionary programme, *if the Churches of Christendom are to reach the Moslem world with the Gospel.* The Cairo Conference (1906) marked a new era in the attitude of Christian missions toward the subject. This Conference, through its reports and the other missionary literature resulting from it, made clear the unity, the opportunity, and the importunity of the task of evangelizing Moslems everywhere. Mis-

sionary leaders felt that the Church was called to a deeper study of the problem, as well as to a more thorough preparation of its missionaries and a bolder faith in God, in order to solve it. To this end there is need for a common platform, a common forum of thought; a common organ for investigation and study.

"As an outcome, therefore, of the deep interest manifested at the World Missionary Conference at Edinburgh in June last, and to conserve, continue and interpret its deliberations on this subject as well as to bind together all those who love Mohammedans and labor for their welfare, THE MOSLEM WORLD greets its readers.

"Its aim is to represent no faction or fraction of the Church, but to be broad in the best sense of the word. Its columns are open to all contributors who hold the 'unity of the faith in the bond of peace and righteousness of life.' It is not a magazine of controversy, much less of compromise. In essentials it seeks unity, in non-essentials liberty, in all things charity. We hope to interpret Islam as a world-wide religion in all its varied aspects and its deep needs, ethical and spiritual, to Christians; to point out and press home the true solution of the Moslem problem, namely, the evangelization of Moslems; to be of practical help to all who toil for this end; and to awaken sympathy, love and prayer on behalf of the Moslem world until its bonds are burst, its wounds are healed, its sorrows removed, and its desires satisfied in Jesus Christ.

"To this end we invite the cordial co-operation of all those who have made special study of any phase of Islam, or who can from their experience show others how to win Moslems to Christ.

"We are fortunate in having as associate editors those who have already won distinction in this field. Mr. Marshall Broomhall, the Secretary of the China Inland Mission, is an authority on Islam in the Chinese Empire. The Rev. James S. Dennis, D.D., is known throughout Christendom for his scholarly contribution on 'Christian Missions and Social Progress'; he is an expert statistician on missions, and knows Islam from long residence in Syria. The Rev. W. H. T. Gairdner, B.A., of the Church Missionary Society at Cairo, is the author of 'The Reproach of Islam,' and ·has been in close touch with orthodox Mohammedanism at Al-Azhar University. Dr. Johannes Lepsius, of the Deutsche Orient Mission, is at the head of the Potsdam Seminary for the Training of Missionaries, and has written much on Islam in Turkey and Central Asia. Dr. Julius Richter was the leading German representative at the World Missionary Conference, is one of the members of its Continuation Committee, and is widely known through his standard works on Missions in India and in the Nearer East. Dr. W. St. Clair Tisdall, of wide experience in India and Persia, is one of the best known English authorities on Mohammedanism. Canon H. U. Weitbrecht, D.D., Ph.D., by reason of long service knows Islam in India, especially the New Islam; while the Rev. E. M. Wherry, D.D., has, in addition to his long experience in literary work for Moslems, written a 'commentary on the Koran' and other books. The Rev. Friedrich Wurz, Secretary of the Basel Mission, and Editor of 'Die

Evangelische Missions Magazine,' has made special study of Islam in Pagan Africa.

"With these words of explanation and introduction this new venture is launched in faith. Because we believe that God wills it, we bespeak for this first number the charitable judgment, as well as invite the candid criticism, of our fellow-missionaries. Unless the quarterly serves them and helps them, it fails in its primary purpose. Only through their united co-operation can the ideal set before us be realized."

Though the Quarterly was in a very true sense the brain child of Samuel Zwemer, the idea long in his mind came to fruition following the Edinburgh Missionary Conference of 1910. A committee was formed which met in London and plans were made for the actual publication. Volume I of *The Moslem World* was issued from London under the joint sponsorship of the Nile Mission Press and the Christian Literature Society for India.

The first number was one of the best in the long history of the Quarterly, as indeed it should have been, for it was the final fruition of thought and prayer over the years, the idea of such a quarterly having been suggested as early as the Cairo Conference of 1906. After the editorials in the first number there is an exhaustive article on Islam in Russia, with statistics and a colored map. Another important article is by Marshall Broomhall on the Moslems of China. Dr. Charles R. Watson writes of the Islamic presentations at the Edinburgh Conference and incidentally tells of the reasons for starting the quarterly. There are some fifteen book reviews in the first number, as well as a survey of periodicals and mission notes. The number set a standard for future years in both style and quality.

During World War I publication from London became very difficult and was transferred to New York under the auspices of *The Missionary Review of the World,* of which Delavan L. Pierson was editor. He was a long-time friend of Zwemer and his help was invaluable from the moment the magazine came to New York.

The difficulties of editing and publishing were formidable, with the editor in the Persian Gulf or Egypt, or often on tours to even more distant parts of the world. Faithful friends did their part and the editor was indefatigable in gathering material. Wherever he went items of interest and articles by experts poured into the offices, so that through the years the Quarterly never missed an issue.

Years later Zwemer wrote in a report, *"The Moslem World Quarterly Review* took a great deal of my spare time, and bound our mission by many ties of correspondence and friendship with scattered workers throughout the world of Islam. In fact the volumes of the periodical contain a brief history of the attempt to evangelize Moslems, not only in Arabia, but from America to North-west China. When I look back also to the six books in Arabic and

the twenty-four tracts for Moslems . . .I can only thank God for the strength
given me for so varied and extensive a literary effort."

The Quarterly avoided political articles and across the years only one article
was barred by a censor in a Moslem land. Year by year the magazine gained
in prestige for its full coverage of both missions and problems of scholarship
in regard to Islam and the lands where Moslems live. There were also many
articles of permanent value by authorities on various phases of Islam and the
Christian missionary task.   In fact, the file of the volumes of this periodical
makes up something of an encyclopedia.   Though an exhaustive index has
never been made of the publication, each volume is indexed and a fairly complete index was made of the first twenty-five volumes by students of Princeton Theological Seminary.   The project was financed by the government
WPA, which was an active institution at the time.

The Moslem World never paid for articles, though it received many of
worth; its support was always a problem. A small fee was paid for the review of periodicals, but neither the editor nor faithful workers in the office
received any remuneration; quite the opposite, they contributed themselves as
well as presenting the needs of the periodical to friends. During the decade
that the editor was a professor in Princeton Theological Seminary, much
time was given to the Quarterly and a closer control was possible since there
was more continuity of residence and frequent trips could be made to the
office in New York City. The financial problem continued to be a difficult
burden. The first twenty-five years of publication ended while the economic
depression was on in America, as well as over most of the world.

In the January 1936 issue of *The Moslem World,* Dr. Murray T. Titus
writes:

> "For twenty-five years THE MOSLEM WORLD has faithfully
> tried to discharge its obligations not merely to those of scholarly in-
> stincts, but to all Christian people with a missionary passion, and even
> to Moslems themselves, by providing them information about their
> religion, and developments in Moslem lands not easily obtainable else-
> where.   In fact, the writer can well believe that editors of important
> Islamic journals in English, which are published particularly in Eng-
> land and India, look forward with more than ordinary interest to the
> arrival of THE MOSLEM WORLD among their exchanges.   For
> some of the world's most able Islamic scholars have contributed to the
> wealth of interesting material found in its pages; as, for instance, Dun-
> can B. MacDonald of Hartford, David S. Margoliouth of Oxford, A.
> J. Wensinck of Leiden, Alfred Guillaume of Durham, S. Khuda Bukhsh
> of Calcutta, Louis Massignon of Paris, H. Kraemer of Java, and W. H.
> T. Gairdner of Cairo.

> "Names such as these suggest a magazine of the highest order, and
> such it has ever striven to be.   Th new Index covering these twenty-
> five volumes, which is now available, shows at a glance the amazing

amount of information contained therein, and the vast range of Islamic knowledge which has been assembled.

"It is abundantly apparent that THE MOSLEM WORLD has even more than met the expectations of those who so daringly, and with so much faith and vision, brought it to birth a quarter of a century ago. Today the need is no less urgent for the existence of such a magazine, than it was at the beginning. In fact, one may say that the need is even greater as we face a still more confusing future Many feel that to discontinue the Quarterly at this critical time, so full of new hopes, would be a serious blow."

Dr. John R. Mott who was one of the best informed men in the world on missions in general and who had conducted a number of conferences in the Moslem lands, said:

"I have no mental reservation whatever with reference to the desirability of the continuance of THE MOSLEM WORLD Quarterly. I cannot overstate my sense of the indispensability of this organ in the period before us."

Especially appreciated by Dr. Zwemer was the comment from the eminent Islamic scholar, Dr. Julius Richter of Berlin:

"I hope the economic landslide will not crash your valuable magazine in its depression. Being the only paper which is handling the complicated and in many directions unsolved questions of the Mohammedan missions, it would indeed be a serious loss if it should go out of existence."

Another milestone in the history of the Quarterly was reached when Dr. Edwin E. Calverley, long a member of the Arabian mission, became co-editor and the sponsorship of the magazine was taken over by the Hartford Seminary Foundation, where Dr. Calverley was a professor. An agreement was signed between Dr. Zwemer and the Institution as to the ownership and continued policy of the periodical.

A campaign attempt was launched to raise a fund in honor of Dr. Zwemer, which would place the Moslem World Quarterly on a more secure financial basis. Though there was good response to the appeal, the fund never reached the projected figure and other efforts were necessary from time to time to keep the magazine out of the red.

Several years later another attempt was made to assure the support of *The Moslem World* through the formation of a Fellowship among those who were interested. There were contributing and sustaining members and others who paid a small fee in addition to their subscriptions. The Committee on Work Among Moslems, of the Foreign Missions Conference also evinced an interest in the magazine and each of the Mission Boards that had work in this part of the world was asked for a certain subsidy. This has put the Quarterly on a rather sound basis of support. During the Second World War the size of the magazine was somewhat decreased and the disruption of regular mail service to different parts of the world cut down the number of sub-, scribers.

When he retired as editor of *The Moslem World* in 1947 at four-score years of age and looking back across the years of publication, in his final editorial the Apostle to the Moslem World wrote:

"LOOKING BACKWARD AND FORWARD FROM THE BRIDGE"

'If ever I forget Thy love
And how that love was shown,
Lift high the blood-red flag above:
It bears Thy Name alone.
Great Pilot of my onward way,
Thou wilt not let me drift:
I feel the winds of God today,
Today my sail I lift.'

"With deep gratitude to God, whose mercy and love have· sustained us in carrying the burden of editorship of this Quarterly well nigh thirty-seven years, we put the responsibility in other hands with confidence that He who hath blessed will bless.

"This number of our Quarterly marks the passing of one editor from the bridge and the standing of another—a colleague of many years in Arabia and at Hartford—at the wheel.

"Looking back to Vol. I, No. 1, dated January, 1911, and tracing the chequered history of our Quarterly through two World Wars and two financial depressions, which proved the death-knell of many publications on both sides of the Atlantic, we realize that the task was a work of faith, a labor of love, and a patience of hope. Had it not been for ardent, praying souls, faithful helpers, and liberal friends of missions to Moslems in Great Britain and America, the effort would have been impossible. We are grateful to the Associate Editors whose names began to appear on the magazine almost from the outset: W. H. T. Gairdner, H. U. Weitbrecht (Stanton), Julius Richter, W. St. Clair Tisdall, and many others besides those now listed.

"In 1938 Dr. Edwin E. Calverley became co-editor and he has now assumed full responsibility under the Hartford Seminary Foundation. For all the earlier years the Quarterly was owned by the editor and published for him at first by the Nile Mission Press and the Christian Literature Society for India, London (1911-1916) and later by the Missionary Review Publishing Co., Delavan L. Pierson, New York (1917-1937). The editor was oftentimes thousands of miles from the place of publication; in Bahrein, Arabia; in Cairo, Egypt; on journeys across the world of Islam; until finally he resided in Princeton, N. J., and later in New York City. The very possibility of such a shifting, awkward and trying arrangement was due, during all these years, to the self-denial of five devoted women who served, some without compensation, often without office space, as secretaries with all the detail of subscriptions, proof-reading, and accounts. They were Miss Lucy Mackenzie of Edinburgh, Miss E. I. M. Boyd, of London, Miss Charlotte B. Vellien, Miss Julia Chester, of Murray Hill, N. J., and for eighteen years, Miss May S. Blauvelt, of Yonkers, N. Y. With a single exception, no contributor nor any of this office staff has ever received compensation; for thirty-seven years it has been a labor of love which we can never repay. Now that Miss Blauvelt and I have retired from our respective tasks I desire specially to pay tribute to her unexampled and exemplary devotion during the long war-years when the life of the Quarterly so often hung in the balance and financial assistance was precarious. The annual deficit was always met by gifts solicited from interested friends.

"Now the transfer of the Quarterly to new ownership and editorship marks, we hope, a new period of life and growth for a magazine older than the Yale Review and *The International Review of Missions,* and which has through several crises survived other periodicals, in English, German, and French, which dealt with the world of Islam but ceased publication."

The editorial then goes on to quote a paragraph from the declaration of intention which was published in the first number of the Quarterly, and continues:

"We nailed those colors to the mast and have never surrendered to compromise nor appeasement in the battle for truth. It is, therefore, a joy to note that the transfer of ownership was on two simple conditions. A slight change in the title—*Moslem World* to *Muslim World*— (not as a mere matter of disputed orthography but to denote at the same time a continuity and a discontinuity of editorial responsibility): and the second condition was that the Hartford Seminary Foundation agree to continue the magazine on the same lines as noted above.

"When an octogenarian pilot is released from the bridge and a new Blue Peter is hoisted, it is but seemly that the name of the vessel be slightly different. We hope and pray that its course may be set by the ancient Compass and the ancient Chart, and that waves and tides may ever prove propitious. And so whether we face calm or storm in the vast world of Islam, we say:

> 'Nail to the mast her holy flag,
> Set every threadbare sail,
> And give her to the God of storms,
> The lightning and the gale.'
> — SAMUEL M. ZWEMER.

For over thirty-five years *The Moslem World* was more than an avocation to Zwemer. In fact, many men would have considered its editorship and publication a full-time job. Though with this man of boundless energy it was only one of many irons in the fire. The Quarterly offered a central medium for the consideration of Islamic culture and an exchange to gather the threads of Christian mission work for Moslem fields over the world and weave them into one design. It was not an easy venture; at times it took full measure of the tenacity which God has granted to the Dutch. But the periodical will remain as a great monument to the man who conceived it, brought it to birth and nursed it through its youth. Always *The Moslem World* magazine was a powerful force in the heart of this Apostle.

II

Christian Literature for Moslems

A long while before the numerous government agencies had made alphabetical organizations common in this country, a notable society was formed which has been known over the years as the A.C.L.S.M. It was called by these letters because it took so long to say or write the full name, The American Christian Literature Society for Moslems.

The work of the society actually began when Dr. Samuel M. Zwemer and Dr. Charles R. Watson, with others, got together in 1910 and formed a group to support the Nile Mission Press. It was through this committee that the sum of $29,200 was raised for the purchase of the building in Cairo which for many years was the home of the Press. By 1915 the work of the organization had grown, and with the desire to extend the work to other Moslem fields, the A.C.L.S.M. was incorporated. From the beginning the settled purpose of the Society was not to publish books or tracts, but to promote the production and use of Christian literature and to finance publication through area committees in the various Moslem fields.

In the year 1943 the officers and directors of A.C.L.S.M. voted to turn over the balance of cash on hand, the good will and the list of subscribers to the Committee on World Literacy and Christian Literature of the Foreign Missions Conference of North America. This Committee had been formed some time previously to make allocation of funds from the Boards and Mission agencies to Literacy and Literature in various parts of the world. Since it also had in view the Moslem world it was felt on both sides that the work of the former organization should be turned over to the more general committee and this was done.

With the passing on of the work to the new Literature Committee, provision was made that all publications for which the A.C.L.S.M. contributed funds would be evangelistic and evangelical in content. From the beginning, the Society insisted that the literature which it sponsored must be evangelistic in purpose, must have Christ at the center of its subject matter, and be conservative in content. In this connection we might quote from the Constitution of the Society:

"The distinctive method of missionary work which this corporation desires to encourage and promote is the use of the printed page, since it is our conviction that this has a unique value as a means of carrying the Gospel to Mohammedans. The printed message finds an entrance into many doors closed to the living witness and can proclaim the Gospel persistently, fearlessly and effectively.

"The members of this corporation believe that the only unfailing sources of moral energy and spiritual quickening which the world needs are to be found in Christ and His Gospel, as accepted and preached by the great body of evangelical Christian Churches. It is therefore agreed that the Christian literature whose production and distribution this corporation shall encourage, shall be of such a character as to be generally approved by those who, acknowledging the divine inspiration, authority, and sufficiency of the Holy Scriptures, believe in one God—The Father; the Son, the Lord Jesus Christ our God and Saviour Who died for our sins and rose again; and the Holy Spirit by Whom they desire to have fellowship with all who form the one body of Christ."

The A.C.L.S.M. attracted to its membership such notable elect ladies as Mrs. Wm. Bancroft Hill, Mrs. Eban E. Olcott, Mrs. Finley J. Shepard, Mrs. William Borden and Mrs. James M. Montgomery, as well as many other consecrated men and women who gave of their time and money to support the work. Dr. Samuel M. Zwemer was the great inspiration and life of the Society throughout its existence and he was ably supported by Delavan L. Pierson, Robert E. Speer, Fennell P. Turner, William I. Chamberlain, James Cantine and many others; among them, of late years, such men as Fred J. Barny and such women as Miss May S. Blauvelt, who was to the end the recording secretary and treasurer.

The annual meetings of the Society were notable events. In 1915, for example, Dr. John Henry Jowett gave over the Fifth Avenue Presbyterian Church for a meeting and appeared on the program with Dr. Zwemer and others. The edifice was packed to overflowing for the occasion and there was a chorus of five hundred voices led by Dr. Tali Esen Morgan.

Local auxiliaries of the Society were formed in many places, and Dr. Zwemer made a number of visits to different parts of the United States to stir up interest and raise funds. On one of these trips to the middlewest $18,000 in cash was contributed to the Society in less than a fortnight.

While the work was promoted with vigor at home, the actual out-reach of the A.C.L.S.M. greatly broadened on the field. In 1918 the work was extended to China, and Dr. Zwemer created a great interest in literature for Chinese Moslems by his visit there as a representative of the Society. When he visited South Africa or Persia or India, or spent time in North Africa, Southeastern Europe, and other Moslem fields, wherever Zwemer went hearts were set on fire with zeal for this cause.

The writer knows that in Iran we had distributed annually in our whole Mission only a few hundred pieces of Christian literature before Dr. Zwemer's visit. In the years following, the circulation mounted to many thousands and a real Christian literature was produced in most attractive

188 *Apostle to Islam*

form. It covered the field from small tracts of a single page to a Bible dictionary in Persian of a thousand pages, and all of these books and tracts go on working across the years for Christ and His kingdom.

Since the actual publications sponsored by the A.C.L.S.M. were always produced by the Literature Committees in the various areas it would be well to call in the testimony of one or two leaders of these committees who know better than anyone else the place of the Society in the actual production of Christian literature for Moslems. Dr. Murray T. Titus of India, for example, wrote:

> "The A.C.L.S.M. has meant everything to the development of our Christian Literature program for Moslems in India during the last twenty years. Without its grants we would not have been able to make any advance at all. Today we have a fairly adequate literature program for Indian Moslems in twelve languages."

Dr. William N. Wysham, who was for many years chairman of the Literature Committee in Iran adds his testimony:

> "Perhaps the best way to characterize what the A.C.L.S.M. has meant to Christian literature in Iran, is that it has served as a constant answer to prayer through the years. Again and again the Inter-Mission Literature Committee prepared a book for publication with no money in sight. Along with our prayers to God for funds went a statement of our need to this Society, and unfailingly the money was made available so that no worthy book ever had to wait long for publication.

> "Through the years a number of most effective evangelistic books and tracts in Iran were sponsored by the Society, and many Moslems have become Christians there after having their first introduction to Christ through these books. Moreover, the effect of the Society's generous grants has only just begun, for through decades in the future these same books will continue to bear witness to Christ in Iran."

Statements such as those above give an idea, from those who know best, as to what the work of the Society had meant throughout the Mohammedan world. Those publications stand as a great monument to the one who has been the heart and soul of the Society, and to the hundreds who have been faithful over the years in giving and in prayer for this truly great work. Not only did the Society sponsor books and tracts in North and South Africa, Egypt, Arabia, Iraq, Iran, Palestine, Syria, Turkey, Albania, China, Turkestan, India, Malaysia, the Dutch East Indies, Cyprus, and Bulgaria, but the various areas were stimulated into a new literature consciousness by visits of Dr. Zwemer. There are many reasons to believe that the near future holds greater promise than any era of the past for effective literature production and distribution in Moslem lands.

The thirty-odd years of the A.C.L.S.M. are an example in our day and generation of what God can do when weak human channels work in accordance with His will. The Society received and expended in the cause of Literature for Moslems more than two hundred and fifty thousand dollars!

Nor was there ever any overhead expense except for office rent and postage. The Society never had any paid executives. Much of the travel expense of Dr. Zwemer was met privately, by special gifts, not included in the above amount.

There is no limit to the good that will be accomplished through the years by this quarter of a million dollars invested in seed for the sower and bread to cast upon the waters. These myriad pages of Christian literature are truly "leaves for the healing of the nations." Last of all, it should be noted that these great ends have been accomplished through the power of consecration, faith and prayer. It was the constant hope and prayer of Dr. Zwemer that many might be moved to continue faithfully this great work which was so well begun by the A.C.L.S.M. in the most difficult of mission fields.

XIV
Of Making Many Books

" 'As a man thinketh in his heart, so is he.' Dr. Zwemer, for many years a missionary to Moslems and a powerful advocate of Missions, leaves no one in doubt as to his convictions. They have been born of earnest study and wide experience. He is neither narrow-minded nor prejudiced, but where a conviction as to right or wrong, truth or falsehood, takes hold of him, there is no will to compromise."

DELAVAN L. PIERSON,
in *The Presbyterian*,
September 12, 1940.

CHAPTER FOURTEEN

OF MAKING MANY BOOKS

As Martin Luther is said to have heaved his ink pot at the Devil, so Zwemer threw the modern ink pot of the printing press at the evil spirits which would retard the knowledge of the Gospel and the Kingdom of Christ in the world, for he believed with all his soul in the value and power of the printed page.

It was said of Raymund Lull that he wrote an unbelievable number of books—hundreds of manuscripts of his works may be found in European libraries to this day. In this particular, as in others, Zwemer ranks as a disciple of his famous precursor in missionary work for Moslems. Aside from a stream of publications in English for over half a century, and many in Arabic, his books have been translated into many languages of Europe and Asia—covering the gamut from Dutch to Chinese.

Since his father had been a writer and poet known widely in the Dutch community, it was natural that Samuel should have a taste for reading and writing. We may quote his own views on this subject, from an essay on "Reading" published in the Preparatory School paper in 1883:

"Many are the pastimes and amusements employed to rest one's body and mind from every-day pursuits. Of all amusements none is so attractive and pleasant as reading. The more we read the more taste we will have for reading; but, as someone has said, 'It is in reading as it is in eating, when the first hunger is over you begin to feel a little critical and will by no means take to garbage' . . . . .

"In olden times books were not accessible to the masses, and knowledge was pent up in cloisters and convents; but in our day the printing press does the work that then was done by the monk's quill."

Is it not possible to discover here the germ of a remarkable literary career?

The first venture in print of a booklet under his own name took place in 1889 when Zwemer was in his middle year in the Seminary at New Brunswick. It was a small book in Dutch under the title "Zendings-Woorden" or "Missionary Words." It contained a chart showing the various religions of the world and the large number classified as "Heathen." There were some sixteen missionary hymns, several being original and others translations. This 32 page booklet was the first trickle of a stream that would reach the printing presses of America, Europe and Asia over the next six decades.

The books may be grouped under three general classifications. First, those concerning Islam and the Moslem World. Second, general works and those on missions. Third, biographical and devotional. A full list of these books will be found in appendix. In this chapter we shall give a brief outline of the material they cover and a number of striking incidents that have to do with several of the volumes.

I

His first major book was *Arabia: The Cradle of Islam*: Studies in the Geography, People and Politics of the Peninsula with an account of Islam and Mission Work. The first edition was published in 1900 in New York.[1] By 1912 a fourth edition was necessary. The work has now been long out of print. It was wrought on the anvil of daily contact with the land and the people as well as from constant study in the white heat of the Persian Gulf. The whole manuscript was written by hand with an old style pen which required constant dipping in ink, and the volume has 425 pages, the longest of his many books.

A treasured letter in the Zwemer archives is one in the personal handwriting of Sir William Muir. He says:

"I have just finished the careful perusal of your admirable book 'Arabia' in the concluding prayer of which I heartily join. I am sure that we all have to thank you for so wide-spread an account of Arabia and its surroundings, and the various peoples and institutions connected with it.

"I see your preface is dated Bahrein: so I address this letter there; and I am glad to see that you have married, and trust that your good lady is engaged with you in your evangelistic work. God help you both and prosper you in your good work.

"I remain with every sympathy in it and your comfort in that distant land. Yours most truly, W. Muir."

The reception accorded by reviewers in America and Great Britain marked *Arabia: The Cradle of Islam* as a notable book. The London *Spectator*, for example, remarked:

"*Omnis Arabia divisa est in partes tres*, might have been the exordium of this book. Its virtue lies in the adjective. *All Arabia* is not treated, as far as we know, in any accessible modern English work . . . . Mr. Zwemer has compiled from previous travels and his own experience a very useful general account of Arabia as a whole, which undoubtedly fills a want in our bookshelves.

"The information is almost always accurate, well-selected, and to the point; and brief as the outline must necessarily be a single small volume dealing with a large subject, the impression is clear and vivid, and the book will teach readers much that they could themselves find only after much research in a large library."

Yet the author had marshalled his facts from the few books in his own library on the island of Bahrein in the Persian Gulf. This was long before

<hr />

1. The publishers and various editions of all books will be found in the Appendix.

oil had been discovered on that remote island or air-conditioned houses had been built by American oil companies. The missionary author had gathered his materials over a decade and written the manuscript in a climate where for months the thermometer is most of the time above one hundred degrees Fahrenheit, and a towel was needed under the writer's hand to catch the constant drip of perspiration. In spite of all other information, the main direction of the book was missionary. Viewed from all standpoints many still consider his first major book as the best Zwemer ever wrote.

One other curious incident in connection with this book should be mentioned. A translation was published in Urdu without authorization. Almost all the distinctive Christian and missionary point of view was omitted and the Urdu version became quite the contrary of the original intention of the author. A letter to the publishers, the "Paisa Akhbar" Office in Lahore, elicited a reply which is both humorous and typical. We may quote from the letter of the translator into Urdu:

"Revd. Dr. Zwemer, Bahrein, Persian Gulph.
Dear Sir:

From your letter I glean that you have not been pleasant but rather annoyed to learn that your book 'Arabia the Cradle of Islam' has been translated in a language in which it is more easily accessible to a people who must particularly be informed of your views. Though I am afraid their apathy does not allow them to be much interested in it as a few hundred copies of the first edition will last for many years to come.

"I confess that I cannot comprehend the reason of your chagrin as authors are often flattered to know that their productions have been appreciated and translated into foreign languages. I believed that you or your publishers never intended to keep it a sealed book for those who could not read English.
Yours flly, Mahbub Alam."

This certainly offers a classical example of the method so prevalent in the Moslem countries, namely side-step and counter punch. The author was no doubt even more "chagrined" than he had been when he realized how he was endeavoring by his objections to keep Urdu-speaking people in ignorance!

The next book to appear was a short life of Raymund Lull, which will be mentioned at greater length later in this chapter, but is noted here as it has to do with Islam as well as being a biography.

Written also on the island of Bahrein, *The Moslem Doctrine of God* was published in 1905. This book is a theological essay on the character and attributes of Allah, as presented in the Koran and in the accepted traditions of orthodox Islam. A second edition of this book appeared in 1924, showing that although a treatment of a rather technical subject the interest continued over a period of years.

Though chronologically somewhat later, a companion volume to the above should be noted here. *The Moslem Christ* was completed in Alexandria,

Egypt, and published in 1912. A second edition of this work appeared in 1927 published by the American Tract Society. The book was also published in German, Arabic and Urdu translations.

Concerning this work we may quote from the contemporary review in *The Missionary Review of the World:*

"Dr. Zwemer has an unusual grasp of the Mohammedan history, religion and character. In his present volume he gives a unique essay on the Moslem teachings concerning Christ according to the Koran and orthodox tradition. A study of the Moslem view of Christ is helpful to all Christians, and is extremely important to those who are working for the conversion of Mohammedans. Dr. Zwemer is always interesting, even on an apparently technical topic."

Islam, A Challenge to Faith was published in 1907 under the auspices of the Student Volunteer Movement. The American edition had a circulation of approximately 16,000 copies.[2] A second edition was published in London in 1909. German, Danish and French editions of this book also appeared. Although it has long been out of print it still remains a reference work that it often used by students.

The author described this volume as, "Studies in the Mohammedan religion and the needs and opportunities of the Mohammedan world from the standpoint of Christian missions." It has continued to direct the thought and interest of many college generations of students to the missionary call of the Islamic world, and has perhaps done as much as any other one book to interest the sending churches in this most difficult field.

At the time of its publication Dr. Fennel P. Turner was head of the Student Volunteer Movement with his headquarters in New York. He saw this and other books of this time through the press and exercised great care all the way from first manuscript to final publication.

In 1919, some twelve years after the publication of *Islam, A Challenge to Faith.* the Governor General of India and the Governor of Bengal issued orders in Council proscribing this book. The National Missionary Council of India took energetic steps against this order, which was then revoked.

In 1915 two books from the pen of Dr. Zwemer were published, the one in Great Britain, the other in America. The former bore the title *Mohammed or Christ.* The volume was made up of lectures that had been delivered in several places. It was the time of the First World War and because there were a number of political references the book was soon withdrawn from circulation.

The other volume was of quite a different type, *Childhood in the Moslem World.* This book was published in New York, but the galley proofs were read during an attack of typhoid in Alexandria, Egypt. The title gives a

2. Letter from J. R. Wilson of S.V.M. of May 8, 1931.

good idea of the contents. The book had a rather wide circulation and was published also in a Danish translation and in Arabic in Cairo.

The Disintegration of Islam was published in 1916. It consisted of the lectures on Islam which had been given at Princeton Theological Seminary and at the Hartford Seminary Foundation. The book was largely written in New York while the author was on furlough in the U. S. A.

In 1919 *A Primer on Islam* was published in Shanghai under the auspices of the Continuation Committee. This small book gave the essential features of Islam and stressed the spiritual need of the Moslems in China. It was translated and published in Chinese.

The Influence of Animism on Islam was published in New York in 1920. It received more than a half page review in the New York Times book section of July 4, 1920, under the title "What is Your Pet Superstition." The material for this volume was first delivered as the Thompson lectures at the Hartford Seminary Foundation; this series was also given at Princeton Seminary. Illustrations of the book gave examples of talismans and amulets from many parts of the Islamic world. Most of the writing of the book was done in Cairo.

There followed in 1923 *The Law of Apostasy in Islam,* which was published in London. The volume was written in Cairo to answer the question as to why there are so few converts from Islam. It is also a reply to certain modern apologists for Islam who had denied that the death penalty was prescribed for those who left the faith. Dr. Zwemer quoted chapter and verse from the Koran and accepted traditions and went on to give many instances of persecution and martyrdom of those who had left Islam because of faith in Christ. The book was entirely documented and even *The Egyptian Gazette* ends a review with these words: "These 'facts' are formidable, and the book merits a most careful study, not only by Christian workers, but also by all Moslems seeking after truth."

The next volume on the general subject of the Moslem world could only have been written as a result of the widest travel and careful observation. The book was *Across the World of Islam,* published in New York in 1929. It was written in New York where good libraries were available to supplement the information the author had gleaned on his travels. The object was to show the very wide diffusion of Moslems in the modern world, with aspects of the Mohammedan faith in view of the awakening which followed World War I throughout the world of Islam. The illustrations were a notable feature of the book, and it was widely circulated in the churches. A second edition was printed in 1932, but the very useful volume has long been out of print.

Studies in Popular Islam was a collection of papers dealing not so much with the theology or ritual of Islam itself as with the beliefs and actual practices of Moslems over the widely separated lands where Islam holds sway. It was issued in 1939, written at Princeton, and published in London and

New York. Some of the material in this volume had appeared in *The Influence of Animism on Islam,* published some eighteen years earlier. The *Studies in Popular Islam* was never so *popular* as many others of Zwemer's books. War bombing destroyed the plates in London.

In 1941 *The Cross Above the Crescent* was published in Grand Rapids, Michigan. The foreword for this volume was written by Dr. John A Mackay, president of Princeton Theological Seminary and president of the Presbyterian Board of Foreign Missions. In the author's words, the book was written to show the "Validity, Necessity and Urgency of Missions to Moslems." In addition it gives many facts concerning Mohammedans in little known areas of the world. It has proved one of Zwemer's most popular books.

A student who read *The Cross Above the Crescent* as an assignment in Missions class said in his review, "There is something of the feeling of standing beside an old rancher and looking from a promontory at all the vast lands he has known intimately, as he points out the details . . . as one reads the powerful argument of Dr. Zwemer."

In 1946 for the Conference on Work Among Moslems held at Princeton, Dr. Zwemer prepared a *Factual Survey of the Moslem World.* The booklet contained a general statement concerning Islam and Moslem lands, together with a number of maps illustrating various features of the Mohammedan world. There were also new figures on Moslem populations, revised in accordance with data gathered by government sources in Africa and Asia during World War II.

The latest book among works on Islam was called *Heirs of the Prophets,* and was published in 1946 in Chicago. The volume grew out of articles written for *The Moslem World* quarterly and other material. It is a discussion of the clergy in Islam. Although the claim is often made that the Moslem religion has no priesthood, the author shows that in reality the ecclesiastics do perform practically all the functions of the clerics in other religions and have even more prestige and power.

The reader may have noted that the books on Islam of this single author were published by a great many firms in America and abroad. The volumes also cover a host of subjects and make an aggregate of wider authorship on Islamic subjects than any writer of modern times. Over almost half a century there was a single basic motive behind these many books, the prayer of Abraham, "Oh that Ishmael might live before Thee!" His passion was to arouse the church to the urgency of missions for Moslems and to claim Moslem lands for Christ.

II.

The books that Zwemer wrote on Islam would certainly make an astonishing total for a lifetime of authorship, but they are only a portion of his literary contribution to Christian life and thought. Under the classification *Missionary and General* we have grouped a second field of interest; for the Mohammedan world, large a subject as it is, could not limit the thought and activity of this inspired writer. His horizon extended to world missions and comparative religion.

Following the Edinburgh Conference of 1910, where missions from most of the world were represented, Dr. Zwemer was asked to write another volume for use as a text-book. It appeared with the title *The Unoccupied Mission Fields of Africa and Asia,* published in 1911 under the auspices of the Student Volunteer Movement, New York. In this review of the unoccupied fields of the world the notable omission is Latin America. Those familiar with mission history will recall that this great field was not represented at the Edinburgh Conference because of certain elements in the Church of England that would not accept the validity of Christian missions to so-called "Catholic" countries. It was under the influence of this feeling that Zwemer reluctantly left out Latin America in his discussion of unoccupied fields. The book was again guided through the press by Fennel P. Turner and had a wide circulation, arousing a great enthusiasm among young people for these fields. The information contained was the direct cause, in several instances, of Christian undertakings being launched in areas which had not been previously occupied by Protestant mission forces. The book also went through German and Danish editions. It contains many maps and illustrations.

Christianity the Final Religion was published in Grand Rapids, Michigan, in 1920. It consisted of a series of addresses given in different places and some of them prepared for audiences which were largely Moslem, as well as for Christians.

In 1923 *The Call to Prayer* was published in London and also issued in a Dutch translation in 1926. Five times a day over the world of Islam the stated call to prayer is heard from the mosque and minaret and in the bazaars. The author uses this fact to dramatize the necessity for daily prayer as the basic and most vital need of the Christian missionary movement in the face of world conditions as they were at the time, and in fact, at all times; the fundamental admonition is ,"Pray ye the Lord of the harvest".

Following the wide discussion in missionary circles caused by the volume *Rethinking Missions,* Dr. Zwemer in 1934 published a rejoinder. It was entitled *Thinking Missions with Christ.* The book took exception to the theological viewpoint of the work which had been published by a commission sent around the world to make a study of missions. The author stressed his strong evangelical attitude toward the basic, the motive, the message, and the goal of missions. The Gospel cannot be watered down but must continue to be presented to men of other religious faiths as good news, an opportunity to escape the guilt and power of sin through the atonement provided by a Divine Christ. The book was written largely in New York about the time that Dr. Zwemer went to Princeton as a member of the faculty in the Theological Seminary.

In 1943 *Into All the World* was published in Grand Rapids. The book centers on the Great Commission as it is found in all the four Gospels and Acts and makes a strong plea for missions on the direct command of Christ. The author takes up the views of textual criticism on various New Testament passages involved and presents very clearly the arguments for the conservative view in regard to the problems of the passages under consideration. The book was written after he had retired from Princeton and resided in New York.

At the close of World War II, when the churches were launching new movements in evangelism, Dr. Zwemer brought out a timely volume *Evangelism Today*. It was published in New York and has gone through five editions. The volume stresses the message rather than the method of evangelism. Of this book Dr. Edward J. Jurji writes in his review for *The Moslem World* that the author displays "penetrating theological acumen, the burning heart of the pioneer, the charity and piety of the saint and the erudition of the scholar."

There remains to mention in this section a book of a somewhat different type. It is *The Origin of Religion,* published in Nashville, Tennessee in 1935. A second edition was issued in 1936 and a third revised edition in 1946 in New York.

One of the reviews is under the title "Anthropology's Change of Front." Another says, "It is an answer to the too easy assumption of that phase of materialistic philosophy which attempts to explain the origin of religion as the result of an evolutionary process." The author takes the position that there existed a primitive monotheism from which many examples of religion show a decline. The book has abundant quoted material from European as well as American scholarship. The treatise is based most of all on the work of the anthropologist Professor Wilhelm Schmidt, to whom the volume is dedicated. The need of such a book was no doubt suggested when the author began to teach Comparative Religion in Princeton Theological Seminary.

III

As a third section of his literary activity we may consider volumes on biographical and devotional themes. The first of these was the life of *Raymund Lull: First Missionary to the Moslems.* It was published in New York as early as 1902. The preface was written by Dr. Robert E. Speer, also one of the most prolific writers of his generation on missionary subjects.

Longer and more scholarly lives of the great pioneer missionary to Mohammedans have since been written, but for many years this little biography was a leader in the field. It was translated and published in Dutch with no acknowledgement and a bare mention of Zwemer's book.

This is interesting enough to merit a copy of quotations from the letters exchanged on the subject. Dr. Zwemer writes:

"3, Kantarat El Dekka, Cairo
12th April, 1928.

Zendings Studie Raad, Oestgeest, Netherland.
Dear Sirs:

I was delighted and also surprised to receive by the last mail a copy of your little Dutch book by S———— called 'Raymondus Lullus.' Delighted to see this message in the language of my father and mother, but surprised that what purports to be an original book by Dr. S————, is really an unauthorized translation. The only reference to my "Life of Raymund Lull' from which the material is borrowed, is found on page 23, where Dr. S———— speaks of 'een mooi bookje' by Zwemer.

"The titles of the chapters, the vignette on the title page, all of the pictures, and most of the material is taken from the original work and yet no credit is given . . . "

There is more of the letter, but this is the essential part for our purpose. The reply came about six months later as follows:

"Dear Dr. Zwemer:

"The Redaction of the 'Lichtstralen' draws my intention upon the fact that in giving a paraphrase of your study on Raymund Lull, I sticked so much to your original writing that the booklet published under my name by the redaction of the Lichtstralen could as well be called a non-authorized version of your study.

"Acknowledging that there is a good deal of truth in that charge of yours, I humbly want to apology, giving you at the same time the assurance that if I failed I did not do so on purpose; but without any intention to do harm to anybody, and in the least place to you . . .

"I admit that in following your publication of the book and paraphrasing entire parts of it, by adopting also your chapter division, the whole makes the impression of non-authorized version. The editor made the mistake worse by adopting the pictures and vignet of the frontespice . . .

"I remain dear sir

"Very sincerely yours,
———— S ————"

The translator was forgiven by Dr. Zwemer, but years later he would remark, "To think that a Dutchman would do that!"

The other biography written by Zwemer was *A Moslem Seeker After God*, published in 1921. The book was an account of the life and the writings of Al Ghazali, the mystic and Moslem theologian of the eleventh century A.D. Zwemer recognized in Al Ghazali, Islam at its best, and considered that such a man was not far from the Kingdom of God. Translations of the book were published in Arabic and Urdu.

We now come to the devotional books, some of which the present writer feels rank with the best of Zwemer's publications in any field. Most of these volumes were the mature product of ripe experience, long meditation and rugged campaigning in the Christian way of life and service.

Taking Hold of God was published in 1936 at Grand Rapids. It is a book on the subject of prayer and takes up the nature of this highest privilege of the Christian, as well as the necessity and the way to power in intercession. In the view of many this is one of the most helpful devotional books they have ever read. This is certainly our own testimony. The book came to us as we were recovering from a severe oriental fever and made a more profound impression than any devotional book we had ever read, aside from the Scriptures.

The review in the Christian Century illustrates the criticism which modern liberal theology often made of Zwemer's books. In part it says:

> "Much excellent devotional material is to be found in these pages, some of it new and much of it unique. The distinguished former missionary to the Moslems, now professor of the History of Religion and Christian Missions at Princeton Theological Seminary, is so enthusiastic, however, to display his conservative theology, that otherwise splendid reflections on prayer lose much of their significance."

> Other reviewers call the book "A Jewel on Prayer" and one enthusiastic review says, "Only a Christian genius could produce such a book . . . as one of the most versatile of Christian statesmen Dr. Zwemer has given to the Church and to Christians generally a most remarkable testimony."

In 1937 two of Zwemer's books came out in Great Britain. The first was *It is Hard to be a Christian*, which went through two editions. It is a purely devotional book and was made up of addresses given at Keswick and other places in Great Britain. Dr. Charles R. Erdman writes: "Every production from the pen of Dr. Zwemer evidences his loyalty to Scripture, his unclouded faith and his devotion to the Gospel of Christ." The second book was published in Glasgow and London. It bore the intriguing title *The Solitary Throne*. It consisted of five lectures, most of them reproduced from stenographic reports.

A review in "The British Weekly" says of *The Solitary Throne*, "It would be difficult to find a book into which there is packed so much fact and force as is contained in Dr. Zwemer's volume. The whole world seems to walk into this book and sit down, and there it invites the consideration of the Christian mind."

Dynamic Christianity and the World Today was written for the Inter-Varsity Christian Fellowship of Great Britain and was published in London in 1939 under their auspices. The book is dedicated to Robert Wilder, who in his latter years was deeply interested in the Inter-Varsity Movement in Great Britain. He and Zwemer had been intimately associated in the early days of the Student Volunteer Movement and so, in the personalities of these two there is a close tie between these two great student organizations. The edition was soon sold out and the World War II conditions prevented a second edition, but at the close of the war Dr. Douglas Johnson, head of Inter-Varsity in Britain, wrote the author that there were still many calls for the book.

A review in the *Chinese Church Recorder* of Shanghai, June 5, 1940, begins: "This book like all that come from Dr. Zwemer is a hundred times worth reading. It is the result of many years of ripe thinking and careful weighing of such truths as are commonly believed among us."

Although the problem of this chapter is to condense an outline of so many volumes into so small a space, we cannot but quote the final paragraph of this book — it is such typical Zwemers:

> "Alas, there are Christians and missionaries today who have lost the art of itineration. Their strength (or weakness) seems to be 'to sit still.' They resemble old King Asa 'who was diseased in both his feet.' Their parishioners might mock them as the Psalmist does the dumb idols: 'feet have they but they walk not.' Automobiles have they but the poor they visit not. If they could realize the relation between the pastor's mileage and the evening congregation or weekly prayer meeting, there would be a revival in their churches."

The Art of Listening to God was published in Grand Rapids in 1940. It was described as: "Studies in some neglected values of life, religion and missions." In the seventeen chapters the author proceeds to take advantage of the wide latitude allowed by such a plan and starting with The Art of Listening to God he goes on to discuss Reading, Church Union, The Choir and the Collection in Church services, the Question of Suicide,[3] the Religion of Ghandi, Mohammed and Calvin. A whole sheaf of reviews before me vary much in tone, from enthusiastic acclaim to scornful castigation. A reviewer from the opposite theological pole says: "The point of view is not so much conservative as antique, not so much Christian as Calvinistic."

From *The Expository Times* we get quite a different idea; "Whatever be the topic he touches upon he writes with clearness, sound sense and ripe Christian wisdom. One of his chapters is entitled 'Life Begins at Seventy.' and this book may be taken as confirmation of that bold thesis."

A book of twenty-six short essays entitled *How Rich the Harvest* was published in New York in 1948. The chapters are studies in Bible themes and missions and are treated with the usual vibrant diction and rich insight of the author.

Early in 1951 a new volume appeared, published in Grand Rapids, with the title *Sons of Adam.* This was Zwemer's fiftieth book. It was a volume of essays on Old Testament characters and was widely read, as the pungent treatment made these men live for our own time.

There remains to mention among the books from the pen of our author a trilogy on the three towering events in the life of Christ, the Incarnation, The Crucifixion and The Resurrection. The first of these books to appear was *The Glory of the Cross,* issued in London in 1928. Three editions were published over a ten-year period. Published in an inexpensive paper edition, it has been one of the best selling among the works of the author. He char-

---

3. This chapter was reprinted by a society in New York and placed in some hotels hoping to prevent suicides.

acterized this book as "from my own heart," and indicated that more people spoke to him of this book than of any other. Arabic, Urdu and Swedish translations were published.

The second volume of the trilogy was *The Glory of the Manger*, which was published in 1940 in New York. The book won a one thousand dollar prize from the American Tract Society in a contest where more than one hundred manuscripts were submitted. Following the Mohammedan custom of giving the ninety-nine beautiful names of Allah, one chapter selects from Scripture a similar number of beautiful titles for Christ and makes a striking exposition of them. The Incarnation is "the greatest miracle of human history."

The final volume of the trilogy was written after Dr. Zwemer had passed the mark of four score years; it was *The Glory of the Empty Tomb*, published in New York in 1947. The author had just become an associate editor on the staff of a New York publisher. His eye was not dimmed nor his natural force abated. He calls upon authors far and wide in support of his argument for an exposition of the resurrection, and seems to see more plainly because of his advancing years across to the other side, to that glorious morning beyond the night of death and the grave. Upon such a note we end the review of his own books.

IV

In 1906 two volumes were written in collaboration with Dr. E. M. Wherry, both being published in New York. They were *Methods of Mission Work Among Moslems* and *The Mohammedan World Today*. Similarly Dr. Zwemer and Dr. Wherry worked together on two volumes for another conference, which were "*Lucknow 1911*" published in 1912 in Madras; and *Islam and Missions* published the same year in New York.

The Nearer and Farther East, in which Zwemer was responsible for the *Near* and Dr. Arthur J. Brown for the *Far*, was published in New York in 1908.

Zwemer cooperated with Annie Van Sommer of London in the authorship of *Our Moslem Sisters* in 1907. The book was published in New York and later appeared in Danish and Swedish translations. A second volume by the same authors, *Daylight in the Harem* was also issued in New York in 1912.

Zig-Zag Journeys in the Camel Country in 1911 and *Topsy Turvy Land* in 1912 were two books for young readers in which Dr. Zwemer collaborated with his wife Amy Wilkes Zwemer; both were published by Revell. They also wrote the mission study book entitled *Moslem Women*, issued by the United Study Committee in 1926. This work was also published in a German translation.

The Golden Milestone appeared in 1939 to celebrate the fiftieth anniversary of founding the Arabian Mission. It was written by two pioneers James Cantine and Samuel Zwemer. In the introduction Lowell Thomas remarks that both of these are still names to be conjured with in Arabia, and especially along the Persian Gulf. The two aged warriors look back across half a century as stewards, who if not so successful from the standpoint of numbers won to Christ, have at least been faithful in the establishment of a mighty service and witness to Christ in the world's most difficult mission fields.

Perhaps nothing would be more fitting as a close to this sketch of the books than to quote from the review of *The Cross Above the Crescent*, written by Dr. Kenneth Scott Latourette of Yale, who says:

"Never in the history of the church has any Christian covered the Moslem world so comprehensively, in study, travel, planning and advocacy of missions to it, as has Dr. Zwemer . . .

"It is always in its relation to Christianity that Dr. Zwemer views Islam. He is passionately convinced of the inadequacy of Islam to meet human needs. He recognizes in it admirable qualities, but he is clear as to the incalculable superiority of Christ over the Prophet, and states his reasons unequivocally.

"Dr. Zwemer has no illusions about the resistance which Islam presents to Christianity. He knows that through the centuries it has won more converts from Christianity than have been lost to its greatest rival. Yet he has no doubt as to the ultimate triumph of the Cross . . .

"One can hear his voice in every page. As in public address, so here, he is never dull."

And so Zwemer has left behind him a mighty highway of print — almost a book a year in English for over half a century. In all of them he sought to glorify his Lord. An incandescent faith shines from every page.

XV

The Years at Princeton

"Uncounted generations of Princeton men loved Nassau Street; they have remembered it as well for its cheerful daily life, its friendly little shops, its stuffy eating-places; and some of them even for its pavements sparkling in the sunlight after rain in early spring. Apartment houses, office buildings, traffic lights and gas stations are doing all they can to modernize it; but for a few hundred yards where, to quote a Princeton poet,

> — towers dream against the sky,
> While round them swirl and laugh and beat
> The tides of youth in Nassau Street,

it still retains some of the atmosphere of its past.

'Seminole' is the time-honored campus nickname of students in the Princeton Theological Seminary. Long ago Henry van Dyke, reminiscent of bygone wilder undergraduate days, wrote:

> "Well the old Triangle knew the music of our tread,
> How the peaceful Seminole would tremble in his bed,
> How the gates were left unhinged, the lamps without a head,
> While we were marching through Princeton!"

Princeton Past and Present,
by Varnum Lansing Collins.

CHAPTER FIFTEEN

THE YEARS AT PRINCETON

In 1918 Samuel M. Zwemer received a cablegram in Shanghai, as he was on his way home to America via the Pacific. The message was from President J. Ross Stevenson of Princeton Theological Seminary inviting him to become a member of the Seminary faculty. After his arrival in America Zwemer taught special courses on missions at the Seminary one term, but decided to return to his work in Cairo.

More than ten years later he did accept a call to the chair of The History of Religion and Christian Missions at Princeton. This time another opportunity had come when Dr. Stevenson met him at a conference in Lausanne, Switzerland. By coincidence there came about the same time a similar call to McCormick Theological Seminary in Chicago. There were numerous reasons which attracted Zwemer to the latter place, but his decision in favor of Princeton was finally made on the basis of a letter from his friend Robert E. Speer who mentioned the dispute over the body of Moses as recorded in the ninth verse of Jude, and on this analogy urged the Princeton appointment!

I

The decision having been made, the missionary termed the move to Princeton as "The Third Milestone." He quoted the lines from Longfellow:

"Each man's chimney is his Golden Milestone:
Is the central point from which he measures every distance
Through the gateway of the world around him."

The first milestone was the pioneering work in Arabia, the second the period of residence in Cairo as a center, and the third was Princeton Seminary. Zwemer wrote of his decision in the little magazine of the Arabian Mission:

"When the call came to leave Bahrein for the larger opportunities and wider tasks of the Nile Mission Press and the training of workers in Egypt, the pull at our heart strings was strong and we left Arabia with many regrets at parting from the circle of the mission. But as we look back over the seventeen years spent from Cairo as a base in travel and thought for the evangelization of the Moslem World, in the preparation of literature and its circulation, in helping forward in some small way the plans of other pioneer missions in Africa and Southeastern Europe — we are convinced that the call was of God. Once again — not suddenly, but by a series of Providences and calls to service — we have moved our hearthstone to a new center where we humbly trust that God will use us for the same task, although in another way".

209

Though he came to the Seminary in 1929, his formal installation as Professor of the History of Religion and Christian Missions did not take place until October first, 1930. At that time he delivered the inaugural address on the subject "The Place of the History of Religion in a Theological Discipline." Though this was a formal and scholarly composition, it did not lack the interest of the human touch as we may glean from the following quotation:

"My special study has been limited very largely to only one of the non-Christian religions and my experience has been in practical evangelism, rather than in the classroom. It is a far call from the camel's saddle in Oman or a seat in a coffee shop in the bazaars of Cairo to a Professor's chair. I count myself happy, however, henceforth to have a small part in promoting those high ideals of the Christian ministry as a world-wide mission, for which Princeton has always stood."[1]

When Zwemer joined the faculty of Princeton Theological Seminary he came to an Institution which was the oldest and largest of this type in the Presbyterian Church U.S.A. For more than a century a portion of every class but three had gone to the foreign field for missionary service and more had entered such service from this Seminary than any other. When Zwemer took the post he joined the Presbyterian Church, which was required of faculty members as this is a Church Seminary, though it trains men from many denominations and has throughout the years been known for the number of students from countries all over the world.

In a typically casual letter Dr. Zwemer wrote ahead that they did not have furniture but would be satisfied with very little. This put the wives of the Faculty to buzzing and a number of things were put in the house which they were to occupy. On arrival they stayed with the family of President Stevenson. Zwemer was ill at ease until other things had been purchased and they were in their new home. They were welcomed by the other faculty families and felt very much at home in the intimate circle of fine Christian people. Each year there were also twelve missionary families from all over the world resident in Payne Hall on the Seminary campus.

A great deal might be said concerning Mrs. Zwemer and what she did in Princeton. She had been the first woman to join the pioneer mission in Arabia and had for years maintained a home of international reputation for hospitality and spiritual inspiration in Cairo. All of this experience she brought to Princeton as one of the faculty wives and became at once a leader and inspirational speaker in many organizations in Princeton and New Brunswick, as well as New York, Philadelphia, and other centers.

Amy Wilkes Zwemer united with her missionary experience and world travel a most incisive mind and wonderful sense of humor. Though most of her own children had gone from the home by this time, she was like a mother to many a student in the Seminary and a wonderful influence of light and good cheer in Princeton life, besides the constant inspiration and support to her husband which she had been across the years.

1. The address was printed in full in **The Princeton Seminary Bulletin** and translated in **The Algemein Missions Zeitschrift** of Berlin.

II

The versatility of the man is shown in the courses offered by Zwemer during his first year at Princeton. The basic course is listed in the Seminary Catalogue for 1929-30 under the title *History of Religion*. The title of the course was not changed during the decade of teaching, though the lectures were far from stereotyped and contained new material from year to year.

The contents of the course covered the Origin and Nature of Religion as well as the history of its development. Then there was a consideration of what might be termed "Comparative Religion," though the teacher did not like this term. Animism, Confucianism, Hinduism, Buddhism, and Islam were considered. Students wondered at the understanding of other religions and the knowledge of their history which the teacher had apparently acquired overnight but when he hit the home stretch there was no doubt that he was on most familiar ground as he taught Islam from the standpoint of the man who had beyond doubt done more than any other, over a period of forty years, to awaken the Christian Church to undertake Moslem Evangelism, and who had seen more of Islam all over the world than any other man. The course was required for first-year students in the Seminary.

The teaching of this course on the History of Religion led to the publication of the volume *The Origin of Religion* which went through three editions over a ten-year period and was widely used as a textbook elsewhere. Zwemer's position is that mankind had a primitive revelation of monotheism and that other religions, from primitive animistic idol worship all the way to speculative and philosophical departures from basic Theism, are tangents away from the original revelation of God.

But the professor was even more deeply interested in the direct missionary courses of his program. Here the basic offering was *Missionary Principles and Methods,* a two-hour course which was required of all students in their second year. The lectures began with the missionary aim and motive, and continued to describe the types of missionary work and the development of the Christian Church on the field. The latter portion of the course was devoted to the education and inspiration of the sending churches to support the world missionary program and to a consideration of church union and the universal, Christian fellowship. Various missionaries from different fields assisted from time to time in speaking of the work in the land of their service.

Elective courses of his program were *History of Missions, Great Missionaries, The Unoccupied Mission Fields, Race Problems at Home and Abroad, Modern Religious Cults, Introduction to the study of Islam,* and *Present Day Judaism and Missions to the Jews.* In the later years he also conducted a weekly *Round Table Conference* on missions, which was attended by missionaries in residence as well as students with a special interest in the missionary enterprise.

As in his writing, so as a teacher, Zwemer was pungent and dynamic. His world travel and contact with leaders of different Churches, at home and abroad, had given him a very wide knowledge so that he was able to illustrate and sharpen the subject matter of his academic courses with personal anecdotes. From very wide reading and a most retentive memory he could supplement his own observations with quotations from literature and facts of history. In addition, his sense of humor came into full play and though he never departed from the serious attempt to prepare young men for the Christian Ministry and missionary service, the natural out-cropping of humor often made the classroom echo with a roar of laughter. Some of his stories were repeated in the Seminary for many years after his retirement.

His subjects were not considered as snap courses, but were elected by many others than those whose special interest was in the field of Missions and Comparative Religion. He was not, on the other hand, known as one who would require more than the proper share of work and time for any course he gave. His material was well organized and clear, in some courses there was an assigned textbook as well as general reading, but in a greater number of instances the main material of the course was given in lectures and outside reading was required in books on the library reserve shelf for the course. Papers or theses were required more often than examinations. His lectures were never dull, and especially for missionaries and those who intended to go to the mission field, there were constantly new ideas and insights. He put in hard work on the organization and gathering of material for his courses, but did not write the lectures once and then read them *verbatim* year after year. They were often as up-to-date as the morning paper.

When he heard that the students had given him the nickname of "Uncle Sam," he was at first somewhat displeased, but later he came to realize that it was in no way a mark of disrespect, but meant that he had established for himself a real place in the hearts as well as the minds of the undergraduates. He was elected a member of the Warfield Club, an organization where a section of the Seminary men had their meals and much in the way of social life—with the meals, and at other times.

The Seminary furnished for the Zwemers the Professor's house on the edge of the campus, at 48 Mercer Street. In Princeton as in Arabia and Cairo and wherever they lived the house was always open to student or friend and many came for counsel and for knowledge as well as for social chat and hospitality. Behind the study there was a room for a secretary and here much of his literary work was done, as well as the editing of *The Moslem World* Quarterly.

Children were often in the house and in the study. One little girl after a visit with Dr. Zwemer, said "Who said he was a great man, and knew a lot? Why he didn't even know who Shirley Temple was." He was soon intimately known by town and gown alike in Princeton. His natural friendliness and ability to strike up a conversation with anyone had been fanned by missionary service and world travel into a warm flame that would light an answering fire in any heart. He made most of his purchases on side streets rather than the shops on Nassau Street which largely served the University clientele. He came to know the trades people and had a pleasant word and often a tract for them. The number of books he gave away always ate up a large part of the royalties on his published works. Railroad men and workers in the grocery store or the milkman were all his intimates—which they became, without seeming effort on his part, just as men in the bazaars of far away places became his friends the first time they met.

His travels over the world continued while he was at Princeton. In 1932 he visited the British Isles. The story of this brief visit might be quoted from "The Christian," the English journal under date of June 2, 1932:

"Dr. Samuel M. Zwemer has been called 'The protagonist of missions to Moslems,' for he is one of the most outstanding personalities in the world in this connection. He is at present on a visit to Great Britain and expects to spend a couple of months in travelling up and down the country and speaking at missionary and other gatherings.

"Those fortunate enough to have secured him include the Church Missionary Society, the British and Foreign Bible Society, the China Inland Mission, the Egypt General Mission, the Wesleyan Methodist Missionary Society, the British Jews Society, the Sudan United Mission, the Student Christian Movement and the British Syrian Mission. He expresses great admiration for the efficiency of Edinburgh House, and Mr. Kenneth Maclennan, secretary of the Conference of Missionary Societies, in whose office his programme was arranged.

"On the completion of forty years of missionary service Dr. Zwemer received a call to the Chair of Missions in Princeton Theological Seminary, and took up his residence there in 1930. This seminary is one of the oldest and largest of the Presbyterian colleges in America, and is well known for its conservative position in theology, the international character of its students and its missionary spirit.

"The story which Dr. Zwemer has to tell today is not by any means a repetition of what he told when in this country seven years ago. Changes are taking place with startling rapidity in the Mohammedan world, and there are ever fresh permutations and combinations. The effects of these changes cannot be safely prophesied and already some seers have suffered in their reputation by trying to forecast them. For instance, it was confidently affirmed that the cult of nationalism had given Pan-Islamism its death-blow. On the contrary, it has led to the increased cultivation of international sympathy between scattered Moslem groups and distant lands. In the Indian press the Palestine situation is warmly discussed and South Africa is keenly interested in Egypt. The unity of the Moslem world is as much a fact as it was before the War."

There was continuous preaching and missionary addresses in churches as well as courses of lectures in other Institutions after his return to America. One of particular significance to him was the address he gave the evening of October second, 1934, at the One Hundred and Fiftieth Anniversary of his Alma Mater, New Brunswick Theological Seminary. The title was, "The Contribution of our Seminary to Foreign Missions."

He was a favorite speaker at summer conferences. Three times he spoke at the Keswick Conference in England and was repeatedly at the Northfield, Winona Lake and other summer gatherings in this country. He also brought the old fire to many student gatherings. At the great Student Volunteer Convention of 1936 in Indianapolis he was introduced as follows:

"Born on the soil, and from that Antaean touch deriving strength unfatigued by the labors of fifty years; missionary to Islamic countries of the Near and Middle East; scholar, distinguished editor; one who has shed bloody sweat of consecrated toil when many of his friends were spilling futile ink, honorable antagonist of Mohammed, who never asked quarter from Medina or Mecca, nor gave any; a man who as a teacher, preacher and counselor has been unsurpassed in our day as an authority on Islam, who has walked the land where Richard the Lion-Hearted matched his strength with Saracens, one who with equal bravery contested for the faith with the mightier sword of the Spirit; one whose call to faith in Christ has echoed through the streets of many a city louder than the call of the Muezzin on the citadels of Cairo. I introduce to you our friend through many years, Samuel M. Zwemer."

While at Princeton a student in one of the missions classes, who himself went to the foreign field, made the life of his professor the subject of a thesis. Some years later when Dr. Zwemer was giving a special course on Missions at Biblical Seminary in New York City, one of the students there carried out a similar project as the thesis for his Bachelor's degree in theology.[2]

III

A project close to his heart during the Princeton years was the founding of a missionary museum. It became an impressive collection. Concerning it Zwemer wrote in an illustrated pamphlet:

"*Visualizing Non-Christian Religions.* Originally museums were thought of as storehouses for specimens and exhibits. Today the educational function of a museum predominates and the curio type of collection is being replaced with material suitable for cultural and practical lines. The museum as an institution of popular education is fully recognized by the atheist propagandists of the Soviet Union. Anti-religious museums, as well as traveling exhibits for anti-religious propaganda, are part of the Communist program.

"The inspiration to have a museum of the history of religion and of missions at Princeton Theological Seminary came to me at the time of a visit to the University of Marburg, Germany. The Princeton Museum is far more modest in its ambitions and attainments. The museum serves to make us understand and interpret the groping after God and the hunger for communication with Him in the non-Christian world.

2. The Princeton student was D. W. Brewington, the one from Biblical Seminary, R. D. Bontrager.

Eyegate has too often been neglected in missionary education, while eargate only has been beseiged. There are facts and truths in the History of Religion that can be more vividly presented in such a way than by lectures and textbooks.

"Some of the non-Christian religions are dying or disintegrating. Invaluable material will soon become rare. The same is true regarding the material illustrative of the early history of the missionary enterprise and the work of the pioneers. As one of the secretaries of the American Board wrote: 'I am glad you are thinking of building up a museum at Princeton, as it is becoming increasingly difficult to secure the right kind of material particularly when it comes to collecting the idols of the polytheistic religions.'"

The most notable acquisition of the museum was the costly collection of Rosaries made by Dr. Cornelius H. Patton of the American Board of Foreign Missions. The alumni of the Seminary and other missionaries sent in interesting material from all over the world. The museum continues to draw scholars from different parts of the world as well as Bible classes and missionary societies and students interested in missions and the development of the non-Christian religions.

During a part of the time in Princeton Zwemer's usual rugged health was not up to par. His trouble was diagnosed as duodenal ulcers, but he recovered from this illness sufficiently to travel to Northwest China. Later, however, in 1938 he was operated upon for a ruptured appendix but recovered rapidly, and when he returned to the Seminary the next semester he told his classes that a newly published book was the first he had written without an appendix!

The writer of this narrative and his family were leaving for Iran and with some hesitation the hospital authorities gave permission to visit the patient soon after a blood transfusion. He was sitting up in bed writing a book review. His greeting was full of cheer and he said, "Say, Christy, have you read my latest book?" We had not, so he instructed us to get one out of the dresser drawer. He inscribed it, "A momentum to the Wilsons as they leave for Persia." How could they keep a man like that down?

It was a happy time in Princeton and one marked by great achievements, but there was also the sudden sad death of his wife, Amy E. Wilkes who had been his constant inspiration and co-worker for more than forty years of service in all parts of the world. After she was gone there was a poignant loneliness as long as he was in Princeton.

The Seminary has a rule of retirement at seventy which is almost like the laws of the Medes and Persians, but Dr. Zwemer stayed on one more year by special action to give some courses after he had reached the mark of three score years and ten. When it was at last time for him to go, Dr. John A. Mackay had come as the new President of the Seminary following many years of missionary experience, and he took over the chair Zwemer had filled for almost a decade with distinction.

XVI

Life Begins at Seventy

"Ah, nothing is too late,
Till the tired heart shall cease to palpitate.
Cato learned Greek at eighty; Sophocles
Wrote his grand Oedipus, and Simonides.
Bore off the prize of verse from his compeers,
When each had numbered more than fourscore years.

"Chaucer, at Woodstock with the nightingales,
At sixty wrote the Canterbury Tales;
Goethe at Weimar, toiling to the last
Completed Faust when eighty years were past."

Morituri Salutamus, Stanzas 22-23,
by Henry Wadsworth Longfellow.

CHAPTER SIXTEEN

LIFE BEGINS AT SEVENTY

When he reached his seventieth birthday Zwemer gave a talk one evening to the Warfield Club at Princeton Seminary with the above title. As was done in so many other cases, this was later worked over into a printed address which was also translated into Arabic and German and, later found a place as a chapter in one of his books.[1]

He began this address by citation of patriarchs and other great leaders of men from Abraham on down to modern times who had accomplished their greatest work after three-score years and ten; then went on to give seven reasons why life should begin at seventy. 1. We should have a diploma from the school of experience by that time. 2. We are near to the river that has no bridge. 3. We have passed our apprenticeship in the school of life. 4. At seventy we can look further backward and further forward. 5. By this time we should know that life consisteth not in the abundance of things we possess. 6. The responsibility to witness for God to the next generation. 7. At seventy the Christian must redeem the time and live in more deadly earnest.

He visited Great Britain again in the summer of 1937 speaking at Slavanka, Keswick and the Edinburgh Conference on Faith and Order, always throwing down the challenge of the evangelization of the Moslem world.

After his retirement at Princeton he continued to live there for a short time, then moved to New York City in 1939. He took up residence at the Carteret Hotel, just off Seventh Avenue on Twenty-third Street. He had pleasant rooms high up above the noisy life of the City. Here he completed *The Glory of the Manger* which won a prize from the American Tract Society. Preaching, writing articles and preparing new publications kept him from staying on the "shelf of retirement."

It so happened that the man who many years before had with Zwemer founded the Arabian Mission was at this time in New York. Dr. James Cantine often invited his fellow pioneer out for an evening. On one such occasion there were two ladies who were friends of Dr. Cantine. One of them, Miss Margaret Clarke, was introduced to Dr. Zwemer and they proved to be friends of like tastes and met a number of times. The friendship ripened into romance, and on the twelfth of March, 1940, they were married in the home church of the bride, Brick Presbyterian Church in East Orange, New Jersey. The ceremony was performed by the pastor and Dr. John A. Mackay of Princeton Seminary. From this time forth the groom

1. The Art of Listening to God, Chapter IV.

had a new name for his old friend Cantine. He caled him "Eleazar," after the servant of Abraham who found Rebekah as a bride for his Master's son. Three years of loneliness and then a home and a heart that made life new again. They lived for a time at the Carteret Hotel and then later in an apartment at 33 Fifth Avenue, New York City. Margaret Zwemer accompanied her husband upon many of his journeys and entered with understanding and interest in his program of missionary speaking, conference address, preaching and literary work.

In addition to teaching mission courses for three years at Biblical Seminary in New York Dr. Zwemer accepted a similar assignment from the Missionary Training Institute of the Christian Missionary Alliance at Nyack, New York. After teaching there seven years he was awarded "the gold key" for service to the Institute.

As she went with her husband hither and yon, Mrs. Zwemer gathered a scrap-book of press clippings and notices of appearances from New England to California and from Seattle to Florida. There were also calls to which he responded from Canada and Mexico. In fact, the release from regular classwork on a full schedule gave him more time for missionary and Bible Conferences as well as commencement addresses and other meetings with students. In looking over the press clippings one is struck at once by the variety of subjects and engagements in widely different types of gatherings. Some of the programs were in Dutch. In Mexico his addresses were given through an interpreter.

It was often said that he had more fields of interest after his retirement than before. He often spoke for the smaller, more conservative groups and was beyond doubt greatly stimulating for them, but in his later years he was not heard so much by the wider-visioned intermissionary and international gatherings. He was still very busy, however. One typical vacation was in a summer month when he spoke at Bible conferences on the shores of the Pacific in Oregon and returning to a similar assignment at a camp on the coast of Maine. In the one month he and Mrs. Zwemer travelled twice across the continent and he spoke forty-five times in regular services, aside from a great number of informal talks and interviews.

One summer he was scheduled to speak at an evening meeting of the annual Princeton Institute of Theology. He gave one of the notable addresses of the program, but we found he considered his days there as something of a rest. The previous fortnight he had taught twenty-eight hours in classes and preached four times in addition at the Winona Lake School of Theology!

For some years before her marriage Mrs. Zwemer had been deeply interested in the *Friendly League for Christian Service*, which maintained a residence for business women at 233 East 17th Street in New York City. It was accomplishing a most useful work in giving young women a place to live, classes in interesting subjects for outside activity, and putting the girls into contact with churches in the City, as well as encouraging Bible study and offering direction in things of the Spirit. As is so often the case, however, the Friendly League was at that time having financial difficulty. Dr. Zwemer was asked to head a committee to raise funds to put the organization on a more sound financial basis. He took up the work with his usual zeal and in a short campaign raised nearly seventy thousand dollars, which reduced the mortgage on the building to meet the terms of the bank which held it, and in addition installed a new heating plant.

It may come as a surprise to those who knew him that Dr. Zwemer was also elected president of the *New York Jewish Evangelization Society*. Though his ardent passion all through life was for Islam, yet he had across the years been deeply interested in evangelical work for Jews as well, in the Moslem lands in addition to contacts in Europe and America.

Dr. John R. Mott had invited Zwemer as a special delegate to conferences on Jewish work held in Budapest and Warsaw during April, 1927. Both of these men were conscious of the close similarity of leading modern Jews to Christ and evangelistic work among Moslems. This is evident from the discussion and reports of these conferences as well as the fact that both men wrote and planned conferences and evangelistic work for followers of the other two monotheistic religions.[2]

II.

When his eightieth birthday drew near it is not surprising that his family circle, grateful to God for so long sparing the life of the father and grandfather, should have desired a gathering for the birthday occasion, April 12, 1947. The happy party was held at the Grosvenor Hotel, near their apartment in New York City. Only Dr. Zwemer and his wife Margaret and her near relatives with some of the children and grandchildren were present.

His friends knew of the occasion of his birthday and from many points in this country and across the seas a sheaf of congratulations came by letter and telegram. Some of these were formal, though affectionate, others were deeply moving because of long friendship and close association in the work of Christ.

For example, his long-time associate in Cairo, Wilbert B. Smith, wrote in part as follows:

"I often think of our years together in Cairo. What fun we had and what difficulties we had. I shall always be grateful to you for the idea that you gave of putting us on to the Nubar Pasha property. It surely was an idea from God, for the place is today quite as suitable and desirable for our work as it was when you led Halcombe, Morrison and me to it in the spring of 1921. The work that has been done in that place through the years I think has been well worth all the investment of time and money. As a result of what we started then, there are some six thousand Egyptian and foreign men and boys

2. For Zwemer's interest in Jewish Missions see Chapters VII, VIII, IX, of his book **Into All the World**, pp. 99-142.

222 Apostle to Islam

in Y.M.C.A.'s in Egypt: in Cairo, Alexandria, Assiut and Minieh. And I know that you are, in no small measure, responsible for the beginnings that were made and, therefore, I want you to know that I shall always consider you a partner in an enterprise that has meant everything to me."

Erick F. F. Bishop of Jerusalem wrote:

"Dear Prince of Missionaries to Moslems: This goes with our love and gratitude for this anniversary and the prayer that the next decade too may fructify as so many of the past. Thirty-one years now it is since you first came into my life and have remained there ever since with our united love."

Among many tributes was this striking paragraph from the letter of Fred Field Goodsell of the American Board.

"I wish I might say something or do something which would make you vividly aware of how grateful I am to our Heavenly Father for the service you have rendered. Your utter devotion, your complete sincerity and your indefatigable diligence have been a great inspiration to your younger colleagues, including myself."

Dr. John A Mackay, President of the Presbyterian Board of Foreign Missions and of Princeton Seminary, said:

"According to a famous psalmist 'The days of our years are three score years and ten; and if by reason of strength they be four score years, yet is their strength labor, and sorrow.' But you are a decade past the three score and ten, and as you cross the threshold of the four score no sorrow clouds your life and your labor is the zest of creative work. It is certainly an inspiration for us lesser and younger men to know that life can begin at eighty, and that one can still look forward to the promise to be as the palm tree by springs of water."

From the leading historian of Missions, Dr. Kenneth Scott Latourette of Yale, came the following word:

"I seem to remember that ten years ago you wrote an article entitled Life Begins at Seventy. Life for you began long before seventy and you crammed the first seven decades with more usefulness than is given to most of us even though we were to attain the age of Methuselah .... For one such as yourself what men call death will be simply an episode in a life with Christ which was begun long ago and will continue with increasing richness through the long reaches of eternity."

Among all the greetings received it may be that both the octogenarian and his family appreciated most deeply the affectionate note written in the distinctive hand of Robert E. Speer on Easter Day, 1947, not long before the call of this close friend to higher service. It said in part:

"My dear Sam: So this week on Saturday you will be four score — and thank God it is not 'labor and sorrow' but 'work and joy.' Thankful you will be, and we who love you will be thankful with you for the way the Lord has led you, and for all that He has given to us and to the Church through you . . . . A four-score blessing 'This is my dear, true, powerful servant Sam!' I can imagine God saying, 'He is one of my best and bravest. Angels take special care of him! Let no harm come to him. Breathe his mind and heart full of power.' That is my prayer for you dearest old friend."

His eightieth birthday did not by any means, however, signify retirement from active service. On the contrary, invitations for his public services in preaching and teaching did not diminish.

In 1949, in his eighty-third year, the mission of which he was a founder observed its sixtieth anniversary at the annual meeting in Kuwait, Arabia. Zwemer received an invitation to attend. Encouraged by the Reformed Board of Foreign Missions and by many friends, his attendance was made possible by special contributions so that he was able to observe the great changes in the New Arabia and bring the inspiration of his presence and encouragement to the mission as it entered the second half of the Twentieth Century.

He and Mrs. Zwemer sailed on the American Export Line for the Mediterranean trip, with their destination Beirut. Though political conditions in the Near East were still somewhat disturbed there was a welcome in Egypt. A day was spent largely with the United Presbyterian Theological Seminary in Cairo. In the evening Dr. Zwemer addressed a gathering of nearly 150 missionaries from most all of the Boards and agencies at work in Egypt. The assembly was in the C.M.S. Cathedral House.

On disembarking at Beirut the traveler preached in the church of the American Mission on Sunday, October 9th. After a visit with friends of the Mission there the couple went up over the Lebanons and on to Damascus by car. From the latter city they flew to Basrah in Iraq. They were now on the ground where Zwemer and Cantine had first established their work sixty years before. But what changes! In the then fanatical cities of Baghdad and Basrah there were meetings with small groups of converts from Islam. In fact, Zwemer wrote that though the scenery of Iraq and the heat were the same as of yore, almost all else had changed.

They flew on to Bahrein, the station which Zwemer had opened. What a transformation he encountered there! Dominating the scene were the great plants of the oil company and hundreds of air conditioned houses. In the Bible shop he drank coffee with grey-beards who had known him on the Island over half a century previously. He was invited to the palace of the Sheikh, who ruled the Island. The host told the visitor that as a boy of nine he remembered seeing people throw stones at him for selling Bibles. Zwemer remarked that there seemed to be a different attitude toward the Bible now. The ruler replied that the old-fashioned prejudices of his grandfather's day had now all been swept away. Zwemer wrote, "The hospitality of the Arab rulers and the oil executives at Bahrein and Kuwait was delightful."

He said that doors once hermetically sealed are now wide open and medical missions hold the key to all of Arabia with the exception of the holy

cities, Mecca and Medina. The friendship of Ibn Saud and the enormous
oil industry on the gulf have wrought a social as well as an economic revolution and have greatly changed religious attitudes.

At the Annual Meeting and celebration of the sixtieth anniversary of the
Mission in Kuwait there were thirty-three members of the Mission as well
as the President of the Board and one of the Secretaries, Miss Ruth Ransom. Their inspiration and the general feeling may be shown by a part of
a resolution adopted by the meeting:

"The Arabian Mission is now celebrating its Sixtieth Anniversary. With
all our hearts we thank God for what has been accomplished in the three-
score years that are passed. We realize that 'there remaineth very much
land to be possessed' and we therefore urge upon the Board with all the
force at our command our conviction that the time has come to begin a
definite advance on all our fronts and in every field of work."

A number of the doors of opportunity were listed, and eight new missionaries were requested; then the appeal proceeded:

"But at this Sixtieth Anniversary we think of development and expan-
sion. Our vision reaches out to the large fields and areas as yet untouched
by the Gospel. We challenge the Board and the Church to send us these additional reinforcements so that we may build more worthily on the foundations laid by our pioneers."

During the meeting Zwemer had an invitation to address a large meeting
of oil company personnel near the new pier from which he was told 600,000
barrels of oil are shipped out daily by tanker.

As he thought back to the meeting after it was all over, Zwemer wrote:
"Challenged by the opportunity for evangelism among both Arab and
English speaking communities, the Mission called for large reinforcement
and for prevailing prayer. The burden of Arabia is Islam, but that burden
is being lifted. God's Providence and His Gospel are at work."

On the return journey three Egyptian pastors arranged a meeting in the
Alexandria Evangelical Church where Zwemer spoke in Arabic to more
than 300 who heard his message with enthusiasm and sang the Arabic hymn
"Christ shall have Dominion."

Soon after his return a letter came from a colleague of the Arabian Mission which we may quote in closing:

"The more we think of it the greater the marvel seems that you could —
after sixty years — be with us and inspire us. As we look back upon the
Annual Meeting we realize that many things which seemed to occupy the
center of the stage will fade, but the inspiration of your presence and addresses will remain. And we are glad that Mrs. Zwemer was with you. The
many kind things I heard said about her would fill a book."

The return to New York was made by the same line and Dr. Zwemer
began at once with renewed zeal to tell the story and make the appeal for
work among Moslems by voice and with pen.

XVII

Home and Family Life

"The Christian home ought to be a church. There should be grace at every meal and family worship at least once a day. Graceless meals surely are not only less than Christian but even not wholly human. 'You don't do as we do at our house, do you?' said a small boy invited to dinner at a neighbor's house where there was no blessing at the table. 'At our house we always thank God and then eat. But you do like my dog Rover. He just eats.'

"And the Christian home is the true school, as it ought to be a true church. Here the most powerful of all educational forces are at work — atmosphere and examples. Through all the interstices of life and time, the truth or falsehood of the tone and temper, the attitude and ideals of the home, seep into a child's mind and character."

— *The Christian Home*, by Robert E. Speer, Page 5.

CHAPTER SEVENTEEN

HOME AND FAMILY LIFE

A Christian home is an inheritance as well as a creation. In the early chapter of this volume we have seen the vision of a home from which the subject of our narrative came forth. It was a Christian home where there was much prayer and many children. There Samuel Zwemer had instilled in his mind and heart the ideals of true Christian life, of sincere piety and hard work. The obstacles against founding such a home of his own were many. Only Divine grace and power made possible the marvelous home and family life which came to this missionary in the lands of Islam.

His home life divides naturally into three periods. There was first of all six years as a bachelor, living with James Cantine most of the time during the pioneer stage of the Arabian mission. Then there was the long period of a real home with Amy Elizabeth Wilkes Zwemer, which ended with her passing to higher service in January of 1937. The third period included several years alone in Princeton and New York City, and then, three years after the death of Amy Wilkes Zwemer there came the new home with Margaret Clarke Zwemer for a decade.

I

The start of their work in Basrah was for Zwemer and Cantine much like that of the Apostle Paul in Rome, "And Paul dwelt two whole years in his own hired house, and received all that came in unto him."[1] The young pioneer saw times when people were prevented from coming in unto them by the authorities and by local religious leaders, but their home was a source of light and spiritual power. There were Bible distributors and converts who lived with them at various times and out of this home of the two young bachelors grew the work of a real station and mission which was to affect much of Arabia and Iraq.

Living was difficult in the small adobe house but the ingenuity of the young Dutchmen soon made the best of it with porches which afforded some protection from the heat and the best possible arrangements for frequent cool baths. On his trip to the field in 1949 Zwemer contrasted this early living with the magnificent air-cooled building of the Basrah Airport!

Zwemer's natural hobby of carpentry, inherited from his father, came into full play and very useful furniture, and even a pulpit for their small chapel were fashioned from packing cases. But one should not think the house was bare or unattractive. In fact, it was considered so comfortable

---

1. Acts 28:30.

that the headmaster of the Jewish school in the city asked permission and came to live with them for a considerable time.

When the annual lease on their house expired they were greatly surprised to find that no other was available. Following a number of refusals they were eventually told that the governor had issued a proclamation that no person would be allowed to rent a house to the Americans under severe penalties.

Years later in telling of the difficulty in finding a place to live Cantine exclaimed, "Man's extremity is God's opportunity." When all seemed hopeless the Persian Consul sent for the missionaries and told them he had a better house for them than the one in which they had been living. In God's providence Zwemer had called on him and given the Consul some medicine which had helped him when he was sick, thus returned the bread cast upon the waters.

How they finally got permission to have a house built for them we should let Cantine tell:

> "Some months later we were able to make a contract with a responsible Catholic Christian to build us a house according to our own plans and on a very desirable location. The terms were not easy, as the sum of $800, paid in advance for a lease of five years, was we thought sufficient to pay the entire cost of building. The money was found at home and sent out, but before it was paid over we naturally wanted the contract registered in the British consulate. There was no objection to this, but when I took the paper to the consulate, I found that it had to be recorded in the local land office. This I thought would be impossible, as we were still on the black list of the authorities, and who would dare to register a building contract for the outlawed Americans? I very regretfully explained to the contractor that the deal was off. 'Oh,' he said, 'you don't know how things are done in this country. Give the paper to me.' Very much to my surprise, he did return it duly stamped and signed, and in due course we had our own house. Being thus recognized as permanent residents, our standing was assured, and we had no further difficulties on this score. A year or two afterwards I asked Yusuf, 'How did you manage to get that registration through?'
>
> " 'Oh,' he said, 'I gave the head man a little present.'
>
> " 'What was it?'
>
> " 'Never mind,' he replied. 'It was not much.'
>
> " 'But I would like to know.'
>
> " 'Well, if you must know, it was a case of whiskey.' "[2]

During this period Zwemer was away a great deal in itineration and exploration. When at home the two men for the most part got along well together and were devoted friends through life, though in many things they had opposite tastes. Cantine loved tennis and other sports and spent all he could save for cameras and photographic equipment. Zwemer did not care

---

2. Cantine, **The Golden Milestone**, p. 59.

for sports and spent all the extra cash he could get for books and spent his recreational time in writing.

Zwemer carried one book with him constantly, which he considered the best book on Arabia available at the time. He had it rebound with blank pages inserted through the book for notes and a cover to resemble the way the Koran was usually bound. He used it as a guidebook on journeys in Arabia. The book was *Arabien und die Araber*, by Albrecht Zahme, Halle, 1875.[3]

On the interleaves are notes in Zwemer's handwriting, sketches, hand-drawn maps, lists of tribes and information concerning places and people visited.

When he came to Sana'a of Yemen he must have spent a sleepless night—as had the author of the book in question and other travelers. On August 18, 1894, he wrote on one of the blank leaves a twelve-stanza poem addressed to the Bedbugs, with apologies to Keating's Insect Powder. Though it may not be a literary gem, it at least shows that in these early days a bit of humor could brighten even the most difficult experience. The pioneers of the Arabian Mission took every hardship with a smile and a prayer.

I I

In an early chapter we have described the miracle of how the Lord provided a wife for the lonely young pioneer when the time came. There at the head of the Persian Gulf, in one of the most impossible places in the world —at an unusual time, when Zwemer instead of Cantine was in residence, she appeared!—the charming Amy Elizabeth Wilkes, the young English nurse, on her way to Baghdad from Australia. Providence having made the necessary arrangements, Zwemer did his part—and rapidly.

Mrs. Amy Elizabeth Wilkes Zwemer was born March 30, 1865 at Wolver-hampton, Staffordshire, England. She studied nursing at Prince Alfred Hospital, New South Wales, and also did Bush Nursing in Queensland. In the manuscript records of the Reformed Board the following sentence appears in her own hand: "The Spirit of God moved me to offer myself to the Lord for foreign work at a missionary meeting, January, 1892, Sydney. Reading F. R. Havergal's *Marching Orders* decided me to offer."

She was one of a group to enter the Training School for Deaconesses in Sydney and was "set apart" by the Primate of Australia, commissioned and appointed by the Church Missionary Society to work in Baghdad.

From the home she founded on the Island of Bahrein, Mrs. Zwemer wrote some years later:

"May 13th will be the anniversary of our engagement. We were engaged seven years ago. It was a Monday morning in Baghdad, sitting on a couch facing the river Tigris. We were looking up Arabic

3. The copy with its priceless notes is now in the Gardner A. Sage library of New Brunswick Theological Seminary, presented to his Alma Mater by Zwemer.

roots at the time, and had two dictionaries, a grammar, and various other books between us."

Modesty forbids her to give the details of how Zwemer got around the dictionaries, grammars, etc., but he did and also overcame many other obstacles. The wife continues in her letter,

engaged *5 days*

"On the 18th of May we will have been married six years, and on May 23rd Katharina will be five years old."

After their marriage they resided for a time in Basrah and then moved on to found the home in Bahrein. In spite of very primitive conditions, the awful heat during a part of the year, the great difficulty of sanitation and the fanatic opposition and superstition—in spite of terrible sieges of cholera and plague—in spite of the lack of the companionship of any other women of her own race—the missionary home which resulted was an almost ideal example to the people of that island and Arabia. After some time other members did join the station. The round of duties of a rich, full missionary life and some of the conditions encountered will be understood from a few excerpts from letters she wrote. Always a great correspondent, here lay another facet of her character and power. She wrote:

"I had an interesting hour yesterday afternoon with ten women in two houses. One of them asked me for a dress. I said: 'Why do you not ask your own people for one? I am a *kafir*.' They shouted all at once: 'No, no, you have the love and mercy of God in your heart: Our people will not give a thing without some return. You people are all good; you see and heal the poor and afflicted, and give medicine and clothes to those in need, and your religion is right!' More and more I find the doors opening and the women ready to listen to the Gospel, and some of them are surprised at what they find written there.

"Last Friday afternoon I went with Mrs. Thoms to see one of my old friends; we stayed an hour and drank tea and coffee (five tiny cups) and also had an opportunity to speak a word. She is one of the women who seem to understand a great deal of the Gospel. While we were there an urgent message came that I was wanted at home. Another old friend had come to see me and had brought six other women with her. She would not go away until I came, for she wanted them to hear the music and the hymns. The women she brought with her were from Hadd, a most fanatical place, near Moharrek, where they stoned the missionaries and colporteurs. Now I think I must try going over there to see if the music, the tea, and biscuits have not made their hearts softer . . . .

"We are now enduring the hot weather and enjoying cold baths when there is time to take a dip in the tub (which I manage three or four times in the twenty-four hours). Sometimes you may be tempted to think you are the leader of a forlorn hope, but do not encourage the thought. We here are often tempted in the same way with the same thought, but just as sure as are the promises of God is the certainty that He will gather out a people for His Name from Arabia. Pray for us that we may not be discouraged, even though we do not see the blade or the full corn in the ear. I have not been able to do any visiting for the last ten days. The children have had fever, sometimes two of them together. Bessie is quite ill again, has had a high temperature for the last four weeks and needs constant attention to keep her alive. She will not take food except by force . . . . The other day I had an open air meeting with a lot of children out on the desert. I gave them a little talk about the love of God in Jesus Christ; they listened attentively and asked questions quite nicely, not in their usual rough manner . . . .

"You know about our little school which is growing slowly but surely. I have given up teaching and the Arabic teacher at this station has this department in hand as well as teaching the missionaries. My husband has been working it up lately, and has succeeded in adding to the numbers of Moslem pupils. There are eight Moslem lads, four Jews, five Christians — and a few Moslem girls have begun to come, but these last are difficult to keep. They come and go for various reasons.

"Bahrein is suffering intensely just now and they seem to be digging graves all day long in the cemetery just near us. The plague has come here and it is reaping a great harvest of victims, as are also smallpox and diphtheria. Our general work is very much hampered, the schools are closed, and people are afraid of us. Lots of false reports are about and someone started a yarn that we threw things up in the air and caused the plague to fall on the people. Dr. Thoms tried to get some of the houses quarantined where diphtheria first started, and that was an awful offense to these *holy* Moslems. However, nothing is being done, or can be done, because the chief of the island does not wish it, neither do the people. The same trouble that the Government has in India, but here we have no "compelling" authority so the people have their own way, and through their gross ignorance and fanaticism, large numbers are dying. One report is that the Christians have brought these diseases in order to kill off the Moslems and make the island Christian. Poor things, we can still pray for them, and believe that in some way God will make this calamity to glorify His Son in this place . . . .

"We have in the hospital one of the colporteurs from Muscat. He is rather sick with chronic dyspepsia, and so he is staying here for treatment. The gist of the story is this: The other day he was sitting on the veranda and heard the strains of a familiar hymn and looking up saw some poorly dressed children coming over the desert with water jars on their heads, going to the well and singing a Christian hymn. It was such a marvel to him . . . . Moslem children singing the praises of the Son of God . . . .

"Have we told you before that the windmill is working finely and is, in its way, an evangelizing agency. Many people are like those in Goldsmith's poem 'And those who came to scoff remained to pray' or something like that . . . .

"Our little boy Raymund Lull is a bonnie little chap; although not a big baby he seems strong and healthy. Mrs. Thoms was a good and pleasant doctor as well as trained nurse. Hitherto on these occasions I have had to fend for myself with the help of an untrained native woman . . . ."

When Peter Zwemer left for America various missionaries took some of the slave boys from his school. The Zwemer family took two whom they taught to read and write and who were trained in household work and honorable occupations. One of them by the name of Solomon, was assigned to the care of the children. He not only did a good job of "baby sitting" but was so thankful for the influence of the home that for years after he left he contributed ten per cent of his earnings to the Reformed Board.

Some years later Samuel Zwemer wrote of his wife Amy in those early days: "For a short time we lived in Basrah and then my wife became the first woman in our Mission to work under circumstances and in an environment of untold discomforts and physical hardships. Naturally strong and self-reliant, she triumphed over everything bravely and hopefully. Our small, uncomfortable, three-room leaky house, without screens in the midst of the town became a center of hospitality for Arab women and children. A trained nurse, she cared for the first patients; she opened the first day school for girls, and 'roughed it' by tours in an open sailboat to Katif and along the Oman coast, not to speak of tours all over the islands. Looking back on those early years, what she patiently endured now seems incredible."

> "Her love was like an island
> In life's ocean, vast and wide,
> A peaceful, quiet shelter
> From the wind and rain and tide
> 'Twas bound on the north by Hope,
> By Patience on the west,
> By tender Counsel on the south
> And on the east by Rest.
> Above it, like a beacon light,
> Shone faith and truth and prayer;
> And through the changing scenes of life
> I found a haven there." [4]

A comment on the impression Mrs. Zwemer made on these tours came from an old Arab with whom Dr. Zwemer had a rather lengthy discussion concerning polygamy. Finally the old man ended the argument with the statement, "Well if you can find me an Arab woman as intelligent as your wife, perhaps I would be satisfied with just one."

Though great sorrow visited the home in the passing so suddenly on the Island of Bahrein of the two little girls, Ruth and Katharina, four of the children survived.

The first American baby born in Bahrein was Nellie Elizabeth Zwemer (known commonly as "Bessie"). After her marriage to the Reverend

---

4. **The Golden Milestone**, p. 116.

Claude L. Pickens, Jr., the couple went as missionaries to China under the Episcopal Board and spent many years of service there with special reference to work for Moslems. There are two sons and three daughters in the family who often visited with their grandfather while they were in college.

Raymund Lull Zwemer was born at Bahrein on the day that his father sent off the manuscript of his book on Raymund Lull. After graduate work at Yale and Harvard he became a member of the faculty in the Department of Anatomy at Columbia University Medical School. He moved from that post to Washington, D. C., and served in the Department of State the National Academy of Sciences and the Library of Congress. There are four children in his family and one grandchild.

Amy Ruth Zwemer was born at Holland, Michigan. She married Homer H. Violette and has four children. Dr. Zwemer spent some of his last months in their home in Alexandria, Virginia.

Mary Moffat Zwemer was also born in Holland, Michigan, and was named for the wife of David Livingstone. She married Dr. Robert E. Brittain, a poet and author. They have two sons.

The fifteen grandchildren and one great grandchild brought great joy to the heart of Dr. Zwemer. Five of them went to Hope College and others to Vassar, Columbia and various institutions of higher learning. Two served in World War II, one in the Army and the other in the Navy, and two are student volunteers with their hopes set on the foreign missionfield.

Wherever the Zwemers were their home was truly international or ecumenical with the Dutch background and the United States and Great Britain represented by the parents. For this reason, as well as for the truly universal Christian spirit so evident, people of all nations seemed a part of the home. Having lived a good deal under British sovereignty, they were strong supporters of the good that Great Britain had accomplished for peoples of the Middle East, while at the same time not being blind to the faults of the United Kingdom in the policies concerning colonies and other peoples. Displayed on holidays and present in the home for other occasions were both the "Stars and Stripes" and the "Union Jack."

During the years of World War I in Cairo their home was a haven for many a soldier or nurse, and both of the Zwemers had their share in work among the thousands of troops stationed in Egypt. Mrs. Zwemer helped to arrange groups to meet the Red Cross trains and visit the wounded in the hospitals, as well as having a share in the opening of the "Anzac Hostel." Dr. Zwemer, as usual, threw himself into work for the troops, in large measure with the Y.M.C.A. In the camps and chapel tents he gave stirring devotional talks and led worship services. To Christians the challenge to reach Islam was always presented by both of the Zwemers, and several future missionaries to Moslem lands came from these war-time contacts.

Through the training of Bible women, visits to Moslem homes, and baby clinics many Egyptian Christians as well as Mohammedan women came into the Zwemer home. There were never any distinctions as to race or class and always time to listen and share in joys or sorrows, to tell a cheering story, or give a word of comfort and prayer.

Like so many missionary families, one of the great problems when on the field was that of the children and their education.

Zwemer himself said from experience that a missionary family was on the *three* horns of a dilemma. At times it seemed all but impossible to keep the children in the awful heat. If the wife went home with the children some would remark that the missionary did not love his wife to let her go like that. If the children were left in the homeland they were thought to be neglected by their parents. If husband and wife both spent more than usual furlough time at home they would be accused of neglecting the work on the field.

This reminded the missionary of the story about the old Arab, his son and donkey. When the boy rode, passers-by remarked how heartless the young fellow was to make the old man walk. When the latter got on, people remarked that the father was selfish to make his son walk. When they both got on other travelers said they were cruel and killing the donkey.

At any rate, through the years in Arabia and Cairo and in America there was a wonderful home life which was notable for at least three things.

First, there was the law of hospitality. Any friend or stranger was welcome in the home for a meal or for tea or a visit. There were no doubt times when such a welcome was imposed upon, but they also entertained angels unawares in the constant stream of guests who entered and left the home. It may be that the family had learned something of the virtue of hospitality from the people of the East, but it went back even farther than that, and was inherited from the forbears of both parents as well as founded upon Biblical and Christian precepts.

The family life was also marked by constant breaks through long journeys or absences. On meeting with them at one time the father remarked to the writer, "We have been dwelling in suitcases with Isaac and Jacob joint heirs of the promise." He also said that if "three moves were as bad as a fire," they had gone through the equivalent of many fires. "Eliminate" was Zwemer's favorite word when a move was made, but his wife always salvaged enough to create an atmosphere of gracious living wherever they were.

Third, there was in the household the constant atmosphere of prayer. When separated often the different members of the family read the same devotional Scripture from the devotional booklet "Daily Light," and though often sundered far, by grace they met daily around the Mercy Seat.

After decades on the field and the years in Princeton, Amy Wilkes Zwemer, the wife and mother, died suddenly and peacefully, January 25, 1937, in the Presbyterian Hospital of New York City, following a heart attack suffered during a missionary meeting.

The Memorial Minutes of the Reformed Board may be quoted in part: "After her marriage Amy Elizabeth Wilkes lived first in Basrah and then in Bahrein. She opened the first girls' school in Bahrein, holding classes in the mission house. Through this and other channels she gained admission to some thirty homes. There too, in 1904, Dr. and Mrs. Zwemer lost their two little daughters within eight days of each other, a sacrifice which deepened and sanctified their rare devotion to work among Moslems.

"Mrs. Zwemer was an active co-worker with her husband throughout his great missionary career. In 1912 they left the Arabian Mission and took up residence in Cairo where they were associated as honorary members with the United Presbyterian Mission in Egypt, while at the same time retaining a personal relationship with our own Board of Foreign Missions. Mrs. Zwemer was co-author with her husband of the two books 'Topsy-Turvy Land' and 'Zig-Zag Journeys in the Camel Country.' The Board would pay its reverent tribute to the consecrated service of this faithful pioneer."

James Cantine, the fellow founder of the Arabian Mission and life-long friend, wrote:

"On tour with her husband or amid the ever-widening circle of friends in Arabia, Egypt and at home, her voice never uttered 'an uncertain sound.' Her hospitable home had warm welcome for the stranger as well as for her associates, and many of the younger missionaries of those days knew her kindly interest and care in times of sickness and trial. And of even more worth, many of us gained through her an added consecration, a heightened estimate of spiritual values and an unfailing confidence in our Master's ultimate victory in Moslem hearts and homes.

"It seems incredible that we who remain shall not again on earth meet her kindly glance nor listen to her cheery words, but we surely have a share in her triumphant entrance into the glory of the unseen, hearing some echo of the Voice that has welcomed her with its 'Well done!'"

III . *remarried 3 years later*

After Dr. Zwemer's marriage in 1940 to Margaret Clarke they were located for most of the next decade in the apartment at "33 Fifth Avenue," New York City. In this new home Margaret was always a charming and gracious hostess and followed the family habit of serving tea to guests. As had been his custom, Zwemer often prayed with their visitors and scarcely a soul entered the house who did not depart with the gift of a book, pamphlet or some other memento. In fact, the books and tracts that Samuel M. Zwemer gave away in all parts of the world would truly reach around the globe and their effects reach off beyond into eternity.

Not long after her marriage Margaret helped in the preparation of the manuscript for her husband's book "The Glory of the Empty Tomb." This volume was dedicated to her in the Latin of Romans 16:2, "For she hath been a helper of many and of myself as well."

A kind Providence allowed Margaret Zwemer to complete with her husband a trip to the sixtieth anniversary celebration of the Arabian Mission. Little did she realize that so soon after the return from the land of those great rivers, the Tigris and Euphrates, she would be called to the crossing of the river which has no bridge.

She became ill soon after the return and died in a New York hospital on February 21st, 1950. Services were held at the First Presbyterian Church, just up the avenue from their apartment and the church which both had attended when they were in the City. 13 years later 2nd wife dies

So twice it fell to Samuel Zwemer to enter into the experience of the Prophet Ezekiel, as recorded in verses 16 and 18 of Chapter 24:

"Behold I take away from thee the desire of thine eyes with a stroke; yet neither shalt thou mourn nor weep . . . So I spoke unto the people in the morning, and at even my wife died; and I did in the morning as I was commanded."

The apartment was lonely after Margaret's passing but many friends continued to call upon Dr. Zwemer there. His hospitality, wonderful humor, and consecration were evident to all. The children and grandchildren visited often, and eventually his oldest daughter and her husband, the Reverend Claude L. Pickens, returned from China. In the meantime, Dr. Zwemer continued his speaking and accepted what may have been too heavy a schedule. His was a nature that could not stand inactivity, and so it was quite natural that as long as he had life he should continue his zest for fellowship and his zeal to preach and challenge young and old with the call of service for Moslems, which continued to radiate through the years from this truly Christian home.

XVIII

Taking Hold of God

"There are many definitions of prayer. James Montgomery crowds four-teen into a single hymn of six stanzas. Prayer is sincere desire; prayer is often inaudible; prayer is hidden fire; prayer is a sigh, a tear; prayer is the upward glance to God; prayer is simple as the lisp of a child; prayer is sublime as God's majesty; it is the cry of the prodigal, the breath of the soul, the mountain-air that invigorates, the watchword at death, the key to heaven and the pathway of our Saviour. To meditate on these definitions alone would lead us into all the wealth of the Scriptures on prayer."

SAMUEL M. ZWEMER,
in *Taking Hold of God*.

CHAPTER EIGHTEEN

TAKING HOLD OF GOD

After following the story of this man the natural question to ask is wherein lay the dynamic of so powerful a life? Certainly it lies within the realm of the spirit and is for that reason elusive of observation or capture and definition. Nevertheless a key may be found in the simple statement, It was a life in God. The motive force came from constant communion with the Creator through His Son Jesus Christ.

The power for his personal life was from the same source as that which enabled the Mission he and his associates founded to take root in the most arid and stony ground in the world.

Zwemer himself wrote:

> "One of the most vivid recollections of the early years of our Mission is of the hours we spent in prayer together, first in the Seminary dormitory, then on the slopes of the Lebanons, climbing to Suk-al-Gharb, and afterwards in Aden and Basrah and Bahrein.. Cantine nearly always turned to one portion of Scripture which became our *Magna Charta* — the first chapter of Joshua. It seemed to us in those days wonderfully appropriate, and God has fulfilled some of its promises to those who followed after. We always coveted the whole of the promised land and our eyes were beyond its coasts."[1]

I

Up to the present we have told the story of the Apostle to Moslems and a number of his accomplishments. We have noted his vast literary production, so now we may stop to look at the man behind the books. He is indeed revealed in many of the volumes he wrote, but this is true in a larger sense of the devotional books than of the works on Islam. Here we have a glimpse of his very heart. The heading of this chapter, "Taking Hold of God," is the title of a great devotional volume from his pen on the subject of prayer.

Together with the Bible, Zwemer himself used over the course of the years *The Private Devotions of Lancelot Andrewes.* While at Bombay he secured in 1905 a copy edited by Alexander Whyte. This was used over the course of many years and as the cover wore out was rebound again and again. Andrewes was the Court Chaplain of James the First of England and one of the translators of the King James Version of the English Bible. His devotions were written for his private use and not intended for publication. They are, however, one of the great classics in this field. Their language is the grand tongue of the King James Version and scarcely any-

---

1. The Golden Milestone, p. 138.

thing aside from the Psalms can offer such depths of confession and sorrow for sin as revealed in these pages. As Zwemer remarked, "Andrewes goes deep. He makes a man feel like an unmitigated sinner."

On the pages of this devotional book are dates and entries and brief references which record the deepest spiritual experiences of the world traveler and missionary to Moslems. Sometimes the notes are in English, then again portions are in Arabic. They record the prayers and tears of a broken heart as well as the record of spiritual triumphs in widely separated times and parts of the globe. The markings on the pages also show how intently the mind and heart of the worshipper had entered into the very soul of the devotional passages as he prayed.

Whenever he came to the Lord's Supper, Zwemer was accustomed to repeat over and over and from the depths of his heart:

> "Just as I am without one plea
> But that Thy blood was shed for me."

His favorite hymn was: "Christian dost thou see them?" written by St. Andrew of Crete (660-732). The hymn is supposed to have been composed when Moslem forces were taking the Christian holy places. Zwemer seldom sang it without tears. His emotions were such that at times tears would come as he sang, or prayed, and rarely also as he spoke. Another favorite hymn was "My Faith Looks up to Thee." He loved to join in all the great hymns and with Christian people of all sorts in praise and prayer.

It was through his efforts that *The Fellowship of Faith for Moslems* came into being in Great Britain. This continues a very strong and active organization in prayer and other forms of effort for the evangelization of the Moslem world. It has recently been actively organized in Canada and the United States. To the annual prayer conference held in Slavanka, England, during June, 1948, Zwemer wrote:

> *"Greetings to the Saints at Slavanka:*
>
> "How memory brings back the occasions when we met together, and the happy hours spent in prayer and Christian fellowship. I am now in my 81st year and have spent sixty years thinking of the Moslem World and its problems! It began when I signed a card in 1886 expressing the purpose to become a foreign missionary! Little did I realize all the way God would lead me into Arabia and Egypt and across the world of Islam, and guide my pen to call out others,

> 'With mercy and with judgment
> My web of time He wove
> And aye the dews of sorrow
> Were lustered by His love.'

"Never have I regretted choosing a hard field and an impossible task. How much has changed for the better, and how many doors have opened in Arabia since 1890, and in all Asia and Africa. God's providence has been so visible that all may see His purpose. We must not lose faith or courage, but be earnest and steadfast and diligent until the going down of our sun — or the rising of His Sun at His glorious appearing."

The tremendous faith which he held was inherited from his forebears, and especially his father and mother, but he had also attained for himself a strength of faith that could remove mountains. Never did his faith stumble at the power of God to do the impossible. By voice and pen he was able to melt mountains of ignorance and fanaticism and through prayer and service he was used to call out and equip bands of men and women for the most difficult mission fields of the world. Such a faith was not gained or maintained without a struggle, as one knows who has seen a list of the spiritual crises of his life made in the writing of his own hand.

His theology was conservative Calvinism and he believed with all his heart in the whole of the Bible as the Word of God, and in the Reformed Faith. He had little patience for the higher critics of Scripture. He said they were like the ants in Africa who would bite the life-germ out of a seed before they took it underground in their anthill, so it could not sprout. He was a staunch Protestant and believed with all his heart in the great doctrines of the Reformation. He remarked that if all the Popes had had wives, like Peter, whom they claimed was the first Pope, they would never have dared to say they were infallible.

His belief in God and His providence was the most real thing in life. His father taught him the Heidelberg Catechism as a boy and he remembered many of the answers all his life. He said, "In every detail of life God has a hand. God is not dead. Christ is contemporary. If every man's life is a plan of God, in looking backward we are conscious of having frustrated that plan again and again by dullness of perception or disobedience to the heavenly vision, but we are also grateful for the strength which was made perfect in human weakness and that Divinity which 'shapes our ends, rough hew them as we may.' "[2]

The Bible was so much a part of his life that thought and word seemed naturally to take the form of Biblical phrase. Though he was always a Bible student his taste in literature was most catholic, running the gamut from missions and theology to James Jeans and Dorothy Sayre. The breadth of his reading may be gathered from the fact that he wrote more than four hundred book reviews published in *The Moslem World* alone! Even when on vacation or in the hospital he would generally be reading several books.

He not only held the evangelical theological position on the Doctrine of God, the Person of Christ, the Person and work of the Holy Spirit and Revelation, but had sharpened these great particulars of his faith on the anvil of discussion with the master minds of Islam. When he said he believed in Christ as the Son of God, he knew exactly what he meant by that. His doctrine of the Virgin Birth or the Atonement had been tried in the furnace and had come out purified and strong. He held his theology not as theory alone, but he lived it.

2. From unpublished notes written by S. M. Z.

In regard to work with Moslems it may be said that he belonged to the older school which advocated a direct approach. But he did not offend Moslem hearers or readers in most cases, for they found he had a very deep and sincere respect for all Moslems and their beliefs and a broad love for them and all men. This love was his fundamental motive and guiding star, even in times of controversy. Only one who has worked in Moslem fields can appreciate the complexity of the problems of mission work there, yet with all of his zeal and straightforward advance he seldom had trouble, but on any number of occasions was received by Moslem leaders with honor and respect. Although he did have a temper, it was almost always absolutely under control and anger was seldom if ever evident, even under tremendous provocation.

He had a remarkable way of getting around difficulties. As an instance, when Zwemer first came to Cairo there were some missionaries who objected to putting copies of the books he had written and the *Moslem World* in the bookroom for general reading and sale, feeling that trouble might be caused among Moslems. He went to the Khedivial Library (now the Royal Library), where he found not only copies of many of his books but bound volumes of the *Moslem World*.

At a tea party and reception given for him in the home of Dr. Julius Richter in Berlin he was introduced by the eminent Professor Carl Becker as follows, "There are many orientalists and scholars in the field of Islam and the Koran, but our guest, Dr. Zwemer, is the world's leading authority on popular Islam from the standpoint of personal observation." This pleased him very much even though his interest in getting individuals and the Church to take up Christian work for Moslems and his desire to himself bear the Message wherever Islam could be found was much deeper than any claim to erudite scholarship. "Popular Islam" is a field for scholarship and Zwemer was probably the foremost authority in it, but this did not in any way minimize his missionary zeal. He was great in both capacities.

II

Physically Zwemer was about six feet tall and of a strong build, his average weight being about 165 pounds. He had the open features of his Dutch ancestry with a rather prominent nose and a twinkle in his eyes which marked the abundant good humor of his nature. His hair was dark and did not turn gray until he was nearly eighty.

He did not care a great deal for athletics and never played golf. He started to play chess at one time, but gave it up as he felt it took too much time from reading and writing. He did not care for sports, or ordinary games, but loved carpentry as a hobby. He did enjoy walking and at one time owned a horse when he worked for the Bible Society. He was born in Michigan but never owned or drove a car in his life — yet he rode camels to far-away places. The only land or property he ever owned was the family lot in the Pilgrim Cemetery at Holland, Michigan, acquired by his father and left him by his sisters.

He was a great story teller and would match humorous anecdotes with a crowd. He had a habit of cutting out stories that pleased him from papers and magazines, and would carry them in his pockets, reading them over until fixed in his memory. When on the road it seemed his store of humor was inexhaustible. Aside from such a fund of humorous anecdotes he could recount his own experiences or tell stories of mission life or travels that would catch and hold the interest of either children or adults.

Zwemer never collected postage stamps, but in many of his addresses he told people that every time they licked a stamp they kissed Arabia. He had read somewhere that the glue on stamps was made from gum Arabic!

He had a nervous disposition; he never learned the habit of the East to sit quietly doing nothing. He said that as a boy he remembered his Mother's aversion to idleness. Whenever there was a moment's hesitation she would say, "Do something." He did appreciate the practice of contemplation in others. He told the story of the old Arab whom he saw one day beside the Persian Gulf letting the sand of the shore run through his fingers. Zwemer asked him what he was doing. "Thinking about Eternity," he replied. "I was just saying to myself that if a bird came once each year and carried away one grain of sand, by the time all the sand on all those shores of the seven seas had been carried away it would be just the morning of eternity."

In fact, Zwemer's actions were at times marked by a needless haste. Had he stopped on many occasions to take more time for thought he would have saved himself a lot of trouble, but that he did not get into more trouble through hasty action was a testimony to the fact that he was purposely relying on Divine guidance at all times. For almost every occasion he was ready a little ahead of time. His wife, Amy, asserted that on the Resurrection Day Sam would have on his robe and crown and be standing waiting for Gabriel to blow his horn.

On many occasions when a program was planned for him beyond ordinary human powers he would plunge into it and trust God to lead him to the right word for the occasion. He would do anything so far as he felt it was for the glory of his Lord.

Like William Carey in India and Robert Morrison in China and David Livingstone in Africa he had indomitable perseverance, especially in the things where he was certain that Christ would be served. Outstanding traits were determination, courage and faith.

A word should also be said about his capacity for friendship and the circle of those whom he knew and loved. In fact, a chapter could be written in this volume entitled "Of Making Many Friends." He did have enemies too, but that was usually because they did not know him.

Among the notable British leaders he knew were Lord Kitchener and Lord Curzon, General Allenby and Colonel Lawrence.

There were deep ties which united him with the mission workers in Arabia and Egypt. He cherished also as great friends Dr. J. J. Lucas, Dr.

E. M. Wherry, Dr. Murry T. Titus and Canon Sell of India. Bishop
Gwynne and Canon Gairdner in Egypt and Bishop McInnes in Jerusalem
were also companions whom he knew well and who shared in his zeal for
the Moslem World. He also mentioned often Isaac Mason and F. H. Rhodes
in China, the Islamic scholars Duncan B. MacDonald, A. J. Wensinck and
Snouck Hurgronje. There was a long association with two notable women,
Miss Jennie De Meyer, the pioneer missionary to the Moslems of Russia,
with whom he cooperated in the occupation of Jedda, and Miss Annie Van
Sommer, an English lady who resided part of the time in Egypt and published the small magazine "Blessed Be Egypt". She had been called "The
Mother of the Nile Mission Press" and opened a summer home for missionaries near Alexandria. She collaborated with Zwemer in the publication of
two books.

Archbishop Temple in England was a respected friend of long standing
and the two men shared a mutual admiration. Fennel P. Turner, Robert E.
Speer, John R. Mott, Delavan Pierson, and other members of a prayer
circle of close friends, together with a host far too numerous to mention,
were his friends and fellow-workers over the years. Concerning such association Zwemer wrote in the preface of a book by his college classmate Dr.
Albertus Pieters:

"The fruit of friendship, like a pomegranate, has many·kernels, as Lord
Bacon says, and he goes on to point out 'how many things are there, which
a man cannot, with any face or comeliness, say of himself? A man can
scarce allege his own merits with modesty, much less extol them; a man
cannot sometimes brook to supplicate, or beg, and a number of the like; but
all these things are graceful in a friend's mouth, which are blushing in a
man's own.' "[3]

III

In June of 1951 Samuel Zwemer returned from the funeral of an elder
sister in Holland, Michigan, to attend the General Synod of the Reformed
Church meeting at Buck Hill Falls, Pennsylvania. There he had the series
of devotional services and though he was ill, delivered his scheduled addresses with great power.

One who was there has said, "The high point of the Synod . . . was in
the towering, impressive figure of Samuel M. Zwemer . . . that giant of the
faith. He is a burning and shining light . . . he came to us out of physical
weakness . . . yet he arose in an indomitable demonstration of the power of
the spirit over flesh . . . We could only stand and marvel at the wonder of
a mind and soul completely under the dominance of the Divine will."[4]

Though the spiritual impact he made in these services was very deep, he
had to go to the hospital soon afterward with a heart ailment. He was back
again at his apartment in lower Fifth Avenue for a time, and in spite of
precarious health he continued to accept preaching engagements. In the

---

3. **Divine Lord and Saviour.** Albertus Pieters. Fleming H. Revell Co., New York, 1949.
4. John P. Muilenberg, missionary from China.

First Presbyterian Church of Schenectady, New York, he was preaching at an evening service when he collapsed and had to be helped from the pulpit. He was taken to a hospital where he had to remain for about three weeks.

For the next several months he spent a good deal of time with his daughter, Amy, and her family in Alexandria, Virginia. He returned to New York several times; once he spoke at a retreat of Princeton Seminary students and kept the annual day of prayer with a few of the closest friends who gathered each year for this occasion.

After a time back in Virginia he was asked to address a missionary conference of the Inter-Varsity Christian Fellowship in New York on February 16th, 1952. He was to have the evening meeting but arrived for the day and also gave a second address in the afternoon. The next day at midnight he was taken by his son-in-law, the Reverend Claude Pickens, to the Presbyterian Hospital; his heart was giving him trouble again.

His first nurse at the Medical Center was one who had been at the meeting and had been thrilled by his burning appeal for missions to Moslems. As was always the case, he made friends with doctors, nurses and patients and brought to many of them a message of sympathy and consolation. There were a great many visitors during the weeks spent in the great institution in upper Manhattan, but the patient was more often than not the one who gave a message of cheer and humor and often joined with his visitors in prayer.

After a thorough examination and several weeks of recuperation, he was deemed well enough to go up to Port Chester, outside of New York, to the Harkness Convalescent Home. On the last Sunday of March he was asked to preach at a service for the other patients there and continued to be a wonderful influence until the hour of his call to higher service.

On Wednesday, April 2nd, 1952, quietly and rather suddenly "the tired heart ceased to palpitate," and thus ten days before his eighty-fifth birthday Samuel Zwemer passed on to be "absent from the body and at home with the Lord."

Of him it might be said as of valiant-for-truth in Bunyan's *Pilgrim's Progress* "when the day that he must go hence was come many accompanied him to the river-side, into which as he went he said, 'Death where is thy sting?' and as he went down deeper, he said, 'Grave where is thy victory?' as he passed over and all the trumpets sounded for him on the other side."

When he heard of his grandfather's death Peter E. Pickens wrote from Korea where he was in the military service:

"It is very sad to think that we have lost a wonderful Grandfather and that the world lost a wonderful preacher. His sermons were well written and well read, but they really came alive when he was up in the pulpit pounding them out with one hand while his other hand held the train schedule. It is wonderful to know that he died peacefully and without pain. When I think of all the times he might and just about did go in the past, I'm glad he went slowly in the golden taxicab to the heavenly train (a reserved seat) and traveled quickly into the State of Heavenly Peace to preach in the Church of the New Jerusalem to the singing of the Heavenly choirs. I'm afraid Grandfather will stir up too much activity until he finds out that Heaven is a place of rest."

William R. Barbour, President of the Fleming H. Revell Company, wrote shortly after Zwemer's death:

"During his late illness he frequently conferred with us and advised with us about various editorial matters. His comments were to the point and were based on an amazing and long experience as a missionary to the Moslems, a professor at the Princeton Theological Seminary, an author, and a preacher of the Word. Around the conference table, in spirit he seemed to be a young man, for his eighty-odd years seemed to mean nothing to him. His ready wit tossed off the years, and to the very end of his life he was an informal, talkative, and friendly person. We urged him, as his family did too, to take life easier; he always agreed and then, as in his last speaking engagement, he would accept a call to preach, extend himself too far and soon would be in the hospital for a period of rest."

On Friday, April 4th, services for Samuel M. Zwemer were held in the First Presbyterian Church of New York City. At this service conducted by the pastors of the church Dr. John A. Mackay paid a remarkable tribute to his colleague and long-time friend. He called Zwemer a "Prince among Missionaries" and spoke of him as "first, the Apostolic Missionary to Moslems; second, the Seminary Professor of Missions; third, the Evangelical writer on Religion; and fourth, the child-like Christian personality." He went on to say on the latter point,

"He was, in the best sense, and in the truest Christian tradition, an everlasting child. In the simplicity of his ways, in the boyishness of his spirit, he ever lived in the beyond, in something that would take place tomorrow. In his years as an octogenarian one could find nothing in Zwemer's spirit which spelt the senility of perpetual reminiscence. There was rather the juvenility of perennial expectation. And so he was buoyant and could also be flamboyant. He was affectionate and inquisitive. He was a ceaseless and inimitable story teller. His letters were extraordinarily human. To the very last, a few hours before his death, he wrote to friends in whimsical mood. He was the everlasting child, child-like and Christ-like to the end, one whose spirit was also apostolic and alert, till suddenly and unexpectedly he passed onward to the other side."

Letters and telegrams of condolence, most of them speaking of his notable accomplishments in the realm of spiritual things, poured in to the bereaved home. After the service in New York members of the immediate family accompanied the body to Holland, Michigan, where a final service was held and interment took place in the family plot of Pilgrim Cemetery.

Buried in Michigan

During the committal service Dr. Albertus Pieters spoke as one who had been closely associated in the same class through preparatory school and college. After reviewing the life he went on to say:

"Now he has passed on after a life fully lived, but though a sad occasion for us it is not a disaster when the shock of grain, fully ripe, is gathered in by the harvester. To that end was the seed planted. The Apostle admonishes us that we Christians are not to sorrow as those who have no hope, but in this case it is difficult to sorrow at all.

"One of the things I myself noted with deepest satisfaction, as I watched and admired his career from afar, was that he never yielded to the fashion of the day in toning down the atoning work of Christ or the peril of those who live without the Gospel . . . He valued the esteem of the learned world, but in such matters he dared to stand upon his own feet.

"We have come together at this time to lay away his mortal remains, a common end to a very uncommon life. We do so not as those who lament a great disaster, but as those who lay the capstone of a completed building, as it is written, 'He shall bring forth the topstone, with shoutings, crying grace, grace unto it.' "[5]

And so another life of major proportions has been written into the annals of the missionary enterprise, the Twentieth Century Acts of the Apostles. It was a life ever vibrant, filled with the Spirit, that of a joyful warrior in a great cause — the greatest cause, down to the last day — on the verge of his eighty-fifth birthday; when he went home — when he was translated to a higher and nobler service.

He stood throughout the first half of this century as the Elijah who called the Christian Church to the winning of the Moslem World. His story is told with the hope and prayer that his zeal and devotion may inspire many a young Elisha to take up his mantle and his task with an equal audacity for God, looking unto Him who is the Author and Perfector of our faith and willing in His power to attempt "the glory of the impossible."

Samuel Zwemer would want this narrative to point others to the Master whom he followed. He would hope that the recounting of his adventures and his devotion might lead others to sacrifice for the winning of the Moslem World, that in the Zwemer Saga there might be an incandescent fire of inspiration to light individuals and the church toward a deeper and far more adequate sense of mission for the world of Islam. As he went forth so would he have his story go forth to pass on the torch to all who read, that they might highly resolve to lift it high and bear it far, until the kingdoms of this world shall have become the kingdoms of our God and of His Christ.

> "O may Thy soldiers, faithful, true and bold,
> Fight as the saints who nobly fought of old,
> And win with them the victor's crown of gold.
> Alleluia! Alleluia!"

---

5. Zechariah 4:7. It may be interesting to note that Robert E. Speer quoted the same text at services for Amy Wilkes Zwemer.

Books by Samuel M. Zwemer

BOOKS by
Samuel M. Zwemer

Arabia: The Cradle of Islam. Fleming H. Revell, New York. 1st Edition, 1900; 4th Edition, 1912. 434 pages. Urdu Translation: Pesa Akhbar, 1910 (Unauthorized).

Raymond Lull: First Missionary to the Moslems. Funk and Wagnalls, New York. 1902. 172 pages.
German Translation: Sudan Pioneer Mission, Wiesbaden, 1912.
Arabic Translation: Nile Mission Press, Cairo, 1914.
Spanish Translation: 1926.
Chinese Translation: 1924.
Dutch Translation: 1928 .(Unauthorized)

The Moslem Doctrine of God. American Tract Society, New York. 1st Edition, 1905; 2nd Edition, 1924. 120 pages.

Islam, A Challenge to Faith. Student Volunteer Movement, New York. 1st Edition, 1907. 295 pages.
2nd Edition, Marshall Brothers, London, 1909.
German Translation: 1911.
Danish Translation: Copenhagen, 1910.
French Translation: Paris, 1922.

The Moslem World: Young People's Missionary Movement of the United States and Canada. Eaton, New York, 1908. 239 pages. (Revised Edition of "Islam, A Challenge to Faith.")

The Unoccupied Mission Fields of Africa and Asia. Student Volunteer Movement, New York. 1911. 260 pages.
German Translation: Basel, 1912.
Danish Translation: Copenhagen, 1912.

The Moslem Christ. Oliphant, Anderson and Ferrier, London. 1st Edition, 1912; 2nd Edition, 1927. 198 pages. American Tract Society, New York.
German Translation: *Die Christologie des Islams,* by Dr. E. Frick, Stuttgart, 1921.
Arabic Translation: Nile Mission Press, Cairo. 1916.
Urdu Translation: 1929.

Mohammed or Christ. Seeley Service and Company, London. 1915. 292 pages.

Childhood in the Moslem World. Fleming H. Revell, New York. 1915. 274 pages.
Arabic Translation: 2nd Edition, Cairo, 1921.
Danish Translation: Copenhagen. 1917.

The Disintegration of Islam. Fleming H. Revell, New York. 1916. 227 pages.

A Primer on Islam. Continuation Committee, Shanghai. 1919. 24 pages.
Chinese Translation: 2nd Edition, 1927.

12 *The Influence of Animism on Islam.* Macmillan, New York. 1920. 246 pages. S.P.C.K., London. 1921.

13 *Christianity the Final Religion.* Eerdmans Sevensma Co., The Pilgrim Press, Grand Rapids, Michigan. 1920. 108 pages.

14 *A Moslem Seeker After God.* Life of Al-Ghazali. Fleming H. Revell, New York. 1921. 302 pages.
Arabic Translation: Nile Mission Press, Cairo, 1922.
Urdu Translaton: 1925.

15 *The Law of Apostasy in Islam.* Marshall Brothers, London. 1923. 164 pages.
German Translation: Guetersloh, 1926.

16 *Report of a Visit to Mesopotamia, the Persian Gulf and India.* Summer of 1924. The American Christian Literature Society for Moslems, New York. 1924. 31 pages.

17 *The Call to Prayer.* Marshall Brothers, London. 1923. 79 pages.
Dutch Translation: Kampen, 1926.

18 *The Glory of the Cross.* Marshall Brothers, London. 1st Edition, 1928. 2nd Edition, 1935. 3rd Popular Edition, 1938. 128 pages.
Arabic Translation: 1928.
Swedish Translation: 1930.
Urdu Translation: 1929.

19 *Report of a Visit to India and Ceylon.* September 23, 1927, to February 28, 1928. A.C.L.S.M., New York. 1928. 33 pages.

20 *Across the World of Islam.* Fleming H. Revell, New York. 1st Edition 1929; 2nd Edition, 1932. 382 pages.

21 *Thinking Missions with Christ.* Zondervan Publishing House, Grand Rapids, Michigan. 1st Edition, 1934; 3rd Edition, 1935.

22 *The Origin of Religion.* Cokesbury Press, Nashville, Tenn. 1st Edition, 1935. 2nd Edition, 1936. 3rd Revised Edition, 1946. Loiseaux Brothers, New York. 256 pages.

23 *Taking Hold of God.* Marshall, Morgan and Scott, London. 1936. 188 pages.
Zondervan Publishing House, Grand Rapids, Michigan. 1936.

24 *It is Hard to be a Christian.* Marshall, Morgan and Scott, London, 1937. 159 pages.

25 *The Solitary Throne.* Pickering and Inglis, London. 1937. 112 pages.

26 *Studies in Popular Islam.* Macmillan, New York. 1939. 148 pages. The Sheldon Press, London.

27 *Dynamic Christianity and the World Today.* The Inter-Varsity Fellowship of Evangelical Unions. London. 1939. 173 pages.

28 *The Glory of the Manger.* American Tract Society, New York. 1940. 232 pages.

29 *The Art of Listening to God.* Zondervan Publishing House, Grand Rapids, Michigan. 1940. 217 pages.

30 *The Cross Above the Crescent.* Zondervan Publishing House, Grand Rapids, Michigan. 1941. 292 pages.

31 *Into All the World.* Zondervan Publishing House, Grand Rapids, Michigan. 1943. 222 pages.

Evangelism Today. Fleming H. Revell, New York. 1st Edition, 1944. 4th Edition, 1948. 125 pages.

Heirs of the Prophets. Moody Press, Chicago. 1946. 137 pages.

A Factual Survey of the Moslem World. Fleming H. Revell, New York. 1946. 34 pages.

The Glory of the Empty Tomb. Fleming H. Revell, New York. 1947. 170 pages.

How Rich the Harvest. Fleming H. Revell, New York. 1948. 120 pages.

Sons of Adam. Baker Book House, Grand Rapids, Michigan. 1951. 164 pages.

Joint Authorship

Topsy Turvy Land: With Amy E. Zwemer. Fleming H. Revell, New York. 1st Edition, 1902. 4th Edition, 1912. 124 pages.

Methods of Mission Work among Moslems: With E. M. Wherry. Fleming H. Revell, New York. 1906. 232 pages.

Mohammedan World Today: With E. M. Wherry. Fleming H. Revell, New York. 1906. 302 pages.

Our Moslem Sisters: With Annie Van Sommer. Fleming H. Revell, New York. 1907. 299 pages.
Danish Translation: Odense, 1909.
Swedish Translation: Stockholm, 1908.

The Nearer and Farther East: With Arthur J. Brown. Macmillan, New York. 1908. 325 pages.

Lucknow, 1911: With E. M. Wherry. Madras, 1912. 298 pages.

Zig-Zag Journeys in the Camel Country: With Amy E. Zwemer. Fleming H. Revell, New York. 1st Edition, 1911. 2nd Edition. 126 pages.

Daylight in the Harem: With Annie Van Sommer. Fleming H. Revell, New York. 1912. 224 pages.

Islam and Missions: Report of the Lucknow conference with E. M. Wherry. Fleming H. Revell, New York. 1912. 300 pages.

Christian Literature in Moslem Lands: With a Committee. Doran, New York. 1923.

Moslem Women: With Amy E. Zwemer. United Study Committee, New York. 1926. 306 pages.

The Golden Milestone: With James Cantine. Fleming H. Revell, New York. 1939. 157 pages.

INDEX

CPSIA information can be obtained
at www.ICGtesting.com
Printed in the USA
BVOW06s1813280317
479153BV00009BA/307/P

9 781258 125202